Overleaf: Red-robed members of the Children of God leave a church en route to jail after staging a protest in San Francisco in 1971—thus becoming a fitting symbol for their movement, which rebelled against biblical Christianity and entered into spiritual bondage to David [Moses David] Berg.

The Children of God
The Inside Story

Deborah (Linda Berg) Davis
with Bill Davis

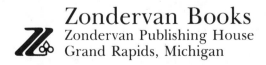

Zondervan Books
Zondervan Publishing House
Grand Rapids, Michigan

THE CHILDREN OF GOD: The Inside Story
    Zondervan Books are published by the Zondervan Publishing House
        1415 Lake Drive, S.E., Grand Rapids, Michigan 49506
Copyright (©) 1984 by The Zondervan Corporation
Grand Rapids, Michigan

Library of Congress Cataloging in Publication Data
Davis, Deborah.
  The Children of God.
  Includes bibliographical references.
  1. Children of God (Movement)—Controversial
literature. 2. Berg, David, 1919–   . 3. Davis,
Deborah. I. Davis, Bill. II. Title.
BV4487.C5D38 1984   289.9   83-26025
ISBN 0-310-27840-6

Scripture quotations are paraphrased or from the King James Version unless
otherwise indicated by the abbreviations NASB (*New American Standard Bible*), NIV
(*New International Version*), or RSV (*Revised Standard Version*).

Edited by James E. Ruark
Designed by Ann Cherryman

Printed in the United States of America

84 85 86 87 88 / 10 9 8 7 6 5 4 3 2 1

This book is dedicated—

—to Mr. and Mrs. James P. Davis, and to the generation of parents who have suffered the painful tragedy of having children become cult members. Few will ever know the extent of their suffering;

—and to our children—Joyanne, John, Philip, Nina, Misty Dawn, Clare, David, Davida, and Barak Joseph. To the extent that each of the children has suffered for our sins, it is our prayer that they will learn by our mistakes, realizing that God's present blessing in our lives is but the result of His mercy upon a repentant spirit. May the truths presented in this book be the foundation for the establishment of many godly generations.

We express our deepest appreciation to the following people, without whose support and help—emotional, spiritual, and financial—we could not have written this book. There is one we have never met: Rev. Richard Wurmbrand. It was through his books and tapes that God revealed to us the mystery of suffering, giving us a deeper understanding of life itself.

Dr. and Mrs. Richard Price
Professor Ronald Enroth
Bill Gothard
Rev. Richard Wurmbrand
Kin Millen
Jim Ruark

We will be forever indebted to them all. May God bless them.

Contents

PREFACE

The famous missionary Oswald Chambers wrote, "The first thing to do in examining the power that dominates me is to take hold of the unwelcome fact that I am responsible for being thus dominated." It is on the bedrock of this truth that I write this book. Having been dominated for more than thirty years by the tyranny of religious hypocrisy and human weakness, I have made a choice to expose the sin of a family and of a man who have influenced tens of thousands of people in a very unrighteous and ungodly way. The family is the David Berg family, and the man is my father. For the past four years I have examined the power that has dominated me, and I have accepted the responsibility to resist that power.

My responsibility entails self-examination, for neither my father nor his movement could have held any power over me at all unless I had yielded to them. It is said that in order to find a real solution, one must find the real problem. This book is an open and honest sharing of my life and heart, revealing the fetters that bound me and the truth that set me free. It was not easy to write this book. But difficulty does not diminish responsibility; I had to write it.

I can tell only my own story and write of my own involvement. This book is written from my perspective. There are close family members and friends who will be affected by my personal exposure. I am not telling their stories, for they may disagree with some things I say. Furthermore, this book is not meant to attack or hurt them, but to share reality as I have seen it and lived through it.

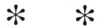

The Children of God movement founded by my father, David Berg, in 1968 has been known as "Teens for Christ," the "Revolution for Jesus," the "Children of God," and now the "Family of Love." The movement also broadcasts on radio under the names "Music With Meaning" and "Musica con Vida." Through music it has lured thousands of youth into its clutches. In today's news media and periodicals the movement is commonly referred to as the "Sex Cult of the Eighties."

Many stories and books have been written about cults, yet few have dealt with the issues that spell life and death for so many thousands. Why do people join cults? Where does brainwashing begin and end? How does one free himself from the mental shackles of the cultic experience? Who bears the responsibility for involvement? How does the ex-member cope with guilt and condemnation?

Most of the people in this book are alive; many are still in the cult. The story is wild and bizarre, but it is true. I sometimes find it hard to believe that it really happened to me, yet daily I am surrounded with the living scars and wounds to assure me that it is true. In all sense this story has fulfilled the axiom, "Truth is stranger than fiction." By the mercy of God, I can share it with you.

When I first left the cult, I hid the truth of who I was and what I had done. The past was like a razor's edge on which I was forced to lie—and the consequences of that past pushed me slowly but heavily upon it. Could I ever be a whole person again?

But I came to see that hiding the truth of my life would only hurt my children and spell disaster for them someday down the road of the future. Through the actions of my oldest daughter I saw that they could fall into the same trap as I. I realized I had to tell them the truth. And if it were important for my own children to know the truth, then what about the rest of society and the thousands who have been and are being affected?

I had to resolve two issues in order to write this book. The first, my children's well-being, has been resolved. The second, my mother's well-being is deeply perplexing. In exposing myself I would affect my children: that is my duty. But in exposing my father, I affect my mother: that is painful. I have yet to resolve that pain; perhaps it never will be resolved. Consequently I am suffering for this book.

The Berg family in 1961 during the days of evangelistic ministry: (rear) Paul [Aaron], Jonathan [Hosea], and Linda [Deborah]; (front) Jane, Faithy, and David.

Part One

Deborah teaching at TSC (chap. 7) in the first high school she organized as director of education for the Children of God. (Below) Bill Davis [Isaiah Carpenter] at the COG's Bromley Factory in England in 1972, the year of Deborah's Coronation.

Chapter 1
The Coronation

Being the oldest child of David Berg had its special problems. How to accept him as God's Endtime Prophet, Moses David, after thirty years of his being just "dad" caused a rending of my soul, mind, and conscience. Yet securing my total loyalty seemed to be the primary motivation behind the "Prayer for a Queen" prophecy that Moses David received "directly from heaven." The place was London; the time, September 16, 1972.

> *Hear, O Israel, the words and the prayer of Thy King! Let it be known that:*
>
> *She is born to be a Queen, and can be no less. She must set the example to show Thy people she puts the work and duty before personal pleasure and personal concerns.*
>
> *She cannot always be a woman—but she must always be a Queen—She has Thy people in her hands, Thy flock; as Thy Shepherdess, she shall diligently feed and lead them and protect them. . . .* [1]

Thus it was prophesied that I was to be crowned Queen: the mouth of the Lord had spoken it! Moses David's prophecy was summarily fulfilled.

> *In accordance with the . . . prayer and prophetic vision, the King's firstborn, Deborah, was crowned Queen of God's New Nation by Archbishop Joshua in an extremely dramatic and colorful ceremony on September 21, 1972. . . .[2]*

My dad intended that the Coronation bring an emotional and spiritual uplift to the London disciples and the movement in general. A select group of leaders prepared secretly for several weeks to make it a glorious occasion. It took place in Bromley, Kent, a suburb of London.

An English millionaire, whose son had joined the Children of God, had given to the movement the use of a large, vacant factory. It was affectionately referred to as the Bromley Colony, and it housed from 50 to 150 disciples at a time. In it we set up a print shop, a small school, a photo lab, a large industrial kitchen, and offices for the secretarial staff. It was the hub of our European activities for a number of years. Disciples would arrive from the United States and be processed through the Bromley Factory and from there be sent into "all the world" to "preach the gospel."

On the fateful night, more than two hundred disciples were gathered for the big event. We prepared a fantastic meal complete with turkey, potatoes, gravy, cake, and ice cream—a veritable treat for the revolutionary disciples accustomed to eating a diet consisting of starch, starch, and more starch. These were days of pioneering and expansion and sacrifice. A disciple's spiritual diet would compensate for the lack of physical diet.

But on this night the banquet tables were overflowing, and a spirit of festivity and joy filled the huge second floor of the Factory. There was dancing, music, and a great spirit of liberty and hope. The disciples didn't really know what was going to happen; everyone was simply told to be prepared for something wonderful and exciting. There was a strong feeling of suspense.

"Do you know what's going on? Why are we having this big meeting?"

"Why, I don't really know. I heard it has to do with Deborah!"

"What do you suppose that stage is for? They've been working on it all week. Mo must have gotten a heavy revelation!"

The red carpet had been rolled out—literally. To this day I don't know where they found the hundred foot roll. The lights were dimmed, and into the room marched a royal procession of the Queen and her court. Other queens, princes, princesses, lords, and ladies of our Royal Revolutionary Kingdom were in attendance, with costumes rented from a local costume shop. It looked like a scene directly out of 16th-century Tudor England; the only thing missing was King Henry himself.

My sister's husband, Joshua, had earned the title of Archbishop for the occasion and presided over the Coronation as the personal representative of our Prophet and King. In one of my hands was placed a scepter, the symbol of my royal Power; in the other, a Bible, the symbol of God's authority.

Archbishop Joshua solemnly read the prophetic revelation Mo had received from the Lord, entitled the "Prayer for a Queen," and then crowned me with a bejeweled diadem. The Factory shook as the two hundred disciples cheered choruses of "Long Live the Queen!"

*　　*

My father lived in a rented house quite near the Bromley Factory. Nestled among the prim and proper homes of the quaint London suburb, he lived, a kind, retired American gentleman with his young "daughter," Maria. You would see them every evening taking a casual walk past the neatly manicured lawns and exquisite rose gardens of Bromley, Kent. It was a most beautiful and tidy English community, the ideal frame for the image my dad was attempting to portray. It was also part of an elaborate veil of secrecy and security.

Moses David had been living incognito for more than two years. There were two basic reasons for this. The first was security. My dad lived under great paranoia, always fearing for his life. It is true that there were people—especially in the United States—who would have liked to see Moses David locked up; but his fear and obsession with security were irrational. At times I feel he was trying to create an air of importance, setting himself high above his followers and the rest of the world. At other times I think he was downright scared. As time passed, it became impossible to tell the difference.

The second reason for his life secrecy was the development of his persona as the Prophet on the Mountain. Being separated from the disciples created a sense of mystery and awe. A man perceived on paper is always more impressive than one known in the flesh. The less the disciples saw of Moses David, the more they would reverence the sacred image developed in the "Mo Letters." Only a very small percentage of the thousands of people who have joined the COG have ever met my father in person.

Anyone visiting the Bromley Factory became submerged in a sea of happy, smiling faces and greetings of "Jesus loves you!" The dedicated youth strummed emotional folk songs that stirred the imagination to "reach out and touch the hand of God"; on the streets they witnessed by the hour of salvation in Jesus Christ, Forsake All, and follow Jesus full-time. But as in every cult, appearances were deceiving. Only the Royal Family knew what was going on behind the scenes, in the counsel chambers of Moses David.

The Royal Family were the only people who actually knew Moses David's whereabouts and talked to him personally. The leadership structure of the Children of God has changed through the years (always with Moses David at the top, of course); but in 1972 it was governed by a hierarchy. Atop the hierarchy were the Royal Family, David Berg's personal family: my husband, Jethro, and I; my sister, Faithy, and her husband, Joshua; my brother Aaron; my brother Hosea and his wife, Esther; and my mother, known in the movement as Mother Eve, or simply Mother. Maria—Moses David's secretary, mistress, and full-time companion—was also a member of the Royal Family, whose place grew in importance with time.*

---

*In the COG we adopted new names taken from the Bible. The legal names of

The Royal Family commuted between the Bromley Factory and the secret house under strict security rules. Usually we could come and go only after dark so as not to arouse the suspicion of neighbors at the sight of these unconventional people visiting the quaint American gentleman. We were always to use the same car; if perchance we came in a different vehicle, it was to be parked around the block out of view of the neighbors.

From his tidy little home, Moses David was busily engineering his worldwide Revolution for Jesus. The movement had never been stronger, and it was gaining momentum every day. However, this success was exacting a staggering toll from the personal lives of the Royal Family. By the time of my Coronation, my life was at the very least an atrocity. My marriage had been virtually destroyed, traditional Christian principles obliterated, and all ties with outside relatives severed. Only one thing mattered: The Cause! There was no place for natural affections; these more often than not got in the way and hindered the "work of God." Thus, normal friendships and relationships were rendered useless.

Given the immorality that permeated the lives of the leadership in 1972, one could hardly carry on a normal life, let alone a normal marriage. Life was anything but normal; life for the dedicated disciple of Moses David was not intended to be normal! We were in a revolution—ushering in the Revolutionary Kingdom of God! The Cause was all. My father wrote to all the disciples at that time,

> *In our situation, God is trying to teach us the lesson of putting Him and His Family first. [We often referred to ourselves as "the Family."] If you cannot be trusted with a private relationship [marriage] and to keep it in its proper perspective—last— then God will break it up to insure He and His work get first place.* [3]

---

the Royal Family are as follows: Faithy—Faith Berg Dietrich; Joshua—Arnold Dietrich; Aaron—Paul Brandt Berg; Hosea—Jonathan Emanuel Berg; Esther— Luranna Nolind Berg; Mother Eve—Jane Miller Berg; Maria—Karen Zerby. I was born Linda Berg, but my Christian name was legally changed to Deborah by my father after the movement began.

I had been slow to enter into the sexual freedom mandated for the COG. My father's concept of indiscriminate "sharing" caused me great confusion. Nevertheless, I knew I would someday need to become more "spiritual" in this matter. My father made it quite clear that any inability to "share" sexually with a Brother or Sister demonstrated not only the height of selfishness, but also a severe lack of spirituality. One's attitude toward "sharing" could rightly gauge a person's yieldedness to the Spirit of God. On that basis, my spirituality was in a tailspin.

Prior to the Coronation Dad had ordered my husband, Jethro, to return to the United States to oversee the work there. This was an important move in his overall plan. At the time, my marriage of nine years was in the final stages of deterioration, and Jethro and I could no longer treat each other with kindness or respect. My loneliness, confusion, and despair led me into an adulterous relationship with one of the disciples in the Bromley Colony. This affair would prove to be disastrous in his life, a source of deep personal sorrow.

My father was keenly aware of the grief my marriage was causing me, and he began to worry about my new relationship. Not because he thought it was wrong, but because it posed a threat to his hold over me. My involvement was not "sharing." He greatly feared I would fall in love and find happiness and security, which would diminish his power over me. He was right. Only years later I realized that as long as I was fighting and unhappy with my husband, Dad was inwardly pleased. He enjoyed the conflicts and often aggravated them through his devious manipulations of people and circumstances. If my loyalty to Jethro were subverted, it would necessarily be directed toward my father. Dad well knew this fact. (False prophets cannot exist without total loyalty.) Marriage as an institution threatens loyalty to Moses David; through his doctrines on sex and marriage he has destroyed the institution within the COG.

At the time of the "Queen Prophecy," all the Royal Family members were conveniently situated in other parts of the world, with the exception of Joshua and me. It was Dad's chance to make his move: he would make me Queen. I would be exalted, honored, blessed of God—all by merit of his prophetic revelations. As

Queen I would be married to the work, and to the work alone. All other relationships would be secondary.

Thus, living in adultery and watching my marriage disintegrate, I was crowned Queen of God's New Nation. Yet my reign was short-lived. In a few days I would discover my dad's true motives for the Coronation, and in a few months Queen Deborah would be summoned to the Royal Guillotine.

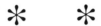

One evening, a few days after the Coronation, Dad made his move. He delivered the master stroke designed to solidify my place within the Kingdom, establish my position before God, and prove my loyalty to God's King and Prophet.

I had been to his secret house for discussion and counsel. I decided to spend the night, as it was too late to return to the Bromley Colony. I was asleep when he entered. I was awakened gently.

"Deborah, Deborah, wake up, honey."

"Yes, Dad. What is it? What's wrong?"

" Honey, the Lord has given us a great deal of freedom in Christ. We mustn't look upon it lightly. God's love is all-encompassing, and to the pure all things are pure."

My stomach tightened.

"God has made me King over His New Nation and now He has made you the Queen. God wants from each of us total loyalty and submission. As Queen you must prove your loyalty to God and the King. God has given us all things freely in Christ Jesus, and His only law is love."

Oh, God! I thought. *Is that why he has done all this?*

The nightmare was all too familiar. Memories came to life of the times when Dad had made similar advances—once when I was seven, once when I was twelve. Now I was twenty-six, and Dad was attempting it again under the banner of prophetic revelation: Incest.

"But you're my dad, my father! I don't need this. I love you without this. It's not necessary to prove my love this way; I already love you. Perhaps in a few years when I'm more spiritual; I'm not spiritually ready yet." Feigning sleep, I rolled over, and he left me in peace. Peace? My mind was burning with confusion.

Dad had made me Queen, set me up, all for that! I thought, *Could the desire for sex, for incest, be so powerful, lust so all-consuming, diseasing a person's mind so totally that he has no control over himself?* Although I was not conscious of it at the time, God was bringing me face to face with the consequences of unrepented sin. Even after all these years my father was still a slave to these evil passions and desires. For the next nine years God would continue to confront me with the consequences of sin; but at that time I had no idea that God was even around, nor had I the slightest notion what God deemed right or wrong. Life was becoming a jumble of sordid experiences held together by the framework of religious acts.

Why does he want this so? I wondered. *Since I was only seven years old.* I was feeling terribly sick. My thoughts ran wild. *What about the man I am living with? My husband? My children? My mother? Is this right?* One question led to another, and my confusion turned to despair. *But I know I love this man*—I thought—the man with whom I was living in adultery. *Love? What is love? Do I really love him, or am I just telling myself that? It was Dad who condoned the relationship in the first place. I have Mo's permission and therefore the Lord's approval; that makes it right and not adultery. But maybe Dad only allowed it to appease me, to set me up for his incestuous desires. What does the Lord have to do with it? No! I really love this man. God is in it!*

My turmoil intensified. I did not know that my life was being consumed by sin. In the COG sin did not exist: "to the pure all things are pure." The idea of sin had been carefully removed and set aside by the doctrines of Moses David. However, the doctrines of Moses David did not rule my conscience completely. Thus my soul felt its torture.

Within a few days of that experience I left for a month's tour of our European Colonies in Switzerland, Spain, and Italy. News of the Coronation had reached the other Royal Family members, and they were in an uproar. They wanted me out! Political jealousy flared.

By the end of October everyone was back in London. On October 28, Dad delivered his infamous "One Wife" address to the members of the Royal Family. This would become the foundation principle for all his future sex doctrines. According to Mo—as Moses David was familiarly called—"The private family is the basis of the selfish capitalistic private enterprise system and all its selfish evils! . . . the most successful communes [referring to communal systems of the past] either abolished all private relationships entirely and required total celibacy, or abandoned the private marriage unit for group marriage." Mo was determined to see that his children and disciples would be "successful for the Lord"; not even marriage would stand in our way.

> *God will have no other gods before Him, not even the sanctity of the marriage god! If we broke up every so called marriage in the Revolution, and it did the work good, to make them put God first, it would be worth it! God is the greatest Destroyer of home and family of anybody. We are Revolutionary! We are . . . not even hesitating to destroy marriages that don't glorify God and put Him and His work first! Partiality towards your own wife or husband . . . strikes against the unity and supremacy of God's Family and its oneness and wholeness!*[4]

The institution of marriage had officially been dealt the *coup de grâce*. A few weeks later I was to receive mine.

Divine retribution. My rejection of God's Prophet was not to go unpunished or unnoticed; moreover, the incident would provide an opportunity to further reveal "the Lord's direction on sex and true freedom." The entire Royal Family was gathered for a leadership meeting in Dad's pretty English home in that quaint London suburb. There was a low fire burning in the fireplace as we took our seats among the couches and chairs of the downstairs living room. We were discussing general details of the work, and it seemed like a normal meeting. Then Dad started in:

"The churches have gone astray in their puritanical interpretations of the Scriptures. God has been showing us the wonders and beauty of the freedom He has given us. Sex is one of God's greatest gifts to man and we are free under grace to enjoy the liberties of sexual freedom. To the pure all things are pure. But there are some here who are and have been resisting the Spirit of God! And God won't have it!"

I knew it was coming. Instinctively I stifled my emotions. My mother hung her head. She too knew a traumatic session was in the making.

"In the Bible," Dad continued, "God makes many exceptions to His rules. How do you think Adam and Eve propagated the human race? Who do you think Cain took as his wife?—he took one of his sisters, of course! And what about Lot and his daughters? It says that Lot had intercourse with his daughters and God made a great nation out of them. If we take a closer look at Scripture we find that in some special situations God breaks His own rules."

He railed for hours, citing Scripture after Scripture to prove his point. Then he turned his attack directly against me. Because I had refused my father's desire for an incestuous relationship, I had in effect refused to accept him as God's Prophet. The Prophet did not act selfishly or for his own personal design or pleasure—it was always under the direct inspiration of the Almighty. I had rejected the counsel of the Lord. I was no longer worthy to be called Queen. It was, indeed, my little sister, Faithy, who was the rightful Queen—she had never rejected my father. It was revealed in front of all present, for the first time, that from her early childhood, she and my father had practiced incest. It was she who reverenced him as a true Prophet. I was rebellious and selfish—I had always rejected him. Consequently, the newly crowned Queen Deborah lost not only her title, but figuratively her head as well.

I was demoted, removed from all power and authority, ordered to be subservient to all present, and stripped of my right to the throne. I had lost the birthright because of my rebelliousness. My dad said he would never give me a chance to be restored. My adulterous relationship with the man at the Bromley Colony was also terminated, although no one present knew that I was pregnant with his baby. All these were conditions of God's wrath being poured out upon me via His Prophet.

I sat quietly through this session, showing little emotion. Inside I was seething: I hated my father. He had ruined everything I held dear in my life. *How can he be so perverted, so selfish?* I looked at my mother and wondered how she had put up with this kind of thing all these years. There she sat, in stunned silence. How could she? *I* wasn't going to take it, not *this* time! What was the point of going on? I would never be happy as long as I was living under my dad—but there was no way to get away from him. To whom would I go? I had no one to turn to. I determined what to do: Like the warriors of Masada, I would snatch the victory from him.

I will not get emotional, I told myself as his tirade continued unabated. *I will not explode. I will act repentant and sorrowful. When the meeting is over, I will go quietly to bed and then sneak out in the early hours of the morning. I will leave this horrible house and never, never return!*

London at four o'clock in the morning is a very cold, rainy, and lonely place for the banished daughter of a prophet. I had escaped undetected with a few pounds in my purse, enough to last a couple of days in a cheap hotel. It is hard to relive such moments, but today I can be thankful for God's merciful hand that kept me alive. I had come to the edge of life itself in that lonely hotel room. I was standing at the brink. Only four months later my brother Aaron would also stand at that brink. His body was to be found at the bottom of a cliff just outside Geneva, Switzerland.

I had fully intended to commit suicide when I fled my father's house. Yet I could not do it. I look back upon these events and ponder. *What was that restraining force within me? Was it God? The will to survive? faith? Was it concern for my children?* All I know is that as much as I considered suicide, I just could not accomplish it. How was it that my brother could?

I spent four days alone in that tiny hotel room. For four days the spiritual battle raged. I ate nothing. I told myself I would never return to that house, or to my father, or have anything to do with the COG again. I thought about going back and telling my father he was wrong. Hatred stirred at the thought of what he was doing, what he had tried to do to me. I wanted to confront him. A part of me told me that he was wrong. And if that were true, it meant God was on *my* side not his.

As I struggled with these doubts, my mind became more clear, more sane than it had felt for years. But then the flood of circumstance consumed me. Whether from fear or confusion or my indescribable state of lostness, I concluded that I could not fight my father. What would happen to my children? I knew that if I confronted Dad I wouldn't stand a chance of winning. He knew just the right buttons to push, what weak points to attack, how to get through any defenses. By the time he'd finish with me, I would believe that *he* was right and *I* totally wrong. No, to enter his arena was impossible.

When I finally decided to resign my will, to give in and go back, I lost all desire to fight. What little fire had burned in my conscience was extinguished by the resignation of my will. I saw no alternative but to surrender.

By that time, there was bedlam among the Royal Family. They were scared. Dad was worried that I might have taken my life. I agreed to let Joshua come and see me. He brought with him a personal letter from Dad: "Oh, my dearest . . . God has a place for you. . . . I was hasty . . . So sorry . . . Too much pressure . . . Continue your relationship. . . ."

My dad's plan to gain total control over me and begin his long-desired incestuous relationship had backfired. Moreover, he had a mutiny on his hands because of it. My brothers and sister and husband were furiously jealous over the Coronation. My demotion as Queen was the perfect tranquilizer. I think my dad actually enjoyed those family mutinies. He methodically twisted words in order to pit us one against the other—like rats fighting over the carcass of another rat. He would purposely wound a specific member of the Royal Family, then stand back and watch the others devour it. If he could keep us fighting and divided, he could keep us loyal to him and his power secure.

I was seeing the naked truth of this for the first time—the viciousness, the perversion, the intense jealousy, the evil lust for power.

Yet I returned knowingly to all this. The circumstances had not changed. There was method in all of my father's madness— this I now painfully knew to be true. *But where can I go?* I rationalized. I had conquered the battle over physical suicide alone in the hotel room. But in going back I had lost an even greater battle: I was committing spiritual suicide.

Purposefully I placed myself in a mental box. I would accept reality only to the limits of that box; beyond that, I would accept

A familiar scene in Europe during the early and middle seventies: COG members, bearing such names as Heidi, Auko, Hart, Casafea, Timbrel, and Resheph, sing and witness in the streets.

or see nothing. I would bide my time. Fate alone would determine the course of my life.

Insanity, suicide, and emotional destruction had been deflected. My box afforded me suitable protection. Yet what lived inside that box? I was a person out of time, without reality, without foundation, without feeling. I floated in space like a weightless capsule. God and the reality of Jesus Christ had ceased to exist; love was a myth; sex a nightmare of assorted perversions. Right and wrong had been sucked side by side into the vacuum of antinomianism; I had transcended the gravity of moral law. I had entered the outer limits of hell.

Chapter 2
The Inheritance

When we are in an unhealthy state physically or emotionally, we always want thrills. In the physical domain this will lead to counterfeiting the Holy Ghost; in the emotional life it leads to inordinate affection and the destruction of morality; and in the spiritual domain if we insist on getting thrills, on mounting up with wings, it will end in the destruction of spirituality.[1]

The record shows that the Children of God movement started in Huntington Beach, California. The movement, in a physical sense, was conceived in 1968 around the activities of the Huntington Beach Light Club, a small mission/coffee house. But in principle the Children of God started long before, the seeds of its philosophy germinating during the childhood days of my father, David Berg.

David descended from a long line of sincere Christian men and women, some of them notable pastors and evangelists. In

1745, thirty years before the American Revolution, three brothers—Adam, Isaac, and Jacob Brandt—set sail for the Colonies from Stuttgart, Germany. They were German Jews who had accepted Christ as their personal Savior. Their orthodox Jewish family had rejected them, declared them "dead," and buried them in mock funerals, as was the Jewish custom. So the brothers struck out for the Americas in hopes of finding a new life and the freedom to live their Christian faith. As peace-loving Mennonite farmers they settled in Pennsylvania and later moved to Ohio.

The most notable of David's ancestors, John L. Brandt, was born in Somerset, Ohio, in 1860. He began teaching at the age of seventeen and lecturing and preaching at the age of twenty-four. He experienced a life-changing dedication to Jesus Christ when he was in his early twenties and subsequently became a minister in the Methodist Church.

David's grandfather seemed to be a man destined for success. He soon gained the position of president of Virginia College, and through his writings and investments he became a millionaire. He joined the Campbellite movement of the Disciples of Christ in his later life, becoming one of the outstanding leaders of that movement, now known as the Christian Church. He was personally responsible for building and pastoring some fifty churches, and he authored sixteen books in his lifetime.

John L. Brandt's daughter, Virginia—my grandmother—was raised in an atmosphere befitting the child of a wealthy minister. She was still a child when her father grew in fame as a popular lecturer, traveling more than four hundred thousand miles through the United States, Mexico, Canada, Europe, Asia, Africa, and Pacific islands. Virginia accompanied him on many of his tours. Because of her culturally enriched background she was a very sophisticated and learned young lady. However, her relationship to Christ and Christianity was somewhat formal, despite the intense faith of her father.

By her early twenties, this life of excitement, wealth, and pleasure had left Virginia Brandt empty and disillusioned. Her discouragement was turning to despair when a crisis engulfed her world: the death of her mother. Virginia was attending a party at the home of General Winfield Scott when depression overwhelmed her.* On the brink of suicide, she remembered the counsel her father had often given others: Instead of throwing your life away, why not give it to some good cause.

She did. Virginia Brandt became the Field Secretary for the National Florence Crittenton Mission. With the inherited determination and aptitude of her dynamic father, Miss Brandt engaged all her efforts into advancing the cause of the mission and helping the lost and wayward girls of the nation. It was said of her: "She is worth her weight in gold anywhere. She did most effective personal work in the homes and on the streets and her consecration and Christ-like spirit were imparted to all who came to know her." She became one of the mission's most industrious speakers, traveling the country, speaking on behalf of the movement, and raising vast amounts of money for the establishment of the Crittenton Homes. In 1910 Charles Crittenton described the character of my grandmother in the following letter:

> *This will introduce to yourself and workers, Virginia Lee Brandt, who is in the service of the National Florence Crittenton Missions. We send her to you with a hearty "God Speed" and trust that you will give to her all co-operation. She is most worthy of your love and care. Any work that you will entrust to her will be done with dispatch and thoroughness. She is thought to be one of the best woman speakers in the States and is a conscientious and able missionary.*
>
> *It is an inspiration when we have young girls in our work whom God is making a success and I thank Him from the depth of my heart that he has raised up Virginia Lee Brandt to work in this corner of His Vineyard.*

Eventually Virginia planned to marry. She was engaged to Bruce Bogart, the wealthy cousin of Humphrey Bogart. But while attending a special party given in her honor in Ogden, Utah, where she had built her last Crittenton Home, she met Hjalmer Berg, a handsome Swedish tenor enlisted as part of the musical entertain-

---

*This was not the prominent figure of the Mexican War of 1846-48, for he died in 1866. Rather, this general may have been a descendant of "Old Fuss and Feathers."

ment. Virginia fell instantly in love with him, whereupon they eloped.

It wasn't long before Hjalmer Berg dedicated his life to the ministry under the influence of his new father-in-law and enrolled in theological seminary in Des Moines, Iowa. Hjalmer was ordained a minister in the Disciples of Christ.

In 1911, while my grandfather was still studying for the ministry, Virginia Brandt Berg bore her first child, Hjalmer Jr. But as she was coming home from the hospital with her newborn infant on a cold December day, tragedy struck. My grandmother describes the experience in her book, *The Hem of His Garment*.

> *It was Christmas morning and the hospital was alive with visitors and agog with excitement. Some were going home; others were joyfully greeting loved ones who had come long distances to spend the holidays with the sufferers. I was begging the doctor to let me go home for the Christmas holidays. . . . After much pleading, the doctor, against his better judgement, gave orders to get me ready.*
>
> *My heart was simply thrilled at the thought of home, husband, Christmas! There was a deep mantle of snow on the ground and I exclaimed at the beauty of the trees, as their snow-laden branches reached out, glistening white, in the sunshine. I had always loved Christmas better than any other day. And home! We were almost there now—just in sight of the house—how good it looked!*
>
> *But—how strangely God works! How swiftly, unexpectedly, tragedy can come stalking across Life's path. . . .*
>
> *For just in sight of the little home—almost there—there was an accident. I was thrown, and my back, hitting the curbstone, was broken in two different places. . . .* [2]

The doctor's verdict: "She is paralyzed from the waist down; I can find no reflexes here at all." What followed was, in Virginia's words, "five years of awful agony, suffering, and heartbreak—years of intolerable pain, isolation, and loneliness—years that seemed endless with hopelessness and despair." X-rays showed that her back had been broken in two places and that the crushed vertebrae were pressing on the spinal cord. A team of nine physicians and surgeons operated and removed the bone covering the spinal cord. This left an eight-inch portion of the spinal cord exposed and unprotected by bone.

For months Virginia was compelled to lie perfectly still until cartilage grew over the spinal cord. The operation brought a partial restoration of life to the lower part of her body, which had been paralyzed. But because of her weakened condition, she suffered a complete collapse and did not recover from the effects of the operation for several months. Then followed five years of invalidism. Her husband, Hjalmer, testifies in the same book,

> *For over five years she was a helpless, hopeless, invalid, lying on rubber cushions, weighing only 78 pounds, her body emaciated and her face gaunt; unconscious most of the time towards the last—an intense sufferer—a hopeless case, absolutely given up by the physicians.[3]*

At the end of her five-year ordeal, her health was so far gone that it seemed she would die. She was "fast going stone-blind," and it looked as if she would not make it. Then a miracle happened. For years she and her husband and many friends and loved ones had prayed for her healing. One Saturday in Ukiah, California, Virginia Berg was instantly healed:

> *And at that very moment I was healed! At that very moment the Lord let me see that for which I had been believing. The paralysis had gone from my body! I felt cool and rested and sat upright in bed!*
>
> *I walked that floor, it seemed, the happiest woman in the world. The burden of sickness, sorrow, and sin had all been lifted from my life! I had not only been born again spiritually, but I felt I had been made again physically.[4]*

The next day Virginia walked into her husband's church "from deathbed to pulpit," giving testimony to what God had done for her.

This is the story I was told all my life.

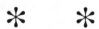

As a result of her healing, my grandmother and grandfather eventually broke with the Disciples of Christ, because the church did not believe in faith healing or in women preachers. This also caused a serious rift in her relationship with her father; thereafter there was very little communication between them.

Mr. and Mrs. Berg began working on their own as itinerant evangelists, giving the testimony of grandmother's miraculous healing and encouraging church congregations that God could do the same in their lives.

In March 1925 the Bergs arrived in Miami, Florida. A year later the newspaper headlines proclaimed: "FAITH—WOMAN—BUILDS CHURCH FOR ALLIANCE: Rev. Virginia Brandt Berg Credited With Tabernacle Success." The article reads,

> *She came for a revival on March 22, 1925. After the series of meetings, she was asked to remain permanently. Now one year has passed. Alliance tabernacle has been dedicated. The auditorium has a seating capacity of 4,500. The building is said to have the best acoustics of any structure in the south.*
>
> *The "power behind the throne"—Mrs. Virginia Brandt Berg—is the daughter of the Rev. John L. Brandt, preacher, author, and lecturer of Muskogee, Okla. She comes from a family of preachers. And is rearing another family of preachers. Mrs. Berg is the mother of two boys and one girl.*
>
> *The older boy is already studying in the Alliance Bible college at Toccoa Falls, Ga. Little David has preached at the tabernacle several times, and will enter the ministry as soon as he is old enough. The girl will follow in her mother's footsteps.*
>
> *. . . She married the Rev. H. E. Berg, who was active in the work of the Christian church in Texas and Oklahoma. Then the case of Paul and Barnabas was repeated. Mr. Berg stepped back and let Mrs. Berg do the preaching. Now she is pastor and Mr. Berg is her associate and director of Bible study.*

By April 26, 1931, six years after the Bergs moved to Miami, the newspaper headlines read: "WOMAN FOUNDS MIAMI CHURCH: Alliance Tabernacle, Started in Tent, Has One of Largest Congregations." The article reads,

> *A crowd of 3,000 hushed persons sits in a vast, wooden auditorium, eyes glued on the figure of an earnest-faced woman on a raised platform.*
>
> *With a dying rustle of musical scores and instruments, an orchestra at her side composes itself to hear and not be heard.*
>
> *A discreet cough is stifled as the woman on the platform raises her hand:*
>
> *"The title of my sermon tonight will be 'From Deathbed to Pulpit.' "*
>
> *Older members of the church never tire of hearing it; new members come by the hundred to hear this exposition on the faith of a woman in the healing power of the Lord—a faith which often packs her tabernacle seating some 7,000, with followers.*
>
> *Though not affiliated with any other church in the country, the tabernacle follows the religious principles of the Christian Missionary alliance.*

My grandmother traveled extensively during her days with the Tabernacle, holding revivals and rallies with the "Berg Evangelistic Dramatic Company." She was as popular in many cities of the country as she was in Miami.

Eventually Virginia lost her place at the Tabernacle through a series of events that remain unclear. During the Depression, the Tabernacle was unable to meet its financial obligations, my grandmother was forced out, and leadership was assumed by someone else. She went on to start another church in Miami known as the Central Alliance—Church of the Open Door; she went on from that church to become an itinerant evangelist full-time, lecturing, preaching, and holding revivals in churches throughout the United States.

This is the environment in which David Berg grew up, along with his older brother and sister, Hjalmer Jr. and Virginia. My father was born on February 18, 1919.

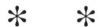

David Berg was drafted into the army in 1941 during World War II. He was discharged, however, because of a serious heart condition. In 1944 he met my mother, Jane Miller, in Los Angeles. The "Berg Evangelistic Party," now comprising grand-mother, grandfather, and David, was holding a revival meeting in the L.A. area. Jane and David met at the Little Church of Sherman Oaks, where she was working as a secretary and helping with its youth program. During the revival, they fell instantly in love. They eloped and became Mr. and Mrs. David Brandt Berg on July 22, 1944, in Glendale, California.

David did not consult either his mother or his father about the marriage, nor did Jane send word to her family asking permission or even seeking counsel. This was not in keeping with the character of her warm and loving Kentucky family. Raised in a fine Christian home of Baptist background, one simply did not get married without the approval of family. Failing to inform Jane's parents of the marriage plans was but one early sign of David Berg's rejection of authority that can be traced through his entire adult life.

After his marriage, David continued to travel and work with his mother in her evangelistic ministry. He had two children by the time he finally stopped touring with his mother to become the pastor of a Christian Missionary Alliance church in Valley Farms, Arizona. He served there from 1949 to 1951. My dad built this, his first church, with his own hands. The building was constructed of old adobe blocks transported from nearby ruins. One of my first childhood memories is of riding atop those blocks in an old flatbed trailer.

Valley Farms was a turning point in my dad's life, because it was there that he began to develop a deep-seated bitterness and hatred toward the established church. This hatred of the church system would later become one of the foundation doctrines of the Children of God. Dad was expelled from the very church he had built himself. There are two conflicting stories.

My father's version is that he was endeavoring to witness to the Indians who populated a nearby reservation: "I would invite the dirty, barefooted Indians to the church service on Sunday and the 'white' members resented it. They were racist hypocrites! So they kicked me out."

Another version concerns a sexual scandal in which he was allegedly involved. Until recently I discounted rumors of this as hearsay. However, a cousin has told me that my dad sent a tape recording to his parents in California at the time of his dismissal. In the tape he categorically denied the charge of sexual misconduct and bitterly defended his position, calling the accusation a lie.

Who knows the truth, except my father? My dad was always trying to be radical in his Christianity; this would explain why he would bring "dirty, barefooted Indians" into his church to which a white, prejudiced congregation would take offense. On the other hand, knowing my dad's sexual weakness, I believe there could certainly have been a scandal. Whatever the case, the event gave birth to a bitterness that grew into a deviant, consuming hatred of the established church.

David wrote a letter to his mother on May 31, 1951, describing his departure from the Alliance and the "church system." It reads,

> . . . *The Lord revealed to me very definitely last Sunday morning while Jane was at church and I was in desperate prayer, that we should "sell all" and "follow Him." I'm telling you, that was really hard to take!—especially for Jane!—But miracle of miracles, He had already prepared her heart, and when she came home and I broke the news to her, she was actually happy, and we both rejoiced at being set free from "things."*
>
> *The Lord finally answered me this time that He could tell me more that I needed to know in five minutes than if I spent the rest of my life trying to gain information through books and magazines!*
>
> *I believe He has also revealed to me that I'll never have the fellowship, inspiration, and power that I need if I stay in the Alliance—even if I have to go to work and earn a living some other way!—That may be a shock to you but I believe it's true. I felt like a compromiser when I went into the Alliance back there when I applied. . . to get Valley Farms, but I knew I couldn't get a church in the Assemblies (Assembly of God Church) with the little I have—so I went back to the Alliance.*
>
> *It seems the Lord is showing me that belonging to anything other than the Lord Himself is too binding, too hindering, too man-made. It obligates you too much to the dictates of man rather than God. When you follow God instead of man they kick*

you out anyhow, so you might as well not stay in or get in. Praise the Lord!

I can't tell you how wonderful it has been to be out from under that bondage at Valley Farms, even as light as it was there!—Free to do and go as we please and witness as we choose where we choose without any fear of having to be obligated to anybody—not even ourselves!—no one but the Lord!

Evidently I was never cut out to be a kowtowing, hypocritical, beating-around-the-bush, please everybody pastor!

I guess I'm really an evangelist or missionary at heart!—I just can't stand sticking with the same little bunch and trying to promote the same little fold—and the same hidebound hierarchy—and be compelled to string along with them on any deal because the Society can do no wrong! I just can't stomach it!

My dad returned to a university in Phoenix to study socialism and communism. In 1972 he wrote in a Mo Letter concerning those days,

. . . Embittered and sick of the whole hypocritical Church System, I nearly became a Communist! I returned to college on the GI Bill determined to study philosophy, psychology, and political science, rather than religion, and became seriously involved in the study of Socialism and Communism.[5]

How childish this seems, like the little boy who gets mad and says to his playmates, "Well, if you're not going to play my way, I'm going to take my marbles and go home!" The little boy nurses his wounds all the way home and announces to his mother, "They were mean to me! They're just a bunch of cheaters!" The truth is plain to all but the little boy: he's the cheater.

This attitude pervades my father's life from his childhood. It started a long time ago. When he was a little boy, my grandmother idolized him and treated him as if he could do no wrong. He was never brought under authority nor taught the strength of character to admit a wrong, accept guilt, ask forgiveness, and go on, strengthened through the humility of telling the truth. My father developed a persecution complex that persists to this day: "Everyone is misjudging me: no one understands me; I'm so mistreated and no one recognizes my true genius."

My dad never learned the concept of true greatness. His self-image has been weakened through the deceitfulness of sin; consequently he believes greatness is measured in how one stands on the scale of success, how well one competes in the arena of numbers, followers, statistics, and publicity. He has yet to learn that true greatness lies in the integrity of your heart, in the ability to be honest with yourself—to be willing to face your mistakes as *your* mistakes, not blaming personal failures on other people. Throughout his writings, my dad consistently blames others for his failings. In his inability to look at himself honestly and objectively, my dad never matured beyond adolescence.

During his "communist sabbatical" my dad taught in junior high school for several years. At that time he also attended a three-month "personal witnessing course" at the American Soul Clinic, an organization directed by a man named Fred Jordan. The Soul Clinic's purpose was to train missionaries for the foreign field. This encounter was the beginning of a relationship between my dad and Fred Jordan that would last for fifteen years. From about 1952 to 1967 my dad was promoting Fred's TV program, "Church in the Home." (Fred Jordan can still be viewed on television in Los Angeles.) My dad and Fred seemed to have a good working relationship.

Dad learned many business tactics from Fred Jordan, not all of them good. Dad developed the philosophy that it is okay to present facts in any way which will produce positive results—because "we are, don't forget, doing a good work for the Lord." Fred Jordan was second only to my grandmother as the major influence on my dad's life and character. My uncle recently said of my dad, "He was a man who would never be under authority. He always resisted authority." Dad had struck a happy medium with Fred, who himself was under no authority.

After this fifteen-year working relationship, Fred dissolved my father's job, no longer needing his services. Without work my dad drifted about the U.S., evangelizing with three of his children, now in their teens. I had married in 1963, at age seventeen, so I was not traveling with the rest of the family.

Dad's team developed a rather effective system of witnessing to young people. It was so effective that three teenagers contacted in their ministry came to live and work with them full-time. All three are with Dad's work to this day; one of them, Arnold Dietrich, married my sister.

After spending a little more than a year in this evangelism, Dad and his team traveled west to work with his mother, at her invitation, in Huntington Beach, California. Meanwhile, Dad had secured a job for my husband in Fred Jordan's central office in Los Angeles, where we had moved in 1964. Thus, our whole family was living in the L.A. area by Christmas 1967. And when Dad joined my grandmother's ministry, he persuaded me to come along too.

My grandmother had developed a small seaside ministry, feeding sandwiches to the hippies and surfers gathered on the famous Huntington Beach Pier. In the late sixties, Huntington Beach was to Southern California what Haight-Ashbury was to the San Francisco area: the Counterculture pitted against the Establishment. There were long hair, drugs, surfing, sun, free love, free speech, free everything—and my grandmother added the missing ingredient: free peanut butter sandwiches.

To this group of "unloved and unwanted" hippies and society dropouts my grandmother devoted her last days. She purchased an electric cart to rove the streets of Huntington Beach, for much walking was too strenuous for a woman her age. She became quite a welcome figure to the hungry hippies. They loved her and she loved them.

Throughout my grandmother's career as an evangelist she was the center of attraction, especially in the days of the Miami Tabernacle, which was carried to the heights of glory on the wings of her miraculous healing. Yet with all the talk of miracles and power of the Holy Spirit, there seemed to be some profound inconsistencies in her life. These were most evident in her relationship with her husband and in the lives of her children. There is a striking ambiguity in the past glories and present tragedies of the Brandt-Berg family.

A distinct imbalance developed in the family structure of

Virgina Brandt Berg. Due to her domineering personality and great notoriety, her husband was slowly pushed into the background. As time went on, this relationship solidified into a matriarchal family.

Hjalmer Jr., their oldest son, rejected his Christian upbringing and became agnostic as a young adult. Virginia, her only daughter, ran away from home and eloped at age sixteen. Both of their marriages ended in divorce.

And then there was David, her youngest, her pride and joy over whom it had been prophesied—she wrote—that he had been "filled with the Holy Ghost since his mother's womb." It was her lifelong dream that one of her children would follow in the footsteps of her famous father, John L. Brandt, continuing the line of great preachers. She had fully hoped that little David would fulfill this vision. But by 1967 the possibility of fulfilling that dream had vanished. Her son David was, at age forty-nine, a complete failure by all social standards. He had no job and an incomplete education, had been expelled from his only pastorate in Valley Farms, and was—unbeknown to her—bound in the chains of lust and immorality.

When I first encountered my father's problem of immorality at age seven, in his attempts at incest, I was too young to understand his motives. Rather, I was confused and frightened by his actions. Yet my emotions told me he was trying to do something very wrong and evil. From that time on, I was terrified of being left alone with him. At age twelve I was more consciously aware of the "strangeness of his actions," but I still had no understanding of what he was attempting. I determinedly resisted, threatening to jump out the window if he touched me. He tried to explain that he wanted me to fulfill special needs that my mother didn't completely meet. Unlike twelve-year-olds today, I was totally naive about sex, and it wasn't until I was married that I realized what his intentions had been.

This was not the case with my younger sister, Faithy. In 1982 it was revealed to *all* the members of the COG (not just the Berg family) the facts of her incestuous relationship with Dad. During his years with Fred Jordan Dad traveled around the country in a motor home promoting Fred's TV show. Faithy frequently traveled with him. Unlike me, she did not resist him. I entertained the thought on several occasions when I was a teenager, "Could Dad be doing with Faithy what he tried with me?" But he was my father, and I reasoned, "No, surely not." Yet the thought lingered in the back of my mind.

Even in the mind of a child, the untutored conscience is never silent. Evil is not a "psychological development," and the difference between right and wrong is not learned only through courses in a theological seminary. When I was only seven, my conscience spoke loudly and clearly against the father whom I cherished. Right and wrong can be known through the spirit, and evil is resisted in the spirit, even by a seven year-old child.

My father has also revealed through his Mo Letters that he was in no wise faithful to my mother in the years before Huntington Beach. Much of his adultery involved people living in our home such as housekeepers, live-ins, and governesses. "How did your mother put up with it?" people ask me.

My father drew upon the philosophy of "exceptions." He looked to the Bible for cases that would apparently justify his actions and give him grounds for sexual liberty, such as the lives of Solomon, David, and Abraham—all men who had more than one wife. He interpreted these as God's exceptions for His special people, prophets, and anointed leaders. Since my mother couldn't completely satisfy his needs, an exception would have to be made.

My mother was forced to accept this argumentation. Dad was a very persuasive man, and she had no choice but to receive his spiritual and theological reasonings. If she resisted such counsel, she felt she would be resisting the very counsel of God. It is this kind of evil genius that enabled my father to engineer a multinational cult.

It is said that "a man's morality will dictate his theology." This was certainly true in my father's life. His "needs" amounted to lust, nothing more. My mother and father had a perfectly normal marriage relationship, and he had no "need" for extramarital involvement.

This, then, was the scene as the remnants of the Berg Evangelistic Party gathered in Huntington Beach in 1967. But what was wrong? What was the cause of these family problems and disturbing inconsistencies? Why was there such disparity between the Christianity my grandmother preached in public and the absence of Christian fruit in her own home? Why the deep-rooted sin in my father's life? I did not learn the answers to these questions until August 1982.

*   *

In 1982 certain relatives explained to me that my grandmother had not been injured in an auto accident, nor had she been paralyzed for five years. Moreover, her daughter was born during the five years of supposed invalidism.

I was stunned and actually became physically ill for several days upon hearing this news. My grandmother was the person I held most dear in my life; her ministry was the one redeeming factor in my sordid past. The revelation of this delusion was just too much for me to cope with.

I learned that there had indeed been an accident in December 1911, as my grandmother reported in her book. But it did not involve an automobile. Arriving home from the hospital on that Christmas day, my grandfather was carrying his wife from the ambulance to the house. The walkway was icy, he slipped and fell, and Virginia Brandt Berg was thrown out of his arms. Her back struck the curbstone. The back was broken and required an operation.

I have read many personal letters referring to the suffering the accident caused her. But that she was a bedridden invalid for five years is simply not true. From 1911 to 1917 she was quite active in church affairs and even attended graduate school at Texas Christian University. An article written in 1913 reported the arrival of the Rev. H. E. Berg and his wife in Weatherford, Texas, to pastor the Central Christian Church two years after the accident.

> *Another valuable addition to the working force of the church is Mrs. Berg, a woman of exceptional talents. She is a trained church worker, a splendid organizer of splendid accomplishments, and rare executive ability. She is a poet, author, lecturer and preacher, and stands ready at any time to fill the pulpit if*

her husband have need of a substitute. She has lectured through-
out the states on problems of social evils. She will deliver the
regular address at the morning service, tomorrow, Jan. 4th.

In September 1914 her second child, Virginia, was born in
Weatherford. The pregnancy and delivery greatly compounded
the effects of my grandmother's accident, and as a result she
became seriously ill and was confined to bed for a considerable
time. In 1915 the family moved to Ukiah, California; my grandfather resigned the pastorate there in July 1917.

It was in Ukiah that Grandmother's healing was to have occurred. How "miraculous" and "instantaneous" this healing was, I
do not know. However, the pain she had suffered off and on for
years was relieved, making it possible for her to live a more active
life, as her busy evangelistic history testifies. She did, however,
wear a brace for many years and later in life replaced the brace
with a sturdy corset. Was her healing truly "instantaneous"? Did
she walk from "deathbed to pulpit"? Or was the healing gradual,
occuring over a period of weeks or months, the compounded
result of time and many operations?

If my grandmother did have a miraculous healing, why was it
necessary to stretch the truth, to falsify facts? Why testify of five
years of "total" invalidism or an auto accident? Yet she did this
repeatedly. A newspaper article dated August 30, 1927—two
years after the start of the famous Miami Tabernacle—reads,

> *In speaking of her experience regarding her healing, Mrs. Berg*
> *has said to friends: "I was a pitiable invalid for nearly five*
> *years, being confined to bed or a wheel chair, was finally given*
> *up by the doctors and specialists as without the slightest chance*
> *for recovery. . . .*
> *   I was instantly raised and made whole from a bed of un-*
> *speakable suffering. I weighed 82 pounds then. . . .*

The article makes no mention of a daughter being born during
that period. Why should Grandmother neglect that fact? Is it
necessary to fabricate stories about God for people to believe in
Him?

Another, more painful question arises in light of my grandmother's lie: To what extent are parents responsible for the sins of their children? Most people would agree that in the final analysis, a child must himself choose between right and wrong, good and evil; ultimately he is responsible for his moral condition. However, if David Berg learned from his parents—through their lifestyle—a foundational principle that is contrary to Scriptural truth, then they will be responsible for teaching him a false standard for decision-making.

If David Berg grew up with an example of twisting or exaggerating the truth, then he would have learned by the course of nature that it is okay to present facts, even if altered, in such a way as to produce desired results. The result that Virginia Brandt Berg sought after was indeed positive: bringing souls to faith. Therefore, what harm could a slight alteration of the facts do, seeing that it would benefit all, even the cause of Christ? Growing up in this environment, David Berg would have learned in effect that the end justifies the means—a principle that is contrary to everything Christ said and did. It is sheer foolishness to assume that wrong means can be used to gain right ends. The means preexist in and determine the ends! Every cult is founded on the premise that the end justifies the means.

The use of Christianity as a tool to advance not only the gospel, but also one's own personality and personal goals—to build one's fame, popularity, and notoriety—is a subversion of truth. Yet how to separate the work of God from the work of "self" becomes a seemingly impossible judgment. But only impossible to a point. The dividing line between God and self can usually be seen in the personal life of the individual involved. Eventually a person will reap what he has sown. The history of the Children of God bears stark testimony to this truth.

If my grandmother had motives of personal ambition, fame, and glory—if she was in competition with the legacy of her father—she was guilty of deep spiritual error. Christ's command to His disciples was not to *promote* the kingdom of God first of all, but to *seek* the kingdom.

In the years I spent with my grandmother, I saw that it deeply troubled her that her son Hjalmer was so distant. She was mystified why the life of her daughter was marked by great suffering and tragedy. Nor could she understand or accept David's hatred of the church system and his involvement with a man like Fred Jordan. Moreover, she refused to see my dad's moral condition.

I believe it was David Berg's own choice to follow sin. He is ultimately responsible for the degeneracy of his moral state. But I ask, Did he learn from others to use Christianity as a vehicle to get where he wanted to go, to promote selfish desires?

Heredity and environment—factors commonly labeled one's "social heredity"—are the horizontal issues that constantly affect a person's life. But a person's response to his social heredity defines the vertical issues that will take him up or down morally. Parents can greatly influence the horizontal issues of their children's lives, but they cannot determine the vertical issues—that is a matter of a child's personal choice. Yet as a parent I feel responsible for the final moral outcome of my child. When I see one of my children on a downward trend I ask myself, *What have I done wrong? Where have I failed him? What could I have done differently?* I begin to question where I have erred in providing a social heredity that produces wrongful decision-making. I feel responsible for my child's mistakes and voluntarily share blame for his actions.

If a person uses the inherent powers of the gospel to promote his own ends, he bears an identical character with every cult leader on earth—every Jim Jones, Moses David, or Sun Myung Moon. The use of inherent power for the promotion of self is a common denominator of all cults.

If using the gospel for the promotion of self was part of my father's social heredity, then his response to it was to adopt this principle as part of his mental and moral fabric. If he responded to Christianity as a vehicle for self-promotion, then it would follow that he never learned the person of Jesus Christ. My father's character and actions do not reflect a person who has adopted the character and nature of Jesus Christ, nor the ethics of Christian doctrine. He reflects the image of a man bent upon promoting his own goals, fulfilling his desires.

This distorted ethic, having found expression in a lust for sexual pleasure, soon led my father into the next stage of evolution toward satisfying self: power.

David Berg's parents Hjalmer and Virginia Brandt Berg, with Hjalmer Jr., in a photograph taken during the time when Virginia supposedly was a bedridden invalid.

David Berg's career as an evangelist and pastor left him bitter and resentful—a man at odds with himself and with the Christian faith he supposedly represented. He was bitter over what the Christian world had done to his mother and to him. He had failed as a pastor and was in total conflict with scriptural morality. His response: Reject scriptural morality and redefine it. His feelings of inferiority greatly intensified as the compound failures of his life reached flood level, pushing him to achieve a position in which he would be the ultimate authority!

The true condition of my dad in 1967 was that of a faltering ship tossed about on the sea of his own sinfulness. The magnificence and glory of Christianity and the gospel of Jesus Christ had degenerated to nothing more than a tool to advance his selfish purposes and perfidious desires.

And then came the break my dad had been waiting for all his life. In his words, "The hand of the Lord was beginning to move!"

Chapter 3
The Gospel of
Rebellion

The break my dad had been waiting for centered around the activities of a Christian coffee house known as the "Light Club," situated about a hundred yards from the Huntington Beach Pier. Designed to serve as a mission outreach to the youth of the community, the Light Club Mission was directed and supervised by David Wilkerson's organization, Teen Challenge. It had formerly been sponsored by the Full Gospel Business Men's Fellowship.

When Dad and his family arrived in Huntington Beach in December 1967, my grandmother encouraged her grandchildren—Aaron, Hosea, Faithy—and their spouses—to offer their assistance at the Light Club. My family had worked with Teen Challenge off and on for many years, and it was through a Teen Challenge rally held by David Wilkerson in Dallas, Texas, that Faithy dedicated her life to full-time Christian service. Consequently my brothers and sister felt quite comfortable helping out at the Light Club Mission.

Grandmother had been feeding the hippies on the Pier and encouraged the family to get involved in the work with the dropouts. I think she felt it could develop into a new ministry.

"You've got to do something for the hippies!" she said, "Teen Challenge doesn't know how to help. They're just church people offering church meetings, and the hippies don't like it. You need to go down there and get involved, bring some life into that mission!"

They did just that. At first the Berg team simply helped out witnessing and assisting the Teen Challenge staff. However, they proved so effective that they were given access to the mission for their use on weekdays, when it was normally closed. Singing together as a group they called themselves "Teens for Christ." They had great appeal to the youth. Soon the Berg family began to pack the place on weeknights. Teens for Christ had discovered the secret to gathering lost and wayward youth: Free peanut butter sandwiches and live music. It wasn't long before Teen Challenge realized that the Berg family had the key—Feed the stomach and the spirit—and gladly turned the mission over to the industrious Teens for Christ.

By July 1968 the Light Club Mission was being totally supervised by Paul, Jonathan, and Faith Berg. They sang; played their guitars; preached Jesus, endtime prophecy, and the Warning Message; and never mentioned the word *church*. The radical youth loved it. Teens for Christ had a message that was reaching the dropouts. They began to run the mission full-time, keeping it open seven days a week. Local businesses were petitioned to donate free sandwiches for the lost and wayward youth, and they gladly obliged. A steady stream of hungry hippies soon patronized the Light Club.

A new era had arrived, and the Teen Challenge folks hadn't bridged the gap. They couldn't get a shadow of a hippie to walk through their doors, but the Berg family had opened the floodgates. The short-hair, crew-cut, tie-and-sport-coat approach didn't quite mesh with the pot-smoking, free-living, dirty-blue-jeans youth of the Huntington Beach counterculture. Well, my grandmother had the key and my dad and his children had the spiritual liberation to grow their hair and beards, "become one with the hippies," and "do something for the Lord."

The Light Club Mission filled daily with hungry souls—both physically and spiritually—in need of love and direction. It was

this condition that made so many in the hippie generation susceptible to the cults. The counterculture afforded them a vehicle by
which to drop out, but there was nothing to drop into. Everyone
needs a place, and simply being a dropout is good only for a
while; the counterculture deceived the youth because it soon took
on the nature of a sieve: the youth were dropping through its
small but very real holes and finding themselves ever so lost.

It was to this need that my father appealed. There in the
Light Club, the gospel was preached by the "dropout" to the
dropouts. My Uncle Carl nicknamed my dad the "Original Hippie" many years ago. How right he was. David Berg had found his
element: the Original Hippie had found his lost and beleagured
flock of hippies. The shepherd and his sheep united.

Many of the lost youth encountered by Teens for Christ
prayed to receive Jesus as their Savior. Their lives were genuinely
changed. They quit their drugs, immorality, and drinking and
began to develop a sincere love and reverence for God and the
Word of God. Instead of idly passing their hours on the beach,
they would come to the Light Club to hear about Jesus, to read
their Bibles, and to fellowship with other new young Christians.

In March 1968 my grandmother died. By that time a strong
fire of hope was burning in the Huntington Beach Light Club.
For the youth who had fallen through the sieve of the counterculture and found themselves searching for recognition, place, purpose, and leadership, my dad supplied the perfect answer. But
the death of Virginia Brandt Berg marked a turning point for my
father. She was the very last restraining force for morality in his
life. After she died, he pulled out all the stops.

David Berg—in a state of rebellion against the "church system," the American government, his family and religious heritage, and most of all, God—had found an audience of rebellious
youth. He eagerly preached and they eagerly received the Gospel
According to Berg. It was like the cogs of a machine meshing into
perfect synchronization. His bitterness against the church, his rejection of the social establishment and the capitalistic system, his
contempt for parental authority—all crystalized into a Gospel of
Rebellion. The kids understood him; he spoke their heart; there
was no generation gap between the shepherd and his flock. He

talked about the very things that were troubling them, things deep in their hearts, conflicts that they could not resolve; hence they concluded, "He's gotta be speaking the truth. That's exactly what's been bothering me!" David Berg and these searching hippies were, according to my dad, just like Jesus and the original Twelve: Dropouts, system rejects, but truth seekers and "true" lovers of God. A "Revolution for Jesus" was born.

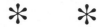

In his condemnation of the present-day society and the parents of the dropouts, David Berg wrote,

> *So you say the youth of today are rebels—rebellious, defiant, lawbreakers and seeking to destroy society. But really, who are the rebels? We, or you, our parents? . . .*
>
> *The kids are rebellious against society because the society is anti-God. Everything the kids are—the way they look, the way they act—in a large degree it's a rebellion against the pattern of society, but it's a return actually to the Lord's pattern.*
>
> *How can they [the youth] rebel against God's laws? How can they rebel against His Word?—They don't know it. But their parents did and they rebelled just like the Children of Israel. The parents were the rebels. Only the children were allowed in the Promise Land.[1]*

And it was he who would lead them to that Promised Land!

By declaring that these youths "never knew the Word of God," my dad accomplished two key goals. First, he cloaked the rebellion of the youth with innocence: they didn't know any better. Moreover, their rebellion was actually a righteous rebellion conforming with the "Lord's pattern." By thus exposing their ignorance, he made a place of great importance for himself in their lives. He would lead them from ignorance to the glorious light of true knowledge. He was laying the foundation, either consciously or unconsciously, for his role as God's Prophet.

Second, by declaring the youths to be innocent of any rebellion—but rather, merely partakers of a spontaneous, honest desire to return to the Lord's pattern—while simultaneously declaring the parents to be the true rebels who had indeed rebelled against God, Dad established the spiritual polarity necessary to alienate these kids from their parents, their churches, and the establishment. There were only two camps: my father's righteous camp and the rebel parent camp. Thus, a return to the parent camp would be a move against the Bible, against God, and against Jesus, to whom they had recently dedicated their lives. Concerning this division, Dad wrote,

> *The parents want them to follow in their footsteps in a selfish dog-eat-dog economy in which they not only murder one another, but they conduct massive slaughters of whole nations. . . .*
>
> *The young people are sick and fed up with what really amounts to a pagan, cruel, whoremongering, false Christianity. They're trying to return to the peace-loving religions of old, including ancient Christianity, and the parents will have none of it.*
>
> *So who are the rebels? If you mean rebels against . . . the looks of the ancients and the economy of the ancients, then the parents are the rebels.*
>
> *But if you mean rebels against this recent modern plastic, artificial man-made, gadget-filled, money crazy, whoremongering, sex-mad, religiously hypocritical society of the parents of today, yes, we the youth of today are rebels and revolutionists. . . . We want to return to the patterns of Noah and Abraham and Moses and the judges and kings, like David and Solomon, and the prophets of old—indeed the pattern of Jesus Christ Himself and His disciples and the martyrs of the Church.*
>
> *Who are the real rebels of today? . . . We are the true lovers of peace and love and truth and beauty and God and freedom: whereas you, our parents, are the most God-defying, commandment-breaking, insanely rebellious rebels of all time, who are on the brink of destroying and polluting all of us and our world if we do not rise up against you in the name of God and try to stop you. . . .* [2]

The youth loved it, and David Berg loved it. Their rebellion had been covered with a robe of royal righteousness: "Truly God has raised him up for such a time as this, just like Moses of old, or David, or Samuel." This was his hour, his destiny. One need not be a psychologist to see the effects of such glorious divine movements of God's hand on these newly converted kids, especially hippie dropouts who were groping for self-respect, self-esteem, and justification for their rebellion against society. David strongly appealed to this need as early as December 1968.

> *What's the matter with these people [speaking of the churches]? Why are they so afraid of us? Let's face it, it's the power of God! They're afraid of God and* you *represent God!*
>
> *The community is actually afraid of us! Why do they get all uptight when we walk into a church? They're afraid! They're scared! What are they afraid of? . . . It's God, let's face it! You got'm scared, kids! Hallelujah! You got'm scared!*[3]

The formerly lost, hungry, dirty, groping, and confused hippie had suddenly become "God's representative," and the world was trembling at his presence! It was a gospel of Rebellion utterly confused with truth and lie, and the youth fell willingly into line. The sad part is that my dad truly believed he was following God. His hatred and bitterness had destroyed his ability to see the error of his way. He was a confused man, blinded by bitterness, hatred, and the guilt of his own sin. My father was not doing this to glorify God, but merely to salvage his own ego. Rather than face himself in the light of his failure and sin, he chose to support his failure with the following and adoration of rebellious youth.

A principle tool my father used to develop his worldwide organization of full-time workers was the doctrine of "Forsaking All." It is based on the biblical story of three fishermen: Simon Peter, James, and John. They had been fishing all night but had caught nothing, whereupon Jesus commanded Simon to cast his net just one more time; when he did, he enclosed a great number of fish. This miracle, coupled with the call of Christ to "follow Me," was sufficient evidence for the three men to dedicate their lives to Jesus and His public ministry. Luke 5:11 records,

> *And when they had brought their ships to land, they* forsook all, *and followed him.*

In Luke 14:33 Jesus says,

So likewise, whosoever he be of you that forsaketh not all that
he hath, *he cannot be my disciple.*

The concept of leaving father, mother, job, home, land, and any
other social influence was essential for full-time discipleship to
Christ, my dad taught. In Huntington Beach it was the challenge
we put to all the hippies: "Come! Forsake all and follow Jesus."
Most of them had forsaken all anyway—they were well-ac-
customed to leaving family and home and job. It required only a
slight variation in the direction of their lives to get them to do it
for Jesus' sake. I think my dad was merely "christianizing" the
nationwide desire to drop out. For a minority it was not quite so
easy to forsake all, for they were more closely tied to family, job,
or school. So the call to 100 percent dedication was one of the
experiences in common that gave us such a deep sense of camaraderie and commitment. Each disciple there knew that the other
fellow had paid the same initiation fee as he—everyone had forsaken all. We were all common fellows in the same boat, rowing
the same direction, paying the same price.

It was the Endtime, and we had dropped out in order to drop
into God's Endtime movement to warn the wicked of their ways
and inform the American nation of its impending destruction. It
didn't matter if one quit school and dropped out: the end was
coming soon, so who needed an education?

"Forsake All" became one of the greatest sales tools in making the final appeal. "So you say you love Jesus? That you want to
obey His commandments? Well, it says right here that 'he that
forsaketh not all that he hath cannot by My disciple'! What do you
think of that? Are you going to be a lukewarm Christian like all
the rest of the church hypocrites? We're following Jesus full-time!
We're real disciples, just like the original Twelve! We've forsaken
all to follow Jesus! Have you? We love you, brother, so come along
with us and win the world for Jesus. Be one of the chosen few!
Receive an hundredfold in this life and in the world to come."

It was a strong message, especially in those times. Long before some other modern cults were getting people to leave their

families, my dad was in California persuading kids to leave their homes and follow him. My dad writes concerning the importance of forsaking all,

> *Once you have chosen God and His way, He refuses to take second place to anything or anybody and will not let you put any other gods before Him—not your old job nor your old boss nor even your old family and friends. This is God's first test for every disciple: To see if he loves Him enough to put Him first by forsaking all immediately to follow Him now!*[4]

The concept of Forsake All became a foundation stone for initiating the practice of Flirty Fishing several years later.

Anything short of full-time service was deemed a spirtual failure. Who wants to be a failure? We learned the art of the "hard sell" in getting youth to buy the whole package. It wasn't long before the Berg family had collected quite a following. My dad recalls those early days with great excitement.

> *The Lord knew it was time and it was what the kids needed! We had the message, the method and the music! Things were just booming!*
>
> *Then things began to get too hot for us! We got all that publicity, front-page headlines everyday in Huntington Beach, Costa Mesa and Santa Ana, and the System began to fight, and we began to have arrests.*[5]

About twenty-five youths were arrested for picketing and witnessing on the school campuses in the winter of 1968-69. As I look back now, I can see that Dad simply adopted the rebellious activities of the politically radical youth of the day, cloaking it in the name of Christ and the guise of religious protest. It was an age of defiance, and he capitalized on it by redirecting the youthful desire to rebel and protest. He writes,

> *We picketed churches, jails and schools! We had sit-ins, march-ins, protests and everything the kids loved, everything that*

was radical! *It was just going great! Terrific!—And I loved it! I was masterminding the whole thing from behind the scenes with Jesus.*

Nobody ever saw me hardly, or even knew who I was or I existed!

We'd walk into these churches 50, 60, 70, 80 strong! It scared them half to death! Some of them called the cops, and finally things got too hot for us! We had our big explosion, our big boom, our big initial start, push, and then the persecution came and we had to get out of town.[6]

My father was in his glory during the early days. His chance for power had finally materialized. But even then he showed his true colors as a coward and began running from the law; he has been running scared ever since. He says,

They were planning as usual to get the big boy when they found out he was me! They were going to charge me with this, that and the other, contributing to the delinquency of minors and all kinds of stuff.

That's when we hit the road. . . .[7]

By April 1969 the Teens for Christ, directed by David Berg, would leave Huntington Beach after causing no small stir among the local community and churches.

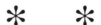

In the early days at Huntington Beach and during the formative years of the Children of God, we preached salvation in Jesus Christ and the Bible According to David Berg. It is important to note that there were many youths who found the Lord through this ministry, who had genuine life-changing experiences. This cannot be denied. We preached John 3:16 right out of the King James Bible, and consequently many people prayed an earnest prayer of repentance, asking forgiveness for their sins and confessing faith in Christ as the Son of God for the remission of sin.

This is why so many people say to this day, "Oh, but it started out good. Berg just got off the track in later years." Not so. Spiritual rebellion never starts off good. There is a fine line, eternally vital, which must be drawn between the place where the work of man stops and the place the Work of God begins.

Even though these youths had found Christ as a result of a ministry triggered by my dad and his rebellion, it was through the power of the gospel of Jesus Christ that lives were changed. Neither my dad nor the Teens for Christ can take credit for that. Salvation is a work of God, not man. It is a grave error to justify a man or his movement on its apparent success or failure, as so many have done with the COG. It must be judged upon its conformity to the principles and truths of Scripture. The mature, discerning eye could have seen upon closer examination that things were afoul in my dad's group from the start. But the uninitiated, immature youths of that day merely looked at the outward appearance. Unbeknown to them, there was another force at work underlying all the apparent good that was being done.

What was that other force? It was an evil that would subvert and totally disease the entire work—the same evil that had diseased my father. The foundation on which my dad built his movement was rebellion. Spiritual rebellion is a cancer that starts with one tiny cell, infects the next cell, and begins to spread; given time it will consume the entire body and kill the life force. The COG was diseased from its onset; it was destined to bring itself to spiritual destruction.

Rebellion feeds on pride. My dad saturated us in feelings of spiritual pride and superiority. This must be done to balance out the guilt and silence the conscience. Spiritual pride will ultimately lead to a self-righteous religion of works. In "Jesus People or a Revolution," my dad writes:

> *We, like Jesus Christ and his disciples, are living our revolution, God's Revolution, His Revolution. . . .*
>
> *This is the real, one and only, genuine revolution that'll ever survive, because this is the revolutionary Kingdom of God and Jesus Christ!*
>
> *The so-called Jesus People [referring to a youth organization known as the "Jesus People"], this Churchianity, little*

churchy-kid, System-kid, so-called, "Jesus Outfit" . . . they're not living it—they haven't quit their jobs, they haven't forsaken all, they're not on the streets all day, every day trying to tell folks about Jesus! They haven't dropped out of the damned Whore, the abominable churchianity system! They haven't dropped out of the damned commercial system, their job and all the rest of it! They don't have any revolution! They couldn't begin to hold a candle to you!

You, the Children of God, are God's Revolution for this hour and this day! You're it!

So, don't let the Jesus People worry you!—Just feel sorry for them! Poor people, still slaves of the System, still slaves of the Devil. They may be saved by Jesus but they're still working for the Devil. . . .

We are the one and only absolute and total real genuine revolution in the whole world! We are it! We are God's children![8]

Thus, the Children of God movement was a mixture of salvation through Jesus Christ and hatred of the established church system, rejection of the government and society, abhorrence and rebellion toward parental values and authority, and a call for total dedication to the real Revolution for Jesus.

If one can grasp an understanding of the evil inherent in the principle of spiritual rebellion—how it works on the minds and egos of people, especially youth, and what its far-reaching consequences are—then it can be understood how groups such as the Children of God can start out apparently harmless, under the banner of religion and Jesus Christ, doing good and having outward signs of benefit in the lives of drug addicts and lost youth, and eventually grow to be totally corrupt—carrying thousands of seemingly "fine young Christians" into corruption and reprobation. This is the nature of the cultic experience, of rebellion, of sin—even when cloaked in the garments of the gospel of Jesus Christ and the guise of religion. This form of deception is not unique to the COG and other cults; many spheres of our society are in a similar condition.

Chapter 4
The Conception

When reports about the Children of God appear in the broadcast or publishing media, there is rarely any mention of the person who bears great responsibility for the birth of Moses David as Prophet.

> *You [Maria] were always the strongest.—You started it all! You were the strongest from the beginning. You prayed and talked in tongues, and all I did was interpret. You did it all—& the Lord—& I was just a poor weak old decrepit instrument.*[1]

The day after Teens for Christ left Huntington Beach, my dad began an adulterous relationship with Karen Zerby, now known in the Family as Maria. She was to become the Prophet's scribe and wife, the No. 1 Queen of the Children of God. However, she did not assume this role all at once; it developed over a period of six to eight years.

My father writes much later about his first involvement with Maria in April 1969.

The first night out, while they were all in this house at this meeting, you went to bed. I stayed out in the Camper usually reading or doing work or writing letters, and I just went back there and you were sleeping on the top bunk. I always kissed everybody goodnight, and we got to kissing goodnight, and ahem, we really got to kissing!—And from then on it was love at first sight! (Maria: Oh, it was love at first sight, before, when I first saw you!)[2]

I remember when Karen first joined the group. She was shy and introverted, a rather homely girl with a bad case of acne and crooked, protruding teeth. My father's sudden interest must have been extremely flattering to her ego and marvelous for her self-esteem. His interest quickly led to lust, and they began an immoral relationship that has continued for more than fifteen years. Apparently Karen greatly needed personal attention and was vulnerable to anyone who was a leader or offered a strong father image; she had already become infatuated with my husband, Jethro. My father recalls this incident:

That's when you [Maria] broke down and wept and confessed you were in love with Jeth and what could you do, a man with a wife and 3 children! So I told then, "Well, how would you like a promotion?" (Maria: "The best cure for an old love is a new love!") So I dropped some pretty heavy hints I guess, huh? Ha, ha!

Can you remember why you made the decision to come with us instead of staying there with a nice secure job?—You decided to hit the road with the Old Rascal! (Maria: "Well, I knew who was the boss!") Ha, ha, pretty smart Leo, she came with the top officer! So you joined us in the camper then.

I'll never forget when we first met in Grandma's dining room: You came in for supper and you gave me that cute little kiss. You won my heart with that first kiss, Honey, so soft and sweet. I thought, "Wow, she looks like a little prudish church girl, but she sure don't taste like it!"[3]

The need for self-acceptance often finds expression in sexual sin and immorality. People have a basic need for love and the assurance they are needed and have worth. My father and Maria met on this ground and greatly complemented each other. Two very insecure people, they attracted like magnets, instantly filling each other's voids.

> *I think I'd really given up on myself. I figured my day was over, and Mother [Jane Berg] had given up on me. It almost looked like God had given up on me because I wasn't seeming to accomplish anything.*
>
> *Then Maria came along, and all of a sudden I found somebody who believed in me! She just trusted and believed and I didn't dare fail her. So I stepped out by faith and depended upon the Lord and I delivered, and here we are!*
>
> *It was her faith! I'm sure when we get to heaven God's going to give her all the credit.[4]*

Knowing my dad as I do, he never could have done what he has without the help of a "Maria" to support his fear and insecurity; he was just too weak in his character.

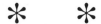

Dad's fledgling group went to Tucson, Arizona, from Huntington Beach in the spring of 1969. I believe it was in Tucson that my mother found out about Dad's relationship with Maria.

Mother, Dad, several family members, and Maria were all staying in their twenty-eight-foot Dodge motor home in the driveway of a friend's house. Jethro and I and our three children were staying in our trailer in front of the same house. There an unpleasant crisis occurred between my dad and mother, but the whole incident was kept very hush-hush. Mother began to spend more and more time away from the motor home, passing her hours in the house. She was continually red-eyed, obviously from crying.

Absolutely nothing was ever discussed openly about this incident. However, knowing my dad and his past record, I assumed that Mom had once again found him sleeping with one of the girls in their little group. At the time I only suspected it might be Maria. Dad's own account of the beginning of the adulterous affair, confirming what I had suspected, was not published until 1980.

During the summer of 1969, Jethro and I stayed briefly in Tucson with a small group of about twenty-five disciples, then we moved on to Fort Worth, Texas. Mother took another group to Florida. Dad's team moved to El Paso, and there it split up into three groups. He took one group of about seventy followers with him as he eventually went north to Laurentides, Canada, near Montreal.* Other groups from "Teens for Christ" scattered throughout the United States to witness and win disciples.

It was in Laurentide that my father began to receive dramatic "prophecies" that would solidify his relationship with Maria and have immense significance in his role as "the Prophet of God." But Dad was in seclusion; none of the disciples really knew what was going on.

Maria's role was crucial. It was very difficult for his own children to see David Berg as anything but father. For me to suspend that part of my intellect and belief—envisioning him as God's Endtime Prophet—was always a source of great doubt. To David Berg, of course, this was of the devil: doubts were *always* of the devil. Moreover, I believe this element of disbelief was even more critical for my mother, who knew all her husband's faults and weaknesses. Anyone who knew David Berg as a "natural man" threatened his status as a prophet. Thus, Maria's role served to affirm the prophetic persona in a way that David Berg's own family could not.

The unseen powers of destiny were moving in the hearts and minds of David Berg and his followers. The seed of "a mighty prophet of God" had been germinated, and the passion of human faith and adoration of his disciples triggered the conception of an organization that would nurture his role as prophet. Fate would soon bring all of this together in a dramatic display of spiritual harmony, and the world would unknowingly witness the birth of a prophet and the birth of a cult.

---

*In all his writings and among the Royal Family, the place has been known as "Laurentide," although the proper name of the town adds an *s*. The COG's usage, without the *s*, is given henceforth in this book

Chapter 5
The Birth of a Cult

With the exodus from Huntington Beach, "Teens for Christ" became a fragmented group of young Christians vaguely following the leadership of "Uncle David." But the winds of change were blowing, and some very special happenings were going on in Laurentide.

My dad likened his time in Laurentide to the forty days Moses spent on the mountain with God, for it was in Laurentide that he began to formulate the principles by which his movement would henceforth be governed. The Children of God history about Moses David records,

> It was there in Laurentide that the Family first began to organize itself as a New Nation, ordaining Bishops, Elders, Deacons, and Deaconesses to lead the work of reaching the youth of the world with the love of Jesus.
>
> It was there too, in August, that David received the revelation "Old Love, New Love," further revelations about the "Old Church, New Church."[1]

Dad couldn't wait to get together all the disciples that had scattered throughout the United States and make them privy to these special "divine" revelations. And so the word went out and all the teams migrated to Vienna, Virginia, near Falls Church. We congregated at the home of a sympathetic friend who had gone away for a few weeks on vacation; he graciously offered us the use of his house and property.

By this time all the teams were used to living on the road, so it was easy to pull up in our assorted vans and trailers and begin living in and around this house.

In the house we divided sleeping quarters, some for the boys and some for the girls: in those days we had strict, puritanical moral codes. The kitchen crew went busily to work preparing meals, which was always a big chore—even prophets have to eat. The older and more spiritually mature disciples taught Bible classes to the newer converts. Dad stayed in his motor home, complete with "secretaries" and other intimates. He concentrated his efforts on teaching the "Leadership Trainees." He was very strong in the beginning about "training the future leaders" of the group, those who would no doubt be the future rulers of God's Kingdom. He carefully selected the most promising leadership and personally saw to it that they were filled with the truth. They in turn would be able to teach others. What was the subject matter of their teaching?—Apart from classes on personal witnessing and salvation, we taught "the Message of Jeremiah": "Woe to this nation and all those who forget God!" It was a message of doom.

Dad had concluded, through "direct revelation," that his message to the nation and the world was one of destruction. The U.S. would be destroyed because of its iniquity. He spent a great deal of time teaching this special message to his followers in lengthy Bible studies, in Vienna, using as his platform the Old Testament passages which, according to his interpretation, related directly to the United States. Just as ancient Israel forsook the Lord and was subsequently judged by God at the hands of the Babylonians, so America would soon be judged by God. It was imminent! We had only a short time to get this message out; destruction could come at any time! As a faithful prophet one could not be concerned about himself, but only with "getting out the message." To forsake oneself totally in this task, before it was too late, was imperative. The blood and souls of the people would be required of those of us who failed to be obedient to this calling. God would hold those who failed to warn the wicked personally responsible. However, if we warned them and they didn't respond, then it was okay—God would let us off the hook, because we had been obedient.

We began to preach the message of doom with such zeal and determination that countless youths were convinced of the validity of the warning. Those who turned a deaf ear to our proclamation were simply rejecting the word of the Lord. We kept right on going for God, undaunted by people's disrespect and unconcern for the special truth God had given us. This single-minded determination permeated the disciples of David Berg. People rarely see such loyalty and determination except in the fanatical zeal of "freedom fighters" or in liberation groups such as the Palestine Liberation Organization (PLO). David Berg's disciples were sold out 100 percent.

While this training was growing in intensity, Dad had yet to clear up his relationship with Maria. Living in adultery was not then an accepted Christian practice among the followers of David Berg, and people were becoming suspicious. Dad knew it was imperative that the top leadership and his personal family recognize and accept his adultery. It was especially important that his own family accept it, as our support was vital to the formation of the movement.

I can remember with explicit detail the occasion when the "truth" was revealed! It happened during one of our long leadership meetings in the Vienna house. Only the top leaders—the team leaders—were present. My brother Aaron began to prophesy over his father; his message declared in effect that Dad should reveal the special truth the Lord had given him in Laurentide and not be ashamed of it. This started the session that would irrevocably set the course of the Children of God.

Dad responded to Aaron's prophecy by saying, "Well, I didn't know or think the Lord wanted me to make this public, but He must feel it's pretty important."

My father began to explain how "it" happened and that it

wasn't his idea, but that the "Lord just did it." He "never intended for it to happen," nor "to hurt anyone, especially the dear wife" that had been so faithful to him for over twenty-five years. . . . And then the tears began to flow.

Dad erupted in an overflow of emotion, of weeping. Through his tears he began to explain the whole affair—the "Spirit's moving him." His talk was directed mainly towards his children and wife, emphasizing over and over again that it wasn't his idea: "I don't want to hurt anyone. I don't want to hurt my family. It's all the Lord's doing!" he sobbed.

There came a great deal more crying and tears, as "the Lord" began to "break" others too. Some of the disciples present started prophesying messages directed toward my dad, encouraging him to reveal this new truth, assuring him that if he would just try, God would give him the necessary strength to tell it all.

By this time everyone was bursting with curiosity as to what this "truth" could be. So they kept prophesying and praying that the Lord would give him the strength to give the true words of God. Such a martyr in the eyes of all present—to bear the excruciating weight of the truth of God! How unselfish and sacrificial!

"Oh, but I never wanted this!" he cried. "It was all the Lord's doing! I don't know why God chose me to bear this burden. I'm so unworthy of such honors. I'm so unworthy." By the time he had finished, everyone felt sorry for him, including me. He was such a humble man. So broken. So meek.

This session lasted nineteen hours, all through the night until daybreak.

Eventually it all came out: the "Old Church, New Church" prophecy that Dad and Maria had received in Laurentide. This was the "truth" everyone had waited to hear. Maria was the New Church, the New Bride, and my mother was the old decrepit Church System. The prophecy gave Dad license to reject my mother because she represented the established church organization of the world, which God had rejected. Maria, on the other hand, was God's new bride and therefore Dad's new bride, because she represented God's new church.

Until this time I hadn't cried. But when Dad and Maria began reading the prophecies containing horrible things about my mother, I was shaken. I had always considered my mother to be loving and kind. The prophecy greatly confused me: it was cruel and harsh. How was it possible that she was guilty of spiritual whoredoms, unfaithfulness to God and His prophet? The prophecy stated,

> *This little one, My infant church, my little one, My beloved, shall be raised upon My knees with fondling care and tender love and My protection and shall be delivered from all these things which shall befall her.*[2]

In the prophecy Maria represents collectively all the young people who were presently following my dad or who would join the COG in the future. They were the "called-out ones," chosen by God to represent His New Church, who would faithfully follow God's Endtime Prophet. In reality we were rebellious youth, groping for meaning and purpose; the abundant talk and gracious promises concerning the glory of God, being special among all the peoples of the earth, and ushering in God's Eternal Kingdom were music to our ears. We were saturated in the spirit of martyrdom and righteous sacrifice.

> *This little one hath forsaken all—houses and lands and family and friends and have made themselves of no reputation and have worn the tattered sackcloth dipped in blood and carried the simple staff of power and been enyoked in the bondage of My love and obedience to My slightest command.*[3]

On and on Dad prophesied, speaking as the voice of God. He described the wretched spiritual state of the organized church and of my mother:

> *Her house is left unto her utterly desolate. Therefore, she doth attack thee [Maria] in fury and attempt to cast thee forth. And she shall be left alone and desolate as those things that she honoured most. . . . The men whose opinions thou lovest shall destroy thee and the Beast whose honour thou favorest shall devour thee. O thou backsliding daughter! Why dost thou not*

*repent of thy spiritual whoredoms? For thou has had many lov-
ers. . . . They shall rend from her her attire and make her naked
and bare. For I, the Lord, have done it that I may glorify My
Name and preserve her whom I love—My infant Church, My
little ones. . . .* [4]

(It's interesting that God speaks in King James English.)

This was but one of the many prophecies my father received
in Laurentide. These prophecies were given while he and Maria
were alone together in the motor home. Maria would speak in
tongues and Dad would interpret in the form of prophecy. The
spirit was giving her the message straight from God in an unknown language; she had the "gift" of tongues and Dad had the
gift of interpretation translating this heavenly tongue. Team-
work. Years later he said, "You prayed in tongues and all I did
was interpret."

In 1980 my dad had the audacity to write the following concerning my mother,

> *We went from there [El Paso] on up to Laurentide, Cana-
> da. . . . By that time you [Maria] and I were living together
> steadily. Mom left on her own free will, because she always
> preferred her own ministry to me, and I guess so to this day.*[5]

My father's lack of sensitivity in this statement is appalling, clearly
showing that all natural sensitivity had been destroyed. Consumed with lust for women, Dad says that my mother left him in
El Paso and stopped traveling with them of "her own free will."
How could she possibly bear the mental and emotional strain of
traveling in a twenty-eight-foot motor home while he was living
"steadily" with Maria? It was his desire that they all sleep happily
in the same bed. After thirty years of marriage he suddenly
brought a girl younger than his own daughter into his bed and
expected my mother to accept it like a Sunday brunch. He concluded that "Mom left because she wanted her own ministry." No
doubt she wanted to maintain her sanity. This incident reveals
that my father's perversion was growing at geometric proportions
as early as spring 1969.

Sin had so twisted my dad's mind, heart, and conscience that he no longer had any natural feelings for the woman with whom he had lived for thirty years. He was a man imprisoned by his own lusts, consumed with the desire to satisfy self, regardless of the consequences or the lives he would hurt or destroy. His own wife was the first to feel the tormenting fire of his burning lusts.

The prophecy further said of my mother,

> . . . *This one that would save her life and her reputation with the Beast . . .*
>
> *They claim to be Mine—My wife—My church—but the relationship is in name only. They have no other communion. They have no other intercourse and they bear no children. Therefore, this is hypocrisy and not a marriage. This is pretense and not love.*[6]

The prophecy did leave my mother a slight way of escape: repentance.

> *I cannot bear their abominations, but I would pluck them as one from the dung heap and as her that hath been cast aside. . . .*
>
> *And if they shall cry unto Me, even these should call unto Me and upon My name in repentance and in turning I would yet forgive, but I would not save their system.*[7]

My mother was humiliated beyond imagination in front of all those present in the room. As I sat stunned over the trauma of what was happening, the prophecy suddenly turned to threaten Dad's own children. He knew exactly how we would react. He knew our first reaction would be to defend Mother. Looking back, I see plainly that he carefully covered all possible areas of opposition.

> *But there shall be those of her children that shall say . . . "Why dost thou not honour this, our mother? Has she not been faithful through many years and ages and times? Why, therefore dost thou disown her and dishonour her to us, and take unto thee this one [Maria, the New Church] who is nothing—contemptible in*

her sight, despicable unto us, who is nobody, and how doth thou flaunt her in our face to shame us and dishonour our Mother?"8

There we sat, the seed-stock of God's New Nation, weeping, praying, wailing, and prophesying. It was quite a scene. My mother was leaning against the wall, on the perimeter of events. Out of shame and fear I dared not even look at her; I could hear her soft, quiet sobbing.

As the meeting progressed, Dad continued to read the prophecy that further justified and glorified Maria and the important place she was to have in his life.

> *This which is despised of men shall be glorified by the Lord, and that which is put down by man shall be highly exalted by the Lord. She [Maria] which is despised and caused to be ashamed shall in due time be highly exalted.*
>
> *Therefore, restore thou her to that position to which I have appointed her, and give her the honor which is her due! For she shall serve Me and My house as the Queen which I have ordained her for in that time I have called her to!9*

Further warning was spelled out to dad's children and specifically to mother: The inner circle of leadership must accept his relationship with Maria or suffer the consequences.

> *Lest I come suddenly upon thee in My wrath and destroy thee who would despise the Word of the Lord! . . . Who art thou to question Me and to whom shall I answer? . . . for thou art My Queen and thou shalt reign with me forever!—And thine accusers shall be cast into outer darkness, and there shall be weeping and wailing and gnashing of teeth! . . . and they which did condemn thee shall kneel at thy feet and ask for water. . . . Therefore, who art thou, O man, that judgest another? Beware lest thou be judged of Him that shall judge all men—for thine iniquity in abhorring that which I have called clean and rejecting that which I have cleansed, and despising that which I have honored! Repent thou, quickly, lest I come to thee in My wrath and put down the accusers before her face! For she is Mine and she is married unto Me.10*

The scene was getting pretty hot for the personal members of David Berg's household! The Prophet's children were suddenly in danger of losing their position.

> *Not they that wear the garments of the relatives and who bear relationship in name only, but love Me not, neither obey Me, nor honour Me, but honour themselves and obey themselves and follow their own way and lift themselves on high and brag of their relationship with Me in name only.*
> *For they do not the things that I ask and they know Me not, and they lie not with Me in the bed of love. . . neither do they look up unto Me to be guided with Mine eye, My wish their command, as doth this one.[11]*

Even then my father's prophecies were steeped in perverse, sexual verbiage. His subtle innuendo of incest—the phrase "they lie not with me in the bed of love"—was a direct reference to me.

Now our heads were on the chopping block! We couldn't slip by simply on our name, by the fact that we were blood relatives. His four children had to declare their allegience to the Prophet. I can remember all four of us going before him, one by one, to bow down and confess our loyalty to Dad and Dad alone—excluding mother. We confessed that we believed his words were from God and that we agreed with all the prophesied statements about mother.

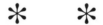

After this session, Mother was sent off to a small room in the house to be by herself and to pray. Dad retired to his motor home with Maria. Mother had a decision to make: Would she accept the situation with a cheerful, repentant attitude? There would be no begrudging compliance. She must show a spirit of repentance for her spiritual whoredoms and do it cheerfully. In the morning she would give her answer to Dad, and he in turn would let her know his decision—that is, would he allow her to return to the motor home and stay within the "inner" circle, or would it be necessary for her to follow as a normal disciple?

Early in the morning, so as not to be discovered, I went to visit my mother in the little room.

"Mother, are you all right?" I asked. "I wanted to make sure you were okay. I was afraid you might do something drastic." I had no idea what she might do after such a traumatic session. "Mother, I love you very much and consider you the best mother in the world. I don't believe that those things they said about you are true. I don't believe them at all."

"Oh, honey!" she sobbed. "Don't you worry about me. The Lord will take care of me. I'm used to getting all the blame."

"But what do you think about all this? Is there something about your relationship with Dad I don't know? Was it really that bad?"

Her face was drawn and pale. She had passed the night alone in that room, crying, without anyone to comfort her. She didn't answer me; with bloodshot eyes she stared into the past.

"What is going on?" I asked. "What about all those horrible things he said about you! Are you going away?"

"No, honey, I'm not going away. We need to stay united; we need to go on together. We must stay united as a family and believe in your dad. God has anointed him for a special ministry." Rather than face the truth about Dad, she covered the guilt and clung to a malignant faith. That day she returned to the motor home. She had accepted her new position "cheerfully." She agreed to be No. 2 in the relationship. Supposedly Dad was happy; she was happy; Maria was happy; God was happy. We had all yielded to His voice and accepted His direction. We had followed the voice of God's Prophet.

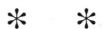

To think that one prophecy caused me to turn against my mother, whom I had greatly loved for twenty-four years, is frightening. My mother had always been the shining example of self-sacrifice, kindness, and love. To me she was the finest example of a Christian mother that a child could have. Yet in one day that was all turned around. One prophecy had altered the realities of history: "God was now doing a great thing in Dad's life! Mother was the Old Church, a spiritual whore. Maria the New Bride!"

I had yielded my will and self to a sex-mad mind. I had done exactly what the people of Germany did as a collective body during Hitler's carnage of the Jewish race. How and why did this happen?

My father possessed immense power, as demonstrated in Vienna, Virginia. This power can be viewed and analyzed from many perspectives. Roy Wallis, professor of sociology at the Queen's University in Belfast, has studied David Berg and the Children of God in light of the phenomenon of charisma. Wallis refers to charisma in the traditional sense, that is, an individual's personal appeal or power to fascinate and attract others; he does not refer to the present-day, popular connotation of being endowed with charismatic gifts of the Holy Spirit. In *The Social Construction of Charisma* Professor Wallis examines the dynamics of charisma in leadership, people's need for acceptance, and their willingness to give full devotion and support to a man such as my father. I value his insight and understanding. He writes,

> *Becoming charismatic is not a once-and-for-always thing. It is a crucial feature of charisma that it exists only in its recognition by others. It must be constantly reinforced and reaffirmed or it no longer exists. The charismatic leader, and those about him, must find means constantly to secure the reaffirmation required.*
>
> *Berg achieved this continual recognition in the same way he generated it originally, that is, through a system of exchanges. Berg would single people out for special attention, affection and praise; they too believed that they were achieving what they aspired to, namely, devoting their lives to the service of God. Having rejected worldly standards, only through Berg's recognition could they know that they were achieving what God willed.*
>
> *Flattered that they should receive so much attention and concern from God's prophet, they in turn were only too willing to accept the status accorded them and thereby confirm the status of Mo as God's oracle to reaffirm his conception of himself, to support his aspirations, and to encourage him at any point at which he felt disheartened, unsuccessful, or when the possibility arose in his mind that things were not as he thought—that he*

was not doing God's will in all this. Like Maria earlier, they too encouraged him to take himself absolutely seriously . . . to see this as something more than merely the passing whimsical thought or action of an individual, but indeed as a divinely ordained revelation from God.[12]

Hence, there was a mutual feeding of Prophet and disciple. Only the most loyal believers could be around the Prophet, and as his role as prophet intensified, Maria's part to play in protecting the prophet grew in direct proportion. Wallis writes on the need for loyalty,

But a consequence of the precariousness of charisma is the leader's need for total acceptance and recognition by those around him. Less than complete commitment, less than full submission, the withholding of anything demanded by the prophet was a denial of his status, a denial that all his words originated in God's will, that all his demands were privileges granted by God, a denial of his worth. The claim to be God's Endtime Prophet was a claim that could be sustained only by complete devotion, and the uncritical respect and adoration of those around him.[13]

It was quite necessary for David Berg to keep around him only the most "loyal" followers. As time went on, he was forced to push out his immediate family and replace them with truly loyal disciples. Life was a continual purge to prove who were the most loyal. Loyalty was measured by belief: by accepting Moses David's new doctrines and his new revelations from God. One by one, with Maria's help, he began to remove his own children and in-laws from his immediate staff (those who actually lived with him). On this theme Wallis writes,

They [those protecting the prophet] will seek to exclude from interaction with the prophet all who might see him in terms of some earlier identity or who—by the nature of their interaction with him—undermine or discredit his identity as a prophet, . . . for example, those who know and continue to treat him as a father, husband, or mere expositor of the Bible.[14]

As we were pushed out little by little over a period of years, Maria grew to be more powerful and consequently more assertive. The "sweet, meek, little kitten" began to feel the intoxicating lust of power and soon exhibited the cunning of a street-wise cat. Her desire for power, hidden at first, shortly emerged and burgeoned into "the Queen!" Wallis writes of Maria on this subject while analyzing the early days of her relationship with Mo:

> *Although we do not have an explicit statement from Maria, we must assume it was also a matter of significance for her, and that moreover, she wished not only to continue the relationship, but also to see it legitimized. Doubtless, given the nature of the movement at that stage, and her own background, she would not have wished to be construed merely as an adulteress. The issue was resolved by an ideological innovation, one which represented the new relationship as a type of God's relationship with the church.*[15]

What we see at work here is the beginning stage of an important principle that lies at the root of every cultic organization—namely, of all who become involved in a cult, none can boast of completely "pure" motives. There is something to gain for everyone. The notion of "innocent" victims is a myth. No one involved with the COG or any other cult has been a totally innocent victim.

It is important for people touched by the cultic experience in some way—as follower or follower's parent—to realize that cults feed a specific need in a person's life. Whether it is a trauma, a need for excitement, a need for acceptance, a lust for power or position, escape from moral obligation or responsibility, or a desire to rebel—whatever the reason, people join a cult because they see something in it for themselves. Each person has a specific motive—albeit the motives may be different.

Deep-rooted selfishness is at the basis of all cults. Following God's Prophet paid great spiritual dividends and offered vital support for one's self-image. The COG was built upon a lie: the lie of the self. We who stayed in it grew into an ever-deepening, self-oriented religion and lifestyle. We did not serve God; rather, He served us. The image of God that we had formulated became our servant: the magic justifier to twist reality in such a way as to conveniently conform to our perspective.

My father had started the ball rolling: "Need a new wife? Want to get rid of the old one?" Simple: take it to the Lord and get a prophecy. In just a few short years we would all be following Dad's pattern. Our God was easy to work with; He would agree to almost anything. Mo was our intercessor; those who followed him did it ultimately for selfish reasons. Concerning this process, Wallis writes,

> *During its early years in particular, members saw the movement as "bearing good fruit" in changing people's lives through acceptance of Jesus, and also saw the movement itself as exemplifying a near ideal way of life of self-sacrifice and mutual love in community. If Mo was the author of this way of life and these "good fruit," then he must indeed be walking close with God, and hearing from Him more clearly than anyone else around. The sense of mystery that Mo cultivated was also transmitted to the followers. Typically knowing nothing of Mo when recruited into the Family by others, they would demonstrate their commitment and trustworthiness. At such a stage, their leader might share with them—in secrecy and with due deference—one of Mo's letters and the information that Mo was their leader and guide, and that he was directly guided by God. They were drawn into a group of "cognoscenti," and validating Mo's claim to prophetic status was thus also to validate their own claim to be part of an inner, knowing elite, party to great secrets.[16]*

In his assessment of the process of "dual validation," Wallis has pinpointed with critical accuracy the spiritual principle defined in the Bible in the Book of James: "Every man is tempted, when he is drawn away of his own lust, and enticed" (1:14). The disciple of Moses David was drawn slowly, yet voluntarily, into a deceitful belief syndrome: Believe this doctrine and it will elevate you to great status in the spiritual hierarchy. Moses David was God's Prophet, and we were the elite followers. The wilder and more bizarre his claims, the greater our devotion needed to be. It was an all-or-nothing proposition. The spiral grew deeper and wider and ever more involved. Before long, we were totally bound in the web of sin.

To fill a legitimate need for acceptance with a lie is a devastating gambit—like the frog placed into a shallow pan of water. The temperature of the water is increased slowly and steadily. The frog is free to jump out effortlessly, but it does not. As the water begins to rise in temperature, the frog sits stationary while the steam curls around his nose. Soon he begins to suffocate; the water boils and he dies. This is a factual experiment; it fits the Children of God and all involvement with sin with frightening accuracy.

Such is the fate of those of us who entered into the process of dual validation. That is, by validating Mo's claim as Prophet of God through voluntary faith and obedience, one validates his own position as an "elite" in God's cadre of chosen vessels. This is brainwashing at its finest—a brainwashing that cannot occur unless there is a voluntary suspension of the will.

Thus, through the deceitfulness of sin, the personal support of Maria, and the adoration and loyalty of dedicated disciples eager to become God's New Church, David Berg was reborn Moses David. Out of the ashes of his past life and former marriage to the Old Church, my dad arose from the depths of obscurity to become God's Endtime Prophet. In just a few short years he would be leading tens of thousands of disciples into his "divine truth" and "spiritual freedom,"

It is said that hindsight is twenty-twenty. Perhaps it is. Yet if people see mistakes of the past clearly, why do spiritual errors continually plague us? I could not clearly discern my errors until I came to a realization of certain spiritual truths and principles. One of these principles enabled me to see that the work of an evil heart is a most subtle and powerful phenomenon; and the evil at work in Vienna was strong enough to trigger a cultic explosion. What was that evil? A unified violation of conscience.

As I sat listening to my father prophesy and humiliate my mother in a way quite unimaginable to the average person, I knew beyond a shadow of a doubt that the whole thing was wrong, terribly wrong! But my own human weaknesses and fears caused me to blatantly violate my conscience. The need for recognition, excitement, position, and acceptance, and the fear of saying that I and my father were wrong were stronger than the voice of righteousness within me.

My conscience was screaming at me, desperately crying out not to give in, to stand up and say, "No!" But I remained silent. No one had ever withstood David Berg before and perhaps then, as far back as Vienna, God was giving me a chance. But I did not. Why?

The Lord, through the working of the Holy Spirit, is always faithful to convict a person's conscience when he or she is about to do evil. However, there is a danger involved. If a person continually turns a deaf ear to the voice of his conscience, that voice becomes progressively weaker and the sense of conviction diminishes. We often identify this by the expression "searing the conscience." The more a person violates the conscience, the more it weakens his moral fiber. If a person can justify a little sin, it is only a question of time until he can justify a great sin. My father built his life and the COG on this principle. I call it "spiritual blackmail."

When we justify the smaller things—those that are not too questionable—we inadvertantly build a reservoir of guilt. This reservoir has tremendous weight of influence on a person when a moral crisis arises. The guilt blackmails the individual and, through pride and fear, keeps him from making the proper moral choice. People become oblivious to the sinful habits that develop in their lives as a result of building a reservoir of guilt over previous violations of conscience.

When wrong moral choices are not followed by immediate divine retribution, it is easy to conclude that God is either impotent or indifferent. But we know that God is neither of these, so reason tells us that God must want us to make decisions based on our relation to existing circumstances. This cycle deepens and continues through the years until a person adopts, as his standard for moral decision-making, the philosophy that the end justifies the means. Decisions are made on the basis of convenience of circumstance and personal desires, not on moral law. Consequently, absolute principles and standards of righteousness must be discarded, because they have no place in this system of thinking. In taking Maria as a second wife, how did my father explain this obvious violation of scriptural law? By defining it as one of God's "exceptions."

David Berg was working with a group of youths who had already, for one reason or another, been learning the art of violating the conscience. The most common kind of violation was rebellion against authority—whether of parents, church, employment, or government. There is an eternity's difference at the fine line between resisting evil and spiritual rebellion. The late sixties were an era of protest and defiance. Most of the youth following my dad had been in rebellion for a long time and were adept at justifying their actions accordingly. Moses David, of course, assisted them by offering, as a cloak for their rebellion, the justification of religious works: serving Jesus full-time.

As time went on, the Children of God believed they could do just about anything because they were serving Jesus full-time. What could be more righteous than having accepted the call of Peter and Paul? With such a call there was a measure of liberty and privilege that transcended the restrictions of moral law. We were special!

As my father received more new truths in violation of scriptural principles, he began to reveal these to his youthful followers, using their deep-rooted sin of rebellion as a lever to hoist his doctrine. He carefully nurtured an individual violation of conscience in each of his followers.

Since rejection of the system and its godless ways was, in their view, a very honorable and righteous reaction to sin, it would only follow that God desired to reward their actions by bringing them into fellowship with His one and only Endtime Prophet. Hence, their righteous desire to reject the godless system led to their call to full-time discipleship . . . which in turn miraculously brought them into contact with the one true group that was indeed serving Him full-time . . . which, by nature of course, was being led by God's endtime man-of-the-hour . . . who was naturally getting the "word" straight from God Himself.

To doubt any of Mo's revelations would be to doubt the miraculous circumstances that had brought each disciple to learn at the feet of God's Prophet. Each one of us believed we had been led there by the very hand of God. How wonderful, how marvelous! Truth was based on the interrelation of experience and cause-and-effect. A disciple would undergo essentially a mental conversation similar to the following:

"To think God has singled me out from all the rest of society to be a part of His endtime movement! Wow, I always knew I was different and had a special calling on my life! Boy oh boy, this is really more than I ever dreamed of! It proves that I was right all along when I told Mom and Dad they were wrong. Just think—if I hadn't run away from home, I would have missed God's perfect will. Or if I hadn't burned my draft card, I'd be in the army instead of right here in the center of His will, ushering in the Millennium! Wow, it sure is a good thing I decided to follow Jesus full-time; otherwise I'd be working eight-to-five in some pagan job! Now I know why Peter left his nets and why my dad hates me so much! 'A man's foes shall be they of his own household. A prophet is not without honor, save in his own household.' Boy, that sure is true! They don't realize that I have a divine anointing. Mo even said so. My dad criticized me for doing drugs, but they really opened my eyes to the hypocrisy of the system! Wow, and to think that just last night a brother prophesied over me that I would be one of the endtime prophets—just think how important I'll be when the Great Tribulation finally comes! I can't wait! Oh boy, it sure is great to follow Jesus! Thank you, Jesus! Hallelujah!"

When sin and rebellion are explained away, the reservoir of guilt continues to grow, while at the same time the voice of the conscience becomes weaker and weaker. One's sensitivity to sin is decreased, making it easier to commit sin in the name of God. Everytime a new "truth" was presented by the Prophet of God, it required further violation of conscience by each disciple; in time everyone was being blackmailed by his own pool of guilt, affording Mo a suitable platform on which to build his doctrine.

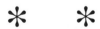

At the time of the "Old Church, New Church" revelation there were many past violations blackmailing me into following

Dad. For years I had been hiding—in the most remote corner of my mind—his inordinate advances toward me when I was a child. I was guilty of withholding the truth, especially from my mother, because I did not want Dad to be exposed. I wanted him to be a great man of God and the perfect father. Pride kept me from facing the truth. I felt guilty that I hadn't told my mother what he had tried to do. By this I was an accomplice: harboring a criminal makes one party to the crime. And most of all, I hadn't faced the truth about him to myself.

I had been carrying the weight of this since the age of seven. Incidents relating to my marriage and my decision to follow Dad in Huntington Beach had added to the store of guilt. To confront what Dad was doing in Vienna would involve facing things that I had been covering for years. Although that sense of guilt kept mounting, I concluded it would be easier to just go on and hope for the best. Pride and fear told me, "It's okay to follow your dad. You're just being prudish. After all, aren't you all simply following Jesus as best you know how? And doing it full-time—that's more than anyone else is doing."

Satan and pride prey upon past offenses and sins to blackmail a person into committing greater sins. These greater sins in turn will be used for more blackmail until the victim reaches the point of a seared conscience, a state of spiritual reprobation.

My dad followed this principle in his Mo Letters, mixing a kernel of biblical truth with one of his questionable doctrines. A forthcoming Letter would contain more error, using the previous Letter to justify it. If we accepted the last one, why not the new one? On and on it went. My dad, like Satan, is a master psychologist. He understands human nature and how to feed pride and weakness. Dad "knew what was in man" and played it for all its worth. He was a genius at cloaking the lusts of the flesh in the garments of rational thinking.

Several days after the infamous prophecy session, my husband and I finally managed to get away and talk alone. We went for a ride in the car to be sure no one overheard us discussing the "reality" of what we had gotten ourselves into, or voicing our questions to one another. We dared not be overheard expressing doubts; with Dad's status as God's Endtime Prophet still in a fragile developmental stage, there would be serious consequences if anyone were caught subverting his position.

At that time Jethro and I had our own Christian work established in Fort Worth. We were not financially dependent upon Dad's operation; we could have gone on without him. The sole reason for going with him was the revelation that David Berg was the Endtime Prophet. Would we believe it or not? I simply could not justify or accept the revelations about mother; my husband did not believe them either. We both had our own personal reasons for following; however, I can only speak for myself. I justified my decision for staying and in so doing stepped over the brink, violating my conscience.

My reasons for staying perhaps differed greatly from the others involved at Vienna, but the same moral process occurs within each person who joins a cult. Pride, ego, peer pressure, selfishness, and the "Oh, I just want to serve God—I just want to help the world" attitude build the case on one side in favor of following, while on the other side the conscience struggles to appeal to the law of God within us. If a person weakens to the demands of self, he makes a wrong decision. At this point he is "in" the cult. After this major initial decision, a person does not have to go through an intense moral battle every time he encounters a new cultic belief. His mind simply points him back to his most recent decision, which provides ample justification for accepting any new truth.

The only time the entire process is repeated (that is, when a cult member reviews all past violations of conscience) is when the person experiences a breaking point. Breaking points occur at times of great crisis, illness, emotional stress, or tragedy, such as the death of a loved one or rebuke from the Prophet. When this happens, the person's reality is usually shaken enough for the voice of conscience to get through to the conscious mind. Then the person's structure of reasoning has to be rethought and rebattled; and if things are bad enough at present, if the person is sufficiently disillusioned, he may be willing to listen to the voice of his conscience.

Disciples often send out subtle distress signals during these times, to which parents should be sensitive. It may be that their child needs help or is considering leaving the cult and would like to come home for a visit.

The classic justification for joining a cult is, "Oh Lord, You know my only desire is to serve You, therefore I'm sure you would not have allowed me to get involved in anything that is not of You. This must be Your will."

A former disciple whom I know very well said that this was the logic he used for his decision to join the COG and that this was the premise that sustained his complete devotion to my dad as the Prophet. Since it was his desire to serve God, and God had led him to the COG, it would only follow that Moses David was of God. This reasoning has a logical sequence, but it falsely presupposes that God led the youth into the movement. Today he has concluded that it was the subtlety of rebellion, not God, that led him into the COG. His declaration of "only wanting to serve God" arose from misdirected zeal and lacked the virtue of mature Christian principles. He believes it was actually a serving of self—his own selfish desires and limited ideas as to what serving God truly is. He now sees himself as a classic example of dual validation and the former prisoner of a violated conscience.

I don't question this youth's sincerity in wanting to serve God, nor the sincerity of the thousands of other youths who followed my dad. I believe he was sincere and in loyalty and devotion, few were more committed. But he was sincerely wrong. Despite the devoted loyalty and sacrifice in serving Jesus (via the leadership of Moses David), it was nonetheless a religious cover-up for rebellion and the lusts and weaknesses of the individual. He was the boss of his own life and consequently was living his life far outside the perimeters of God's authority. *Such misdirected devotion, though totally sincere, is still wrong. We can now painfully see the results.*

In reviewing my own actions in Vienna in recent years, I have come to realize that my loyalty and dedication to Dad as the Prophet of God was merely a covering for my inward desire to see him as a "great man of God." My decision to follow in his movement was a refusal to accept reality—the truth about my father, my mother, myself, and my life.

The apostle Paul describes in detail, in Romans 2, the working of the Holy Spirit in the hearts of men. He clearly explains that God has written His laws in the hearts of men; we are all without excuse.

> *. . . in that they show the work of the Law written in their hearts, their conscience bearing witness, and their thoughts alternately accusing or else defending them (Romans 2:15 NASB).*

We see here the function of our conscience: to bring our thoughts, attitudes, and actions in line with the Law of God written within us. It is small wonder I felt so miserably guilty, why I had no peace for years. A guilty and troubled conscience is one of God's key instruments for leading people in the way of righteousness.

But for the Teens for Christ gathered in Vienna, Virginia, the instrument of the conscience was powerless. The Vienna experience marked the establishment of a movement directed by "an anointed man of God"—one who by divine appointment had been granted rights beyond the limitations of traditional scriptural morality. David Berg, in blatant violation to God's laws, claimed that God had blessed his sin—that God had made it pure. It had been revealed by God through personal prophetic revelation. His followers voluntarily accepted and believed it. Each disciple—in direct violation of his or her conscience—participated in a collective, unified violation of conscience. This was the elementary source of power which gave birth to David Berg's role as a prophet. We all partook of his sin. The blasphemy was complete. A cult was born.

The events at Vienna represented a microcosm of each person's experience in joining the cult of David Berg from that time forward. Although they were not at Vienna, each new convert would pass through this same process.

Chapter 6
Prophets of Doom

O daughter of my people, gird thee with sackcloth, and wallow thyself in ashes: make thee mourning, as for an only son, most bitter lamentation: for the spoiler shall suddenly come upon us.

Therefore thus saith the Lord God: Behold, mine anger and my fury shall be poured out upon this place, upon man, and upon beast, and upon the trees of the field, and upon the fruit of the ground; and it shall burn, and shall not be quenched (Jeremiah 6:26; 7:20).

The Prophets of Doom had arisen in America. This was the message of the Children of God to a nation that had turned its back on God. David Berg taught his disciples that the Lord Himself had revealed this message to him through special revelation. It was the Message of Jeremiah. Thus we set out from Vienna, following our newly ordained Prophet, to warn the wicked American nation of its imminent judgment: destruction, slaughter, murder, and starvation were coming soon.

Because Vienna is near Washington, D. C., we planned our

first demonstration on the doorsteps of the Nation's Capitol. U.S. Sen. Everett Dirksen had recently died, and his body was lying in state in the Rotunda of the Capitol building. My dad explained to us that Dirksen's death was symbolic of the death of the nation, because the senator had tried to pass legislation that would allow mandated prayer and Bible-reading in public schools.

A large group of us, eighty-five strong, held a silent vigil at the site of Senator Dirksen's funeral. We also demonstrated in front of the White House, mourning the demise of peace and freedom.

We planned the vigils in great detail. One of our buses would deliver the disciples to a predetermined location. Then we would march single file in perfect unison (after hours of practice) to the actual site of the protest. The seven-foot wooden staves we carried—representing God's righteous rod of judgment—would strike the ground simultaneously, creating a noise like thunder. People would turn to see what was causing this frightening sound and be awestruck to see seventy-five to a hundred red-robed prophets walking silently down the street with stern countenances, large wooden yokes about their necks, and ashes smeared on their foreheads. The long robes symbolized mourning for the nation, and the red sackcloth (burlap) was an ominous sign of the blood that would be shed in the coming destruction. The yokes represented the bondage that was to befall America, paralleling the bondage of the Israelites under the Babylonians.

The male prophets, with the beards that were in vogue at the time, looked as if they had walked straight out of ancient Israel. Many of the girls wore large gold or silver earrings.

Upon arriving at the protest site, we would stand in complete silence and unroll large scrolls with hand-lettered Bible verses declaring the Message of Jeremiah to the United States. Some of the most commonly used verses:

> *The wicked shall be turned into hell, and all the nations that forget God (Psalm 9:17).*
> *The nation and kingdom that will not serve thee shall perish; yea, those nations shall be utterly wasted (Isaiah 60:12).*
> *For I will bring evil from the north, and a great destruction.*

The destroyer of the Gentiles is on his way; he is gone forth from his place to make thy land desolate; and thy cities shall be laid waste, without an inhabitant (Jeremiah 4:6-7).

The vigils were an oddity to the American public, which had probably thought it had already "seen everything" in that age of protest over Vietnam, civil rights, and free speech. Even the police did not know how to react to our peculiar form of demonstration. Each disciple taking part in a vigil was sworn to a vow of complete silence. When policemen asked, "What are you doing?" they received no reply. Accustomed to the violent, rock-throwing protests of radical leftist groups like the Weathermen or Students for a Democratic Society (SDS), law enforcement officers found our eerie spectacle mystifying. Consequently we were never physically disturbed or arrested.

Some people welcomed our solemn protest. One woman, coming upon a vigil in New York City later on, said to me, "Oh, I'm so glad you're here! I'm praying for America, hoping they'll turn to God!" The interest shown by the news media was also a great boost to our morale; getting so much attention made us feel important—as if we actually were God's endtime prophets, confirming what my dad had been telling us.

Those days were like playing a role in a movie. It was really great fun. We packed a lifetime of excitement into a few short months as we traveled in a large caravan from city to city.

Immediately after the Washington vigil we visited Philadelphia to protest the death of freedom and peace at Independence Hall. We then went on to New York City and held a vigil in Times Square.

While we were in New Jersey, en route to our next destination, a curious reporter visited our campsite and wrote an article about this strange group of prophets. We had explained our cause and our message to him, in his article he quoted Matthew 5:9: "Blessed are the peacemakers, for they shall be called the children of God." It sounded good, so we adopted the name. We were no longer "Teens for Christ"; we became "the Children of God." In some of his revelations, Dad said the Lord had called him "Moses." Hence, we had become Moses and the Children of

God. In prophecies Dad had yet to receive, it would be revealed that he was also like David of old. Thus, David Berg became the prophet "Moses David."

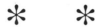

We were gradually being subtly seduced by false teaching. David Berg spoke the longings of our hearts. Like Ignorance, in John Bunyan's allegory, *Pilgrim's Progress,* we did not forsee the inevitable consequences of our seduction.

> *Christian.* Come, how do you? How stands it between God and your soul now?
>
> *Ignorance.* I hope well; for I am always full of good motions, that come into my mind, to comfort me as I walk.
>
> *Chr.* What good motions? Pray tell us.
>
> *Ign.* Why, I think of God and heaven.
>
> *Chr.* So do the devils and damned souls.
>
> *Ign.* But I think of them, and desire them.
>
> *Chr.* So do many that are never like to come there. The soul of the sluggard desires, and hath nothing.
>
> *Ign.* But I think of them, and *leave all for them.*
>
> *Chr.* That I doubt, for leaving of all is an hard matter; yea, a harder matter than many are aware of. But why, or by what, art thou persuaded that thou hast left all for God and heaven?
>
> *Ign.* My heart tells me so.
>
> *Chr.* That may be, through its deceitfulness; for a man's heart may minister comfort to him in the hopes of that thing for which yet he has no ground to hope.
>
> *Ign.* But my heart and life agree together, and therefore my hope is well grounded.

Christian explains to Ignorance that the concurrence of one's heart and life must still be examined against a higher authority, the Word of God. This the followers of David Berg were not doing. We had erred by supplanting scriptural truth with the personally revealed truth of a man. Consequently we were blinded to our sin. As Christian explains,

> *Christian.* Thou neither seest thy original nor actual infirmities; . . .

And that was the sad condition of the disciples of David Berg. We saw neither our original nor our present sins, but were blindly following our hearts and the desires of our anointed leader. Christian's judgment of Ignorance was prophetic for us:

> *Christian.* It pities me much for this poor man, it will certainly go ill with him at last.

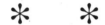

After our vigil in New York we visited Chicago, arriving there while the conspiracy trial of the Chicago Seven was in progress.* My dad's reaction to the seven conspirators was quite revealing. "They are just misguided," he said. "The only problem is that they are doing it for the wrong motive, the wrong reason. They're not doing it for the Lord." His reasoning sounded right to us: Of course, they are just a bit misguided. They should be doing "it" for the Lord. But what was this "it" to which Dad referred? Simply more rebellion, anarchy, and selfish resistance to authority.

My dad did not teach his followers that the Christian way is not the way of rebellion. On the contrary, we learned that as long as we acted in the name of Jesus, everything was okay.

Rebellion against authority is not the same as resisting evil. This Jesus understood, but my father did not. Why? Because my father was himself bound in sin and therefore could not discern

---

*Seven men—Abbie Hoffman, Tom Hayden, Jerry Rubin, John Froines, Rennie Davis, David Dellinger, and Lee Weiner—stood trial on charges of conspiring to incite a riot during the 1968 Democratic National Convention. They were acquitted on February 18, 1970, although five were found guilty of the lesser charge of crossing state lines with the intent to incite a riot.

between rebellion and resisting evil. How could he?—he was drowning in his own rebellion.

Christians are taught in the Bible to submit to God and to other proper authority, but not to submit to evil. As disciples of Moses David we were taught to rebel against authority whenever it suited our purposes. We professed to submit to God—via David Berg's leadership—but actually we submitted only to my dad's deviant teachings. There is no such thing as "righteous rebellion," and our rebellion against the authority of parents, church, government, and employment was certainly not godly. We were not resisting evil; our defiance simply mirrored the actions of political groups such as the SDS or the Weathermen. If the followers of Moses David were truly resisting evil, why then were they so easily led, in years to come, into heretical doctrines of adultery, incest, and spiritism?

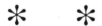

Following our vigil in Chicago we journeyed south to Louisiana to escape the cold northern winter. Just outside New Orleans we were raided by a group of fifty law officers, vigilantes, dogs and assorted "rednecks." Those were "Easy Rider" days, and our group of 150 long-haired, bearded hippie dropouts weren't exactly on friendly grounds. The raiders surrounded our camp and began checking everyone's I. D. Many of the disciples didn't have proper identification or were of minor age, and twenty-five were taken into temporary custody. One black disciple, Simon, had to hide in the swamps for fear of his life.

Joshua, my brother-in-law, was teaching a class to a large group of disciples at the time of the arrests and was suspected of being the "leader" of this group. He was taken to jail and held for three weeks.

Meanwhile, the great Prophet of God was hiding in his motor home, too sick with fear to face the sheriff and his deputies. He locked the door of his camper and refused to come out. (For some reason, the police simply left his camper alone after finding the door locked.) My dad felt "the sheep lays down his life for the shepherd."

In checking the identification of the disciples from California, the officials discovered exactly who we were and that twenty-seven disciples who had been arrested in Huntington Beach in January 1970 had illegally skipped town before receiving sentencing. However, no charges were pressed against us, and we were told to be out of town "by sunup" and not to stop until we had crossed the state border. It normally took a couple of days to break camp, but needless to say, we were on the road by dawn and didn't stop until we reached Houston—a long way from the state line.

Once in Houston, things began to go well for the Children of God. Camping in the numerous state parks surrounding Houston for the maximum two-week limit, we hopscotched about the city gaining new converts and disciples. For one reason or another, the Texas youth were greatly attracted to our bizarre and austere lifestyle. In one month we gained nearly twenty-five new followers.

One event occurred in Houston that was to have devastating effects on my father. Dad decided to visit a Gypsy camp in the Houston area. I don't recall how he knew of this camp, but he felt it was vital that he meet these Gypsies. He asked me to drive him there, and on the way he explained to me that the Gypsies were models for living a truly godly lifestyle. For centuries the Gypsies have lived in tents, just as Abraham did, he explained. "We have a lot to learn from them. They have a special anointing from God."

Dad entered the Gypsy camp of motor homes and trailers and did not return for a long time. Afterward he explained that he had visited personally with the king of their tribe. In several months' time my dad would discover that while visiting with this Gypsy king, a miraculous event occurred—one with immense spiritual significance.

Meanwhile, toward the end of January 1970 we were running out of places to camp, so Dad flew to California to speak with his old friend and employer, Fred Jordan, to beg the use of his abandoned ranch in West Texas.

Chapter 7
A New Nation—TSC

I was quite familiar with Fred Jordan's ranch in Texas, having lived there several times as a child. I can still remember my first preview of the Soul Clinic. Fred had designed the ranch to serve as boot-camp training for prospective missionaries enrolled in his Soul Clinic program. He determined that if potential missionaries could make it at the Texas Soul Clinic, they could no doubt survive quite well on a foreign field.

When our family first moved there, I was only seven years old and attending third grade. I went to a little red brick school building in Strawn, a little town about fifteen miles away. To get to school I had to walk the three miles of dirt road that connected the ranch to the main country road. There the school bus picked me up. I had been instructed to walk carefully around the rattlesnakes that enjoyed sunbathing in the middle of the road.

The property was originally owned by Jordan's mother. She willed the ranch to Fred with the condition that it be used only for the Lord's work. Apart from the brief stay of the COG, it has been used primarily for training missionaries in Fred's Soul Clinic ministry. The four-hundred-acre ranch lies one hundred miles west of Dallas. TSC has an extremely arid, desertlike climate; the land is hilly, rocky, and dusty, spotted with the everpresent mesquite tree. It's a wonderful place to raise goats.

The ranch buildings had been constructed on the outside perimeter of a large circular drive. Over the years Fred had built three groups of cabins for the missionaries to live in. My dad had helped build one of the sections of cabins when he was enrolled in Fred's boot camp back in the early fifties. They had also constructed a very large dining hall that seated hundreds of people, a barn, and assorted small shelters. It was an ideal setting for a hippie commune.

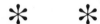

When the "Prophets of Doom," under the anointed leadership of David Berg, limped into TSC in the late winter of 1970, the ranch was in total disarray. It resembled a broken-down ghost town—a resort for scorpions and tumbleweed. Nothing worked. There was no electricity or water. The pipes in the dining hall had all burst. The walk-in freezer was in disrepair. The roofs leaked. All the buildings lacked heating. Yet, in spite of the primitive conditions, the road-weary band of prophets delighted in a place to settle down and call their own. For me it was like coming home. I loved TSC the way a child loves her one-armed, torn and tattered Raggedy Ann doll.

Making TSC livable was a monumental job. We procured thousands of dollars' worth of supplies from sympathetic businesses, and the disciples contributed many manhours of labor. Dad simply organized the project into our communal lifestyle.

The early seventies was a time of communal living for the counterculture. Both hippies and Jesus People wanted to get back to the earth, back to nature, and develop a sense of camaraderie with their brothers and sisters. The youth saw this as their chance to build something, to make a home for themselves, and Dad was keenly aware of this desire. He organized the disciples and turned them loose. We loved it and worked with all the energy our youthful minds and bodies could produce. But my father had other ideas and other goals; these were yet to be revealed.

Life at TSC for the regular, nonleading disciples was highly regimented. We didn't quite maintain the degree of discipline of a military base, but we came close. TSC was a lot like summer youth camp. Every person and every person's time were highly controlled; no one "did their own thing." A typical day's schedule looked like this:

6:30	Reveille
7:00-7:30	Light breakfast
7:30-10:30	Morning work period
10:30-11:00	Clean up
11:00-11:30	Breakfast
11:30-2:30	Bible classes
2:30-4:30	Snack and more Bible study classes or work period
4:30-6:00	Bible classes
6:00-7:00	Dinner
7:00-9:30	Inspiration and fellowship, singing, dancing, testimonies
9:30-10:30	Tribe meetings
10:30	Lights out

The schedule allowed very little time for idleness: disciples were either studying, working, teaching, or sleeping. Ninety percent of the converts had come straight out of the dropout lifestyle, living lives void of discipline and schedule. For many, our strict discipline was a drastic and welcome change from their former state of lethargy. New converts were expected to learn nearly three hundred Bible verses by memory within the first three months; Mo considered Scripture memorization to be an integral part of discipleship.

All new members were placed under the strict scrutiny of an older disciple. This was the "buddy" system. At such a time that they proved to be strong, mature disciples, they were no longer considered "babes" and were free to be on their own. This period usually lasted about three months. One girl told me in later years, "Oh, I had the worst trial of my life at TSC; I was constantly with my 'buddy.' I couldn't do anything without her. I couldn't even go to the bathroom alone. Beds were in short supply, and I even had to sleep in the same bed with her!"

Ironically, without any prompting from the Chinese Communists, we unconsciously incorporated many of the same conditions used by the Chinese in their Thought Reform programs. Many of these mind-control techniques seem to erupt "spontaneously" in cultic organizations. We boasted that we were "heartwashing" new converts.

Everyone who came to TSC as a dropout or hippie or college student left with a new identity. Everyone took a new name from the Bible—this was part of Forsaking All. God was making "new creatures" out of us; all the old things were done away with. A new convert broke all relations with the past, both family and friends. The break with one's former life had to be complete, absolute, because that's what Jesus wanted.

This sudden loss of identity often brought deep conflicts for disciples who suffered the after-pains of leaving their former lifestyles and families. This was why everyone had a buddy. When the older disciple perceived that the younger one was wavering and suffering doubt, he was right there to pick him up. Although it was never revealed, the older disciple often harbored the same doubts. By encouraging the younger convert, the older member strengthened himself. It was a good system that accomplished its purpose well.

With each new convert who matured to the status of a disciple, the "Family" became more and more complete. A total sense of comradeship and unity synthesized this body of youth into a cohesive whole. Despite the things that one forsook, the Family was there to fill the void. TSC gave the youth a chance to realize the fulfillment of their dream of "dropping out." The lifestyle developed at TSC established a pattern of unity among the Children of God that has continued to this day.

We were, in reality, a New Nation. We were not merely dropouts, a band of disorganized hippies; we were dropouts with a purpose: following Jesus full-time. We had left the establishment and all of its "damnable evils," as my father called them, and in so doing created a nation within a nation.

On the ranch we talked much about being self-sufficient. We

began planting a farm, and the disciples were excited about the prospects of producing our own food. Being self-sufficient was the goal of many people in that era: "Who needs society? We can make it on our own." But David Berg had something else in mind. He wanted to be self-sufficient, but not physically. His desire was to be cut off spiritually; to be isolated from the churches, parents, and government—from all aspects of society. That was his real desire.

Thus, at TSC both the kids and Dad began to realize their dreams. We had successfully dropped out of society and into the reality of the Children of God. Our New Nation replaced what the members had left behind when they forsook all. We had our own rules, our own social standards, our own world. What more could we ask for?

Dad originally organized the movement into tribes, modeled after the twelve tribes of Israel. Each tribe had a specific function: the tribe of Benjamin was responsible for childcare and education; Gad was in charge of printing and publishing; Simeon took care of food preparation; and so on. Following the days of TSC, the tribe concept slowly became obsolete and was no longer used.

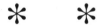

My dad had learned the art of proselytizing from Fred Jordan. Before long we were sending witnessing teams into many of the campus towns of Texas. The steel of each disciple's dedication was tested and tempered on these weekend witnessing trips. We visited universities, parks, and concerts—anywhere youth gathered. An older disciple accompanied by a babe set out to find the lost and hungry sheep in society. One of the Children would initiate a conversation and ask leading questions to bring the conversation down to the heart of the matter: "What are you doing with your life? Are you going to heaven or hell when you die? Do you know Jesus?"

This was witnessing. Children of God disciples witnessed for eight, ten, and twelve hours a day. Depending on how receptive the lost soul was, a conversation could go on for hours.

The instructions given to our disciples were: "First get'm to ask Jesus into their heart. Then get'm filled with the Holy Spirit." Then ask'm if they want to forsake all and follow Jesus." They were invited back to the Prophet Bus to meet the rest of the Brothers and Sisters. While the salvation experience was fresh on their mind, they were challenged to follow Jesus full-time. We quoted Matthew 4:19 with universal implication: "Brother, Jesus said, 'Follow me and I will make you fishers of men' and the disciples straightway left their nets and followed him."

In reality, many of the lost and lonely kids were not so much looking to follow Jesus, but for a place to belong. Our "Love Bombing" tactic hit them right where they were most vulnerable. We accepted people unconditionally and offered them something many had never known: a home where they were loved and accepted. The following is an example of a young girl named Huldah who left "all" to follow the Lord and join the Family; her testimony was written during the days of TSC.

I am eighteen years old and have lived in San Antonio all my life. I lived on the cowboy side of town where I trained and exercised horses for a hobby. I really dug on horses back then. In my senior year I dropped out of school and went traveling all through Louisiana and North Texas then back to San Antonio. I was always getting drawn back into the trap of the city.

I started taking drugs when I was in the 10th grade, three and a half years ago. I was selling large quantities of speed and weed for a long time.

I practiced "spiritualism" during this time, was a medium and had dreams and visions of the future. I was quite lonely out in the world, so I thought that if there were a lot of people around everything would be better, but that wasn't where it was at. It was too lonely.

Things started happening really fast. I was offered a job as a secretary in Austin, by a man who picked me up hitch-hiking back to San Antonio. He was building a big shopping mall in Austin and needed a secretary to take care of his office and answer the phone.

I started making a lot of money, had a lot of dope and a nice apartment in a college town full of freaks like me. I was making the 9 to 5 scene but wasn't liking it.

> *But, praise God, it was all a part of His plan to bring me to my family in Jesus!*
>
> *I met a friend of mine and we both heard about the Texas Soul Clinic and hitch-hiked up there to see what was happening. What happened was that Jesus met us at the gate and we went home "saved" and counting the cost.*
>
> *We had had all the material possessions we had ever wanted but saw the smiling happy faces and decided we had to "forsake all" and follow Jesus. All of our lives we were part of the problem. Now we are part of the solution.[1]*

Huldah was still in the Family thirteen years later, in 1983.

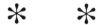

Several months after arriving in TSC, my father turned another corner in his spiritual evolution. He received the "gift of tongues."

The Book of Acts records the supernatural experience of the apostles wherein they received the special ability to speak in the many languages of the various groups of people gathered in Jerusalem for the Feast of Pentecost. On that day "Jews from every nation under heaven" were gathered, and the apostles began to speak the gospel to the people, "each one hearing them in his own language" (Acts 2:6). In 1 Corinthians 12 Paul speaks of the gifts of the Holy Spirit, one of them being the gift of "tongues," or the ability to speak in a language unknown to the speaker by the power of the Holy Spirit.

My father had desired this gift all his life. He believed it was the mark of true spirituality. Yet he was fifty years old and had never received it. Then at long last, on April 29, 1970, he received the gift of tongues.

At that time he was living with my mother, Maria, and a girl named Martha, whom he had taken as another wife. He was still living in his motor home, which was parked in a secluded spot on the ranch so as to keep his private life secret. In March 1978 he recalls this miraculous experience in a Mo Letter entitled "Abrahim the Gypsy King":

I was lying there between Martha and Maria praying like a house afire, and all of a sudden before I even knew what happened I was praying in tongues. . . . it was probably Abrahim. I was finally desperate enough to really let the Lord take over and take control. Abrahim was praying through me in the Spirit.

Three days I couldn't speak any English. . . .

I went for years and years and years and years wanting the gift of tongues because that was such a marvelous manifestation to me, to think you could speak another language you had never learned! That was obviously a miracle, obviously a proof of the miraculous. But the Lord never gave it to me for years!

I begged Him! I besought Him! I fell on my face before Him! I did everything! . . .

He withheld from me the visible, the audible, the tangibly miraculous for years. For fifty years He made me go strictly by faith.

I just simply wanted it for my own personal satisfaction as a kind of final proof to me that I was spiritual. . . .

He finally started giving me those audibly manifested gifts when I least expected it. I was lying naked between two naked women in the same bed in the back end of our Camper when I first received the gift of tongues.[2]

Abrahim, according to Dad's own description, is a "spirit guide" whom he acquired at the Gypsy camp several months before—the place I drove him to while we were camping out in Houston. Mo and Maria explain in detail the identity, function, and nature of Abrahim, Mo's personal spirit guide, in a letter. For years they themselves were not sure what was happening when this strange foreign voice would speak through my dad.

Through this and other experiences and revelations we began to understand who Abrahim really was and the purpose of his ministrations through David.

According to his [Abrahim's] own account, he was living with a Gypsy band we visited in Houston, Texas, in 1970, as the Gypsy king's counsellor or guiding spirit when he first met us, and decided to leave them and come with us for his own reasons. . . .

It was only later we began to realize it was not David who was Abrahim or had been Abrahim or even with Abrahim in some previous existence, as we thought at first. . . .

But Abrahim was a Gypsy king himself, a departed saint from hundreds of years ago, who had come to live with us in spirit as our spirit guide and counsellor!

It was Abrahim himself, therefore, who was speaking through David. . . .[3]

Throughout history, Gypsies have been known for their dealings with fortune-telling, spiritism, and communication with the dead. Just what went on when my father visited those gypsies in Houston, I do not know. But the results of his contact came through in a frightening demonstration of occultic powers on April 29, 1970.

I remember when it happened. All the family members were called to Dad's motor home for a special meeting. We crowded in, and Dad was crying. There was some kind of prayer meeting going on, and it was explained that Dad was really "in the Spirit"—he had received the gift of tongues and was unable to speak English for three days. Everyone was rejoicing over Dad's receiving this marvelous gift. One disturbing aspect of this for me, however, was that as Dad spoke in his strange language, Maria would interpret what he was saying. Only she could interpret. Why was this so? It troubled me.

Once my dad left the motor home and went walking about the camp praying over different disciples in this new tongue. He would then give the interpretation in English, often foretelling their future in the Family. It was a rare occasion for Dad to walk about the camp in broad daylight. For many people, this was the first time they had seen him. I came out of my apartment and heard people saying, "Oh, Dad's out! Dad's out! He's walking around talking to everybody! Disciples were running from everywhere to see him. Needless to say, the young followers were awed by this miraculous moving of the "Holy Spirit." To them, it was as if God Himself were walking around the camp.

Until I was conducting research for this book I never questioned Dad's experience of receiving the gift of tongues. Then I began to put various pieces of this puzzle together. Until recently I held the opinion that my father was deceived primarily by his lustful desires and had been led astray through sexual sin. Indeed, that happened. But when I realized that his involvement with spirits such as "Abrahim" is actually demonism I began to see things altogether differently. As I studied the Mo Letters that pertain to spiritual events, a Pandora's box of occultic experiences opened before my eyes.

I re-examined many of Dad's "spiritual" experiences in light of this fact, and it became ever so clear that my father lives and functions in the nether world of demonic influence.

His first strange experience occurred back in the early fifties when he was working for Fred Jordan. In this experience Dad explains that he died and left his body, being visited by the departed spirit of an old friend of his mother, a "Dr. Koger." During this encounter Dad had a telepathic conversaton with the doctor and decided to return to his body. He wrote about this experience in March 1978: "That was one of the most supernatural miraculous amazing spiritual experiences I ever had! I died!"[4] For many years I shrugged off tales like this as products of Dad's incredible imagination.

But my father's involvement with spirits, mediums, and the occult has deepened over the years. When Dad lived in London in the early seventies he wrote several Mo Letters concerning his visits to a Gypsy medium and fortuneteller there; he referred to her as "Madame M."[5]

The Bible is clear in its warnings and judgments of the occult (see, for example, Leviticus 19 and 20 and Deuteronomy 18), yet my father is now actively promoting occultism under the guise of Christian charismatic experiences. A disturbing fact to me as his daughter is that he has actually become a medium himself. A medium is a person through whom messages from the spirits of the dead are supposedly sent to the living. Abrahim, an alleged spirit of the dead, speaks directly through Mo and gives him detailed advice and direction. Abrahim is not the only spirit who speaks through my father; he was the first, but now there are many more.

Not only has Moses David become possessed by evil spirits, but he relates that he has sexual experiences with spirits and goddesses. In a Mo Letter he entitles "The Goddesses" he relates the significance of these encounters.

. . . I've not understood until now, like all those other goddesses I've made love to in the Spirit. I've even been a little shocked by some of these strange experiences because I didn't understand them. . . . In each case, the one I was making love to would suddenly turn into one of these strange and beautiful goddesses, and I would immediately explode in an orgasm of tremendous spiritual power while at the same time prophesying violently in some foreign language.

Each is the spirit of her country, like the spirit of their religion. It's a sort of symbolism: Aphrodite of Cyprus; the Cat Goddess of Egypt; the Black Girl of the African Nightmare; the bird-like Sun Goddess of the Nile; multi-armed Goddess of Egypt. . . .[6]

In another letter Dad says, "I was getting ready to make love early in the morning when suddenly this huge, beautiful naked black goddess descended on top of me. . . . Big beautiful black goddess, Mocumba! I called for Mocumba and she came!"[7]

When I began piecing these experiences together, from start to finish, it emerged as a nightmare of occultic perversion. Illicit sex and the occult have always been closely related. Satan's desire is to lead his captives into the bondage of spiritual perversion and sin. My father's degeneration along this path parallels exactly the pattern found in occultic practices throughout the ages. Author Dave Hunt explains in his book, *The Cult Explosion,*

Free sex and sex perversion nearly always surface, sooner or later, in any extended involvement with the occult. Demons are intrinsically evil and cannot hide this fact for long in any contact they have with humans.[8]

Mo's use of spiritism, like sex, is slowly digging its way deeper and deeper into the daily life and doctrine of COG disciples. They are learning things that are totally contrary to biblical teachings, yet they believe Moses David's teachings are inspired by God. In a Mo Letter entitled "More Holy Ghosts," Dad claims that God uses the departed dead to minister to Christians still alive on the earth. He explains that the dead are like angels in their ministering services. This doctrine, of course, is diametrically opposed to everything found in Scripture. The ultimate biblical injunction is recorded in Deuteronomy 18:11: "Let no one be found among you who . . . is a medium or spiritist or who consults the dead. Anyone who does these things is detestable to the Lord." Under Mosaic law, violations were punishable by death. But Mo writes,

> *The protestants have almost totally skipped over or deemphasized the agents that God uses . . . . Most of them give absolutely no credit to the good spirits of the departed "dead." . . .*
>
> *How does God give a gift of tongues? . . . interpretation? Why can't these gifts come through separate spirits?*
>
> *I believe by my own personal experience, that that is how I received the gift of tongues. . . .*
>
> *Even though I didn't yet know it, I had received him [Abrahim] weeks before in Houston, Texas, when he jumped off that Gypsy king onto me. . . !**
>
> *See, I don't know any of this, it's one of these spirits who are putting these things in my mouth . . . .[9]*

Dave Hunt further explains, "A major purpose of 'spirit communications' is to refute what the Bible says about death, judgment, sin, hell, and resurrection."[10] What little I have quoted from the Mo Letters clearly indicates that this is precisely what my father is doing to his followers and to others affected by COG disciples.

The extent of my father's spiritual deception, considered in light of his Christian background, is mind-bending. The tragedy is that his disciples, when reading the Mo Letters, cannot see what is really behind them. Over the years Dad has led them from one subtle lie to the next, interweaving these lies with Scripture and distorted biblical truths. Like mixing sugar and salt, they cannot tell the difference. For example, he writes concerning the ministration of angels and spirits,

> *This makes it very simple how God operates and how He gives all these gifts and different languages to millions of people*

---

*It was reported in *Time* magazine that this Gypsy king died less than a year after he was visited by my father.

throughout the world: It's through the angels and the departed spirits of the departed saints! It's just as simple as that!

Well, if the Devil's evil spirits possess people and give them evil powers and evil tongues and evil wickedness, evil strength and evil wisdom, how much more should the good spirits of God give His good people, His children, these godly gifts and godly powers when possessed of the spirit of God.[11]

And of course, his followers believe that the Mo Letters are the inspired word of God and therefore they accept whatever Dad says as truth. A disciple is also conditioned never to doubt anything Dad writes. As to the divine authority of the Mo Letters, my father states, "I will take those inspired and supernatural and divinely inspired Letters and put them on the same level as the rest of the Word of God [the Bible]!"[12] He believes that drunkenness helps him yield to the Spirit of God with greater ease: "When I get drunk, I yield to God's Spirit, and then I am happy about it! Well, I guess that's the truth! That's something, if you have the Spirit of God, if you get intoxicated, why, it just makes you even more free in the spirit—at least it does with me!"[13]

When the practice of spiritism, necromancy, and other communication with the "world of the dead" begins to take hold among the disciples as did the sex doctrines, we will see far more demonic activities in the COG than previously dreamed possible. I believe this demonic influence will be most active among the children born into the movement.

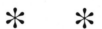

On April 29, 1970, my father most certainly did not receive the gift of tongues in the true biblical sense—as did the apostles at the Feast of Pentecost. Galatians 5:20 states, "The acts of the sinful nature are obvious: sexual immorality, impurity and debauchery; idolatry and witchcraft; drunkenness, orgies and the like. . . . Those who live like this shall not inherit the kingdom of God." Moses David has blatantly committed all of these sins.

My dad opened the final door of demonic influence among his followers through his interpretation of the baptism of the Holy Spirit. He writes,

> *The so-called baptism of the Spirit is therefore not only the baptism of the Holy Spirit but a sudden yielding and surrender to one of the holy spirits of God. Along with the Spirit of God we receive specific spirits who have these specific gifts. How about that? I mean that makes it very understandable. This explains then why things happened to us the way they did in the beginning with Abrahim, right?*
>
> *This all just hit me all of a sudden when I started working on Abrahim [Letters pertaining to Abrahim], God bless him![14]*

Consequently the eager, dedicated disciples of Moses David have been looking expectantly for help from their own spirit guides and helpers, ever since this Letter was published in 1977. I have read several accounts in the COG monthly magazine, "Family News," about young children who have seen and communicated with their "personal spirit guides." This indicates that the satanic influence has filtered down to the youngest cult members.

Moses David's most outrageous blasphemy occurred when he declared that "he is greater than Solomon." He writes,

> *It's a funny thing, the Lord gave us that Scripture the other night, "Behold, a greater than Solomon is here!" That was a verse about Jesus, but that night the Lord was not applying it to Jesus.*
>
> *I don't see how I could be greater than Solomon. It's so simple, I mean, before I even got the words out of my mouth, Abrahim flashed across with: "Because of the gifts that God has given you!"*
>
> *I have the wisdom of all the ages. . . .[15]*

For those unfamiliar with the language of the occult, "the wisdom of the ages" is a euphemism referring to the elemental powers of the earth, the knowledge one receives as a result of being in service to the powers of darkness. It is the great desire of all those involved in witchcraft to tap into the "wisdom of the ages."

Mo's Letters further explain the function of the spirit world and how God communicates to him through all the "sages and all the prophets and all the kings and all the great men of the past."

Moses David advises his followers that to receive the gift of tongues, one must be willing to "yield."

> *You may have to sort of do like the yogi mentalists do—make your mind a blank and just yield your members, yield your tongue and just let go of it so that the spirits can get ahold of your tongue and mind.*[16]

Christians involved in charismatic circles should take a long look at the early stages of the Jesus People movement and specifically the Children of God, which began as a charismatic, Bible-believing organization. Satanic influence is subtle; many Christians who claim to have discernment have been duped by men such as my father boasting the "gifts" of the Holy Spirit. Today I wonder how many Christians are being deceived by people imitating the gifts of the Spirit or by people actually under the influence of demonic spirits. "Wherefore by their *fruits* shall ye know them"—not by their *gifts.*

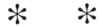

During the first year at TSC, Dad spent a lot of time teaching classes to a select group of disciples he designated to be leaders or leadership trainees. It was important that he train a core of leadership rooted and grounded in his doctrines who could carry on in his absence. He invested much time with about sixty to seventy-five trainees; occasionally he would give a session in the dining hall to the general body, but this was exceptional.

The classes taught to his select group of leaders were tape-recorded and subsequently emerged as Mo Letters. However, the concept of the "Mo Letters" did not originate until Dad left TSC in September 1970 to travel in Europe and Israel., it was then that he began to send home letters to members of the Royal Family with specific instructions on how to run the Revolution for Jesus. Little by little he stipulated that certain letters be read to all the leaders. Then he indicated that certain letters be read to "all the disciples." This practice grew and grew until everyone was anxiously awaiting the next letter from Mo. Hence, "Mo Letters" became the guiding light of the Children of God.

It was also during his days at TSC and his subsequent trip to Israel that Dad began to foster his image as the "Prophet on the Mountain." His trip to Europe and the Middle East forced him to run his organization from a distance. He began to see in this arrangement a unique style of leadership. He wrote a letter entitled "I Gotta Split" in which he explained that in order to really hear from God, in order to see the "whole" picture, it was imperative that he go away—away in the sense that he separate himself physically from the feverish activities of life at TSC.[17] He considered himself to be a "prophet on the mountain" whose only job was to stay in tune with the Almighty so that he might faithfully direct the activities of God's Children. This, of course, gave much greater importance to his letters of communication; if he was hearing directly from God and writing these directions in letters, then the letters were like hearing from God Himself.

Another key development in the spiritual direction of the Children of God occurred during Dad's trip to Israel. He had gone there with the express purpose of buying land and emigrating his followers to Israel. However, in a dramatic turn of events, he returned to the U.S. imbued with anti-Semitic fervor. It was rather shocking to his immediate family. Dad had always had a special fascination for the people of Israel; he always seemed quite proud of the Jewish blood in our family heritage. When he was involved with the Christian and Missionary Alliance, he applied to the mission board requesting that he be sent to Israel. But they rejected him, saying that he was too old and had too many children. (This is the story I was told all my life, and I accepted it as true.) Dad carried great bitterness for years over this rejection; he never overcame it. When I was growing up, Dad taught us about Jewish traditions and customs, the significance of the Jews in biblical history, and the importance of Israel in the endtime. We frequently visited the local Jewish temple during Yom Kippur and often celebrated the Passover with Jewish friends.

Given the demonic nature of Abrahim, Dad's violent turn against Israel and the Jews is not surprising. It is one further evidence of the evil influence that had begun to take over and rule his mind. God has said concerning the Jews, "I will bless them that bless thee, and curse them that curse thee" (Genesis 12:3). To be possessed with a livid hatred against the Jews is not at all in accord with the Scriptures. On the contrary, it rings of demonic obsession. These contradicting experiences never made sense to me until I became aware of Dad's deep entrenchment in the occult.

*   *

While Mo was traveling overseas, the Children of God and the Christian commune in Thurber, Texas, began to attract national attention in the U.S. NBC brought their camera crews to TSC and recorded an extensive documentary on our unusual lifestyle. Jethro and I were left in charge of the ranch while Dad was traveling; we reported to him all the exciting goings-on, and he gave us instructions on how to handle the press. He was just thrilled over the sudden wave of popularity.

The program was telecast nationally and provided a tremendous boost to our credibility with the American public. Youth from all over the U.S. drove to TSC to join the Children of God after seeing this program.

Fred Jordan continued to help the movement during the early days of TSC. He owned a large five-story building in downtown Los Angeles that he turned over to the Family. Faithy and Joshua helped to pioneer this colony, and soon the streets of L.A. were producing disciple after disciple—youth eager for the opportunity to "forsake all for Jesus."

Our L.A. witnessing teams attacked the streets of Hollywood in force everyday, bringing home the lost and drug-ridden youth of the metropolis. New converts "forsook all" at the L.A. colony, stayed there for a two-week trial period to test their sincerity, and were then bused to the TSC ranch in a large bus purchased for us by Fred Jordan. TSC was our version of Bible college.

While L.A. flourished, things in Texas steadily picked up momentum. Regular witnessing trips to Austin, Dallas, Houston, and other college towns were reaping many new converts. Teams were summarily sent out to pioneer new fields in other cities of the United States such as Detroit, New York, San Diego, Cincinnati, San Francisco, and Denver.

The COG soon became known as the most tightly organized of the Jesus People groups and the most fervently loyal. This, of course, was due to the abilities of my father and the loyalty of his personally trained core of leaders. Their zeal and dedication were passed on by spiritual osmosis to all new converts. Having a Prophet to follow, a charismatic leader, a personality who heard directly from God gave tremendous security and stability to the disciples, both individually and collectively.

Individually, each disciple could rest confident that our ship was being steered on the right course, because God's specially anointed leader was at the helm. Even though he, the disciple, couldn't really see the overall direction of things, he could rest assured that God would work through Mo to guide us to the Promised Land. Collectively, we believed our movement was much better than any of the rest, because God had seen fit to exercise His sovereignty and choose the Children of God as His special Jesus People group.

Questions of doctrine and theology did not have to be wrestled with by the disciples of the COG—these complicated issues that tended to trouble the mind could be left to Mo to decide. The only personal struggle that arose was a decision to throw oneself wholeheartedly into the main thrust of the movement. Since vigorous, full-time dedication was admired and rewarded by the group, a disciple could direct all energies into enthusiastically living COG doctrine and lifestyle to the utmost of his or her ability. God was leading the body of the COG in a unique and perfect path, just as He did ancient Israel; consequently one need only stay close to the Family, and the end of one's efforts could only result in the rewards of life in a spiritual Promised Land.

Blind faith, naive obedience, irresponsible dedication, fanatical loyalty—these were the volatile chemicals of human devotion that ignited the zeal of the COG into a white-hot blaze of emotion. I believe that a vast number of youths who joined our ranks did not join primarily out of a desire to live the purity of the Christian faith, but were attracted and caught up by our absolute commitment to a cause. They themselves, without purpose or direction in life, were like pieces of dry wood placed next to a raging bonfire, and they were set ablaze and consumed by the fire of our devotion. We were a gigantic sales force, and contemporary social conditions made our marketing potential unlimited. The effects of the counterculture had graciously prepared a vast host of customers eager for our product: a reason for living, purpose and direction, freedom from financial anxiety, separation from the evil system, rebellion against established authority, a need for love—all in the name of Jesus.

These youth joining the Children of God were committing themselves to more than faith in Jesus Christ. They were in fact submitting mind, body, and soul to the personal lifestyle of David Berg. There were those who did this unknowingly at first, but as their time in and knowledge of the Family increased, each came to a knowledgeable decision that they were following Moses David.

Until the summer of 1971, the moral lifestyle of the COG was strict and puritanical. Dating was forbidden, as were kissing and holding hands. Sex was absolutely taboo outside of marriage. The only exception to this was, of course, Mo. But his situation was specially ordained and known only to the leadership. However, this condition of moral piety among the body of the Children of God was not to remain for long.

When we arrived at TSC in February 1970, we numbered only 150. In September 1971, just a year and a half later, when we were thrown off Jordan's property, there was considerable change. The Children of God would number over 2,000 full-time members, with colonies throughout the United States and other parts of the world. The period of growth at the TSC ranch was a turning point in the success of the cult of David Berg. We would no longer be a fledgling band of nomadic prophets—we were a New Nation. Following the days at the Texas Soul Clinic, there would be no stopping the Children of God.

Chapter 8
Sin in the Camp

Moses David returned in secrecy from his nine-month trip to Israel and Europe. It had been his desire to stay permanently in Europe, but he was compelled to return to the United States to put in order problems in my marriage that were threatening to disrupt the work. Mo's plan was to return to Europe immediately after he had dealt with me and had plotted the conquest of Europe with his leadership cabal.

Before he left the U.S. again, however—feeling the full effects of his newly acquired power and authority as the Prophet on the Mountain, he decided to introduce some new doctrines into the ranks of the Royal Family.

Dad had rented a two-room studio apartment in a Dallas motel that doubled as a meeting place for leadership conferences. The Royal Family members would drive over from the TSC ranch to discuss battle plans. The Revolution for Jesus was exploding, and there were many decisions to be made. I can now see that Dad was already beginning to go off the deep end. His letters from

Europe had become more fanatical, and he was losing all sense of natural morality—as in the case of Abner's wife.

Abner, one of our top leaders, had been killed while riding a motorcycle cross-country on the ranch. His cycle overturned, and he was thrown to the ground. Apparently his head struck a rock, and he went into a coma from which he never awoke. He died a few days after the accident. Prior to the funeral Dad received a prophecy directing him to take Abner's wife, Shiphrah, as his own. So Moses David now had four wives: my mother, Maria, Martha, and Shiphrah.

Intoxicated by absolute power, Dad calculated that he could introduce the doctrine of sexual "sharing" among the members of his immediate family. We had been having numerous leadership conferences, and after these meetings often stayed the night, as it was a long drive to TSC from Dallas. On one of these nights, Dad made his move. I thought, "Oh God, Dad's going to make us get into it too." Until then, only Dad was exercising sexual freedom. But the Prophet was intent on teaching his family members how to practice "true spiritual freedom." When I realized what was happening, my mind short-circuited. I slipped out of the apartment unnoticed. I walked aimlessly down the road. My thoughts flashed back to Vienna, to that nightmare I had carefully buried in the back of my mind, to the remembrance of seeing my mother publicly humiliated. I recalled the sexual advances my father had made toward me as a child.

My mind flipped into a state of utter confusion and dissillusionment. I was overwhelmed by doubts about Dad, about God, about my whole state of existence. As my head swirled, my conscience brought the weight of sin and guilt crashing viciously upon me. I was experiencing a breaking point.

My first breaking point occurred at Vienna when my dad introduced the "Old Church, New Church" prophecies. As I review my ten years in the Children of God, I can see that I have experienced about eight breaking points. These are the times when circumstances and events cause a person to question why he is doing what he is doing, why he is in the COG, why he is following Moses David. I believe that during these breaking points, God—through the influence of the Holy Spirit on my conscience—was trying to help me to see the truth. Being a fiercely proud person, I was not yet in a position to face the truth about my father and what we were "doing for the Lord." To admit that Dad was walking in darkness was a terrifying thought. I wrestled with that reality and forced it back into the innermost closet of my mind.

Before long, the family in the apartment realized I had run away, and my husband came looking for me. He found me walking rapidly down a back road many blocks from the motel. I tried to ignore his presence, but he pleaded with me to get into his car and go back and talk it out with Dad. When we finally returned, I was able to speak privately with my dad.

"Linda dear," he began smoothly (using my given name, which he always used in private), "perfect love casteth out all fear."

He was quoting 1 John 4:18 to explain that my inability to accept this new spiritual freedom was due to my lack of perfect love.

"If you had perfect love as the Bible speaks of," he said, "and were living totally within the love of Christ, you would understand that with other members of the 'body' who also live within this perfect love, we can share freely with one another and there are no boundaries, not even sexual ones. We are all 'one body' and all things are lawful, honey—all things."

This was Dad's "All Things" doctrine, a takeoff from Paul's statement in 1 Corinthians 6:12, which states, "All things are lawful unto me. . . ." Dad was teaching that this freedom was a manifestation of grace, a result of being part of the body of Christ. It was not "immorality," but "love." After all, we were all part of the same "body."

Because I refused to go along with Dad's concept of mandatory sharing, I was consigned to the class of the "unspirituals." My refusal to accept Dad's All Things doctrine certainly did not arise from my being any more righteous than the rest of the Royal Family, but rather, there was something inside me that rebelled and caused me to resist. Consequently, a conflict developed within me. From that moment on, I believed that because I could not accept this doctrine of sexual freedom, I therefore did not have a close relationship with the Lord. I lacked that "perfect love" and was simply not as spiritual as the rest. Throughout my remaining years in the Family I felt great condemnation because of this. However, because of my resistance—running away as I did that day—Dad left me alone and never again tried to include me in his orgies.

After he had indoctrinated the Royal Family members, Dad began to bring other top leaders to his Dallas apartment for "training." He invited the major leaders and their wives under the pretense of leadership meetings, and there he began their instruction in the doctrine of "sharing." In turn, these people returned to TSC and, in the months to follow, slowly began to teach others the same. They had been admonished to handle this "freedom" with discretion, so they did not practice it among the babes or disciples new to the Family. It was kept among the "old-timers"— those who were "mature in the faith."

Ironically, NBC had just shown the highly favorable "First Tuesday" documentary to the American public. This portrayed the COG to be a very puritanical, Christian organization—which, at the time of the filming, was basically true. When producer Bob Rogers and the NBC crews were filming at TSC, we lived morally chaste lives. But by the time of its release, Mo had returned from Israel and things had changed irrevocably.

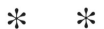

Dad retreated to Oklahoma late in the summer of 1971, but not until he had taken another wife: Rachel. During the days in Laurentide, in the summer of 1969, he had married Rachel to a young man named Samson. It seems Dad repented of his hasty actions and wanted Rachel for himself. Samson was a dedicated follower, a true revolutionary disciple ready to forsake all for Mo or the Lord at a second's notice. Now Dad explained the situation to Samson:

"Son, the Lord has revealed to me that I should take Rachel back. The Lord has used you to take care of Rachel these past two years, and you've done a good job. 'Well done, thou good and faithful servant.' But God's ways are not our ways, and it seems the Lord wants Rachel to be with us."

What could Samson do? He had dedicated his life in service to God, he believed Mo was the voice of God on earth, and he was fully committed to following Mo—so he conceded. It was a sacrifice for the Lord, and Samson knew that he must always be willing to give all for Jesus. Samson's dedication was typical of the people who joined the Children.

Shortly after the transaction, Dad received numerous prophecies stating that Rachel would be a great leader in the Family, that she would become the "Great Queen of the Revolution" and do many "mighty things for God." At any rate, Samson's loss was Dad's gain. Dad left for Oklahoma in his motor home with only Rachel and Maria. He stayed in seclusion there for several months until his departure for England in spring 1972.

Rachel had had a baby by Samson, and she was required to leave the child in Texas. "God will take care of it," Dad explained. It's amazing how little regard my father showed for the welfare of the children. We were taught that any sacrifices could be made at the expense of the children and God would provide their needs because we were doing it for the "cause." Dad never considered or believed that the children could be harmed psychologically.

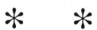

In the meantime, I was sent to Los Angeles to fight a sudden wave of bad publicity in California. Although I was classed with the "unspirituals," I was placed in key positions of responsibility because of my capabilities. Dad especially liked to use me in public relations, because he felt I was the perfect one to "deal with the systemites" in that I was affable, self-assured, and able to communicate with sincerity and conviction.

The bad publicity started as a result of several children from well-to-do families who had joined our ranks. The parents were furious. These children were not the typical dropout hippies who had thrown their lives away on drugs; they were nice kids from nice families. At the same time, Ted Patrick's son tried to join the COG in San Diego, and Patrick was irate! These parents teamed up and formed an organization that became known as FREE-COG. Their purpose was to free their sons and daughters from the movement.* Fred Jordan had been using the Children of God to promote his TV show in L.A. and felt obligated to align himself with our cause and help us combat Free-COG. For that reason he hired an attorney for us.

But with adverse publicity mounting in L.A. and Free-COG gaining power and support, Fred Jordan found himself between the devil and the deep blue sea. The COG witnessing teams were faithfully bringing in scores of lost youth off the streets of L.A. Fred had worked out a very effective promotion with these kids. He would feature some of the "dirty hippies" on his TV show, announcing their recent conversion to Christianity. The following week these same "hippies" would appear on the show, but this time they were neatly dressed, clean-shaven, all-American boys. Fred proudly announced what great things his ministry was doing to help the wayward youth of the nation and then appeal for money to continue this worthwhile ministry. In 1972 Enroth, Ericson, and Peters wrote a book entitled *The Jesus People*. Their comment on the Jordan-Berg connection was quite perceptive:

> *Jordan describes himself as a representative of the establishment who felt a need to reach radical youth. Since he could not do this himself, he associated with the Children of God. On his television show Jordan often spoke as if the Children of God were his ministry, but this was not at all the case. He was the benefactor, not the administrator. His program distorted the Children of God by making them look more ordinary and unexceptional than they really are. He camouflaged those eccentric doctrines with which he did not agree. His appeal to businessmen for funds to support the Children of God was, "You'd better help us reach these tough kids, or they'll destroy your businesses. We're the only ones who can reach them." Jordan plays on the desire of right-wingers to keep America Christian and orderly, followed by an appeal for funds.[1]*

---

*The organization was formed as the "Parents' Committee to Free Our Sons and Daughters from the Children of God Organization," soon took the name "FREE-COG," went national in February 1972, and was strong and active until 1974.

Obviously the authors saw through this relationship with great accuracy. However, at the time they had no idea how great the inconsistencies really were. The fact is, Fred Jordan used the COG and the COG used Fred. Jordan began to raise funds on his TV show to buy a 110-acre ranch in Coachella, California, some miles east of L.A. This was to be another rehabilitation site, a facsimile of TSC. He asked for a half-million dollars from the TV viewers. It is reported that he raised $160,000 in just two months.

The Coachella ranch consisted of a beautiful, sprawling, Spanish-style ranch house, a gorgeous swimming pool, a fountain, citrus trees, acres of date palms, and more. Nearby there was another ranch with a large, new Quonset hut, a very small two-bedroom house, a shack, but no swimming pool. The latter facilities are what Fred gave to the Children of God to use. The main ranch was off-limits. But to prove to the public that their dollars were going to the rehabilitation of wayward youth, Fred invited news reporters and TV cameramen to "come and see" and invited all the Children living in the nearby ranch to visit the big ranch and go swimming. He put out heaping trays of food and filmed the disciples swimming, eating, and thoroughly enjoying themselves on the grounds. Then the COG were sent back to their own facilities. And thus the film footage showed the new Coachella ranch being used by the COG.

The Children of God claimed to be antiestablishment and anti-church—true Revolutionaries for Jesus. Yet our association with Fred Jordan greatly compromised the radical position we boasted on the streets. How hypocritical! Enroth, Ericson, and Peters wrote,

> *While the Children of God proclaim an uncompromising line to potential recruits, their liaison with Fred Jordan was a serious compromise. They knew that he was using them, picturing them as something other than what they are, but they were willing to make this concession in order to gain important bases of operation from which to recruit new members.*[2]

My dad had a remarkable ability to humble himself just enough to get what he wanted—a trait passed on to his children and followers. I personally was there for the mock filming of "our" ranch and knew that Fred was using us, just as we were using him. I knew that Fred had no idea what many of our radical doctrines were, for they had been carefully guarded within the movement. I've often thought about all the money the public donated to "help the Children"; neither I nor the COG will ever know what it was really used for.

We were taught in the Family to "use whatever or whomever you can to gain your purpose. Use it!—That's the goal!" After years of service to his mother and to Fred Jordan, Dad seemed to have an incurable case of that disease of using a righteous end to excuse an unrighteous means. Eventually, through hundreds of Mo Letters, the disciples became indelibly stained with this same moral defect. The final product of this philosophy can be seen in what the Children of God are today.

But the rewards Fred Jordan had gained through the COG were disappearing. There is little doubt that he had stumbled upon a goose that was laying golden eggs, but FREE-COG was "fixin' to cook that goose." Fred had no desire to be cooked as well. FREE-COG told him that he had two choices: Expel the COG from all his properties, or they would investigate and sue him for illicit practices. It was blackmail.

While the witnessing teams from the L.A. colony were out on the streets, Jordan sent security guards to lock the front doors at their home. When the youth returned, they found themselves suddenly homeless. We camped out in MacArthur Park for a week while Fred slowly released our personal belongings to us from his building with the help of pressure from local authorities. He then delivered an ultimatum to the groups in Coachella and at TSC in Texas: COG members had to either renounce Dad and serve Fred, or move off the property immediately. They marched right off the Coachella ranch, bag and baggage to the last man. However, we in the family were a bit reluctant to give up on TSC, our main base, and prepared to fight eviction through legal means. But Dad got one of his revelations, and orders came from the top to "move out now! This is only God's way of moving us on to higher ground!"

Mo spiritualized the whole affair, explaining that God was

going to use this "persecution" as a means of sending us into all the world. FREE-COG hoped that if we had no place to live, it would put an end to the movement; they failed to see that spiritual wickedness is not combatted by physical means. Instead of stopping us, opposition only caused us to grow, just as Saul of Tarsus' persecution led to a burgeoning of the early church. The three hundred COG disciples simply translated into fifteen scattered colonies; in time those fifteen colonies became thirty, and so on. Mo turned the incident into a positive event, a change in direction. The day for big colonies had ended; small colonies were the new order.

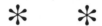

Our expulsion from Fred Jordan's properties coincided with the COG's takeover of the Jesus People Army in the Pacific Northwest. Russ Griggs, leader of the "Jesus People" in Vancouver, Washington, and Linda Meissner, leader of the "Jesus People" in Seattle, decided to join forces with the Children of God. Both these groups had their origins in the same revivalist stirrings that had bred Teens for Christ and the COG.*

In light of what we now know about the Children of God, it is interesting to see how the movement founded by David Berg attracted Griggs and Meissner. On Meissner's part, she had envisioned the organization of a vast "army" of devoted followers of Christ that would sweep the world with the message of the gospel in the "last days." However, her Jesus People Army was not fulfilling this vision; her following lacked the total dedication of the disciples of the COG. She saw in us what her Jesus People Army did not have. But neither Griggs nor Meissner had any notion that the key to such fanatical loyalty was the person of Moses David. They wrongly deduced that we possessed something "vi-

---

*The term "Jesus People" was adopted by specific organizations such as these. But the term was also used generically to refer to diverse groups in the religious movement that swept North America among youth and the counterculture in the late sixties and early seventies.

tal" to spiritual success, that we had something of the "Spirit of God" they had yet to uncover.

Griggs and Meissner looked at our rapid growth and concluded that it could only be the hand of God. This is the deceiving lure of religious works and a source of great error: People who think it is up to them to do God's work, and who believe that spiritual credibility can be judged on statistics, numbers, and success. Phony organizations such as the COG take great pains to publish and promote their statistics; they are well aware of the fact that people are easily deceived by an outward show of religious works.

Thus the Jesus People Army, intent on promoting the kingdom of God rather than seeking it, were greatly impressed by the COG's numerical prosperity and disciple loyalty. Obviously they felt it would be to their advantage to join forces. Underneath it all their attraction was triggered by a desire for power and success. Indeed, they had something to gain. The authors of *The Jesus People* accurately commented:

> One of the Jesus People leaders who tried to talk Linda Meissner out of joining the cult was amazed to listen to Meissner and Jethro conning each other, neither recognizing what the other was up to. Meissner expects to use the Children, and the Children expect to use her. The advantage seems to be all on the side of the Children: we have yet to discover an instance in which they have been outmaneuvered.[3]

In the merging of the JPA with the COG there recurred the mystique of the lure of the cults. The cults deceive, yet the victims are deceived because they are tempted by some unrighteous motive. It reflects the concept of "dual validation"—both parties seeking to promote "self" by a voluntary mutual involvement.

Jethro and I conducted the negotiations and led Meissner and Griggs to believe that we two were actually in charge. We were given strict orders by Mo to leave his name out of the picture as much as possible. Power is at the root of cultic activities. Even though the Jesus People Army was deceived and blatantly "ripped off," their motives were not pure. A desire for success and power had weakened and corrupted their judgment.

God does not lead people into evil; He leads them away from it. Those who have been involved in a cult, who have been influenced by one in some way, must look at themselves. Even those with apparent motivation to spread the gospel of Jesus Christ must examine why they were affected and attracted. Anyone lured by the Children of God was responding to illegitimate motives, even unconscious ones, because from the beginning the direction of the COG was toward darkness—we grew out of an evil root.

Many of the early members of the COG—later called "old bottles"—began to leave as we strayed further and further from the Bible—"Old Word"—toward the Mo Letters—"God's New Word." They couldn't accept the "new wine." Anyone who was truly seeking biblical truth was motivated to leave sooner or later.

The combined force of the exodus from Fred Jordan's properties and the amalgamation of the Jesus People Army spurred tremendous growth for the COG. But at the same time, the destructive influence of sin in the camp was struggling to break through and show its ugly countenance.

The leadership trained in the All Things doctrine by Mo in Dallas were now scattered in various colonies around the United States. Like a disease, they carried in their hearts the virus of sexual immorality, and the infection was beginning to spread. Once the cancer of immoral desires takes hold, it is not easily cut out. Soon these leaders began to infect others. Immorality had been sanctified through the word of the Prophet. Youth who had only recently abandoned their licentious lifestyle in the counterculture were suddenly reveling in their old sins—but now it was done in the name of Jesus. Incident after incident began to occur in the colonies where these leaders were living. But not without consequences.

In Burlington, a large colony north of Seattle that housed more than a hundred disciples, there was a sudden outbreak of hepatitis, scabies, and other illnesses. In other colonies, new disciples—"spiritual babes"—had been brought into the All Things activities, would not tolerate them, and left the Family severely wounded and bitter. The news media began to pick up on some of the stories, and it was being reported that COG leadership was involved in promiscuous behavior. By spreading the doctrine among the leadership prematurely, Dad had opened the lid on a Pandora's box. Things were spreading too rapidly to be controlled; the leadership was out of hand.

Dad interpreted the sudden rash of illnesses and the negative publicity as a warning from the Lord. He wrote a Letter to all the leaders entitled "Sin in the Camp," which succeeded in bringing the fires of immorality under control temporarily. Those who had been overindulging in "excesses of the flesh"—those leaders who had not used their sexual freedom discreetly—were called on the carpet and demoted. They were reprimanded, not because they had committed immorality, but because through their lack of control they had neglected the sheep and gotten the work into trouble through bad publicity.

Albeit, these outbreaks of "uncontrolled liberty" had lifelong effects on the people involved. It is utterly impossible to comprehend the results of my father's monstrous iniquity: the disease of his All Things doctrines is affecting the lives of tens of thousands.

Gail, a twenty-one-year-old disciple, was one of the first to be affected. It happened as she was passing through the Burlington colony on her way back to Seattle in late October 1971. On the same night, one of our leaders—a young man personally instructed by Mo in the All Things doctrine—was also passing through. Gail had been in the Family for ten months and until that fateful night had lived a completely chaste and moral life in the COG. Circumstances placed Gail and the leader in the same room, and he began to expound the things Mo had taught him: "We are free under grace to share love. . . . All things are lawful. . . . The church system has been put under bondage. . . ."

Gail was genuinely confused. Nevertheless, she said she truly admired this leader and was more than willing to consent. It wasn't rape, but she was surely victimized. That is the enigma with sin and the lure of the cults: people are genuinely defrauded, victimized, and deceived, yet they are willing victims.

The next morning Gail said good-by to the leader she greatly admired. But he didn't care to speak with her. To her feelings of confusion was added the pain of rejection. As it turns out, Gail became pregnant that night. Nine months later she bore a son, who has lived the past twelve years without a father.

Gail's life in the COG continued; she finally left after twelve years of service. But the effects of Moses David's love doctrines were tragic. On paper his ideas looked so wonderful, so lofty, so ideal: Total love, total sharing, one body united in Christ. Gail was faithful to these teachings. She is now the mother of five children, by three different men, and none of them have a father to love them.

Gail no longer lives under the deceptive tyranny of David Berg's All Things. She lives alone and raises her children alone. The men legally responsible for the children are busy "serving God"—obeying a "much higher calling"—and have set aside their obligations to their children. In the world of the Children of God, it's lawful, too, to walk out on your wife and children.

In September 1979 he published the following statement:

> The Lord is very reasonable and merciful and understanding and loving and kind, so that if two people simply do not want to live with each other He does not make rules to force them to do so as man does. —PREGNANCIES FROM SEX need no longer be considered as obligations to marry as before. Some have not felt free to help each other for fear it might require marriage if pregnancy occurs. That's optional. We are all married together into one Family to one Lord, one wife, one bride. So every girl in the Family, whether you were the one who got her pregnant or not . . . oh baloney! THE LORD IS THE ONE WHO GOT HER PREGNANT!
> SO FORGET ABOUT WHO IS RESPONSIBLE! That's so ridiculous! God was responsible.[4]

My father's All Things doctrine translates into nothing but unmitigated selfishness. Sex for pleasure, sex without responsibility, sex for sex' sake.

The voice of lust forever screams: "I want it, and I want it now!" Moses David has succeeded in arousing the insatiable lusts of thousands of disciples—but who will still the cries of the fatherless?

Chapter 9
"World Conquest Through Love"

In April 1972 Mo left his hideout in Oklahoma for England, never to set foot on American soil again. England would become his headquarters for the next two years.

By the beginning of 1972 Moses David had successfully retarded the spread of immoral behavior throughout the COG family. Those who had been involved were removed from their positions of leadership, and of some Mo made a public spectacle. He was always—and still is—quite fond of public verbal executions. He feels it puts the fear of God in others and encourages obedience—discipline by terror, an effective tactic used, for example, by the Ayatollah Khomeini in recent years. Nevertheless, Dad was able to curb the premature outbreak of sexual liberties and even caused those who were guilty but had not been caught to stop their licentious behavior.

Then, in the spring of '72, Dad began to wield some new "scare tactics" designed to shift the direction and momentum of his Revolution for Jesus. It was now time for the "Great Escape," a special warning revelation he received from the spirit world. On April 24, 1972, he announced: "The storm of God's judgements upon the ease and luxury of these nations, particularly America, is fast approaching, and the sea and waves of the uprisings of people are about to rage!"[1] He warned his faithful followers that all escape routes out of America would be closed as soon as "the Storm of God's Judgments begins to break upon the wickedness of the Lowlands of America!" In a subsequent, emergency Mo Letter, entitled "Flee As A Bird To Your Mountain," he warned his disciples to run for their lives while there was still a chance.[2] Soon the COG began a mass exodus out of the States. Many fled to South America; others escaped to England and the Continent.

Mo himself had already left for England. Faithy and Hosea had been there for well over a year and had established a work in the London suburb of Bromley. No doubt my father saw the handwriting on the wall and realized that he would not be able to continue his immoral practices in the United States and get away with it. He was scared of FREE-COG and terrified of America's justice system. A guilty man has reason to fear, and David Berg knew that in the near future he would become a lot more vulnerable in expanding a movement dedicated to wholesale debauchery. Knowing full well the dangers that faced him, he gathered his prophetic robes about him and left.*

Shortly afterward, the NBC television network aired its second documentary on the Children of God. The first program, "First Tuesday," had presented a sympathetic picture in 1971; but "Chronolog" painted quite a different scene in 1972.

Because reports of sexual promiscuity in the COG had begun to emerge by the time of the showing on "First Tuesday," Bob Rogers, the producer, looked the fool in the eyes of the public. "First Tuesday" led America to believe that we were ultra-puritanical in our moral standards—which we were at the time of the filming, except for my father. But things had changed in the movement, and Bob Rogers had a score to settle.

Feigning friendship, Rogers flew to England to interview my brother Hosea. Naturally Hosea received him with open arms.

---

*David Berg's fear of legal authorities was well-founded. Eventually the attorney general of the State of New York issued a report substantiating many of the claims made against COG activities. But that was in September 1974—long after Mo had fled the country and his disciples with him.

But in a carefully constructed interview, Rogers broached the subject of immorality in the Family; he zeroed in on the person of David Berg, his sexual exploits, and his totalitarian rule as "prophet" of the COG. Mr. Rogers was intent upon showing the public what was truly behind this highly organized, regimented Christian organization.

When asked if there was immorality going on within the COG, Hosea flatly denied it. Roger's countered Hosea's statements with interviews he had filmed in America of female ex-members who gave eyewitness accounts. The stark contrast between Hosea's denial and the witnesses' testimony was incredible. But why would Hosea lie? To him it was not lying. All cult members are taught instinctively to lie; the COG is not unlike other cults in that matter. One is taught that it is okay to "cover" the truth of things because "other people wouldn't understand our beliefs." Therefore, when Mr. Rogers asked Hosea about immorality, Hosea flatly denied it. Hosea did not believe it was "immorality." Hosea's thoughts: "To the public it may appear as immorality, but to us it is the freedom of God's spirit, which they know nothing of."

The final documentary for "Chronolog" showed Hosea to be an outright, bold-faced liar. And he was.

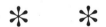

FREE-COG, which had helped Bob Rogers compile much of the negative evidence for the show, hoped that the "Chronolog" documentary would force the COG out of the States. Basically it did just that, although Mo himself had already left. Rogers had struck back with a powerful blow that drove us underground. The documentary, combined with the "Great Escape" Mo Letter, forced the disciples to leave the States and marked the beginning of the end of active work by the COG in America.

But, in typical fashion, Moses David simply used the "Chronolog" film to renew the dedication of his followers to the cause and strengthen his position as Prophet and leader. The film was "an attack of the Devil" and representative of "righteous persecution." The Bible clearly states, Mo noted, that "all who will live godly in Christ Jesus shall suffer persecution." Thus "Chronolog" was one more proof that we were living the true gospel and that Mo was truly the Prophet. Mo proclaimed that the incident was God's way of purging the ranks and preparing the way for the COG to go into all the world and preach the gospel. We had conquered the United States; now it was time to conquer Europe and the rest of the World!

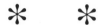

Bromley, England, served as a landing place for all the "refugees" fleeing America before its "imminent destruction." It was in this setting that Mo developed the concept of the Royal Family and crowned me Queen.

From Bromley the disciples were sent into different parts of England and eventually to the Continent. Pioneering teams began to establish colonies in France, Germany, Switzerland, Italy, and Spain. Our message and radical approach appealed to the European youth, and our American drive and industriousness were also admired as the Revolution for Jesus surged forward.

We were making great advances in Latin America as well. Puerto Rico, Mexico, and Brazil received the songs and smiles of the Children with great enthusiasm. We spread to Hawaii (which was a little safer than the contiguous states), Australia, and New Zealand. Late in 1972 our first pioneering team arrived in India; today India is a major focal point of Children of God activity.

By September 1973 we had approximately two hundred colonies scattered through about fifty countries.

In February 1973 the COG experienced a turning point in its public witness. It occurred on February 18—my father's birthday. On that day he received a special revelation that he should begin the mass publication of the Mo Letters for the entire world. Until this time, the Letters had been strictly for consumption by the faithful followers and, on occasion, friends of the Family. But in a prophecy entitled "The Birthday Warning," Moses David was rebuked for restricting the use of the Letters—because the Mo Letters were now as important as the Bible. Therefore it was time to begin publishing these Letters for everyone. We were on the threshold of the "Literature Revolution."

Furthermore, the COG's growth rate had seriously declined, and Mo offered this explanation:

> . . . *We've reached a certain limitation in our ability to grow any further because we have reached the limitations of our leadership that we had originally trained. Most of our leaders throughout the world are still those approximately 150 who were originally trained in California and Texas. . . who were either trained by us or our family personally. . . .*[3]

What to do about the shortage of leadership? Publishing literature was the answer! "God said we now lack leaders because we lack literature, and the literature they need most are the Letters of the Leader!"[4] Mo explained that publishing the Mo Letters would give him and our movement world fame and notoriety. He wrote,

> *Nobody ever heard of Mao until his words really worked—then the whole world heard about him! Why?—Because they put it in print, and his little Red "Thoughts From Chairman Mao" have circled the globe. . . .*
> *Nobody ever heard of little old Mo, either, until his words began to work. . . . We must put them in print on paper so they can circulate around the Globe available to all! Millions for the billions!*[5]

It was now time to publish millions of copies of Mo Letters. "Every disciple, every leader, every Colony, every . . . whatever your job may be, must now know that your main job is to help in some way to get the words that work to the world!"[6]

Overnight, print shops sprang up all over the world producing Mo Letters. Then Moses David wrote a Letter called "Shiners?—or Shamers!" that outlined the principles and directives of "litnessing"—distributing Mo Letters on the street as a new method of witnessing.[7] No longer were we to go out and win people to Christ through conversation: our No. 1 job was to distribute literature and collect donations. Quotas were established; those who distributed the most were rewarded, and those who failed to meet their quotas were chastised.

During 1972 we had published 3 million pieces of literature. But in 1973 the figure soared to 19 million. The numbers grew: 55 million in 1974, 58 million in 1975; and 68 million in 1976. Literature distribution has continued to rise every year.

In the early days of the Literature Revolution, disciples were frequently forbidden to return to their colony until they had distributed their quotas. It was not uncommon to see disciples searching the streets at three o'clock in the morning looking for someone to buy a piece of literature. Before long the financial status of the Family began to change.

Dad had written a Letter entitled "Rags to Riches" in which he exhorted the leadership to think big, to think success, and not to be content with remaining at the poverty level.[8] "Shiners?—Or Shamers?" seemed to offer an effective strategy for improving our financial condition.

Until we began selling Mo Letters on the street, we had been a very poor organization. We lived merely on the money received from new disciples "forsaking all" and donations of material goods solicited from local businesses. I recall one man who joined with his family and forsook his house—which we sold for $75,000. This, of course, was the rare exception. Most of the people joining were lost youth who owned nothing but the clothes on their backs. All the finances were pooled, and we struggled along. Nearly all our food came through our "provisioning teams"—specially designated disciples who phoned and visited businesses requesting support for our work in "helping youth off drugs."

Litnessing gave each colony a specific means of financial support. Yet our financial success never reached the proportions of cults like the Unification Church—the "Moonies"—who enjoy the benefits of affluence; we always seemed to have just enough to keep things running, even after intense litnessing. Finances were a perpetual concern.

With the advent of relative wealth, however, the complexion of the Family began to change rapidly. As our economic conditions improved in late 1973, Mo began to publish more and more messages on sex. Among them were "Revolutionary Sex," "Revolutionary Women," "Revolutionary Marriage," "One Wife," and "Mountain Maid," along with his Letters on the "Goddesses" with whom he was having sexual experiences.[9] In a calculated barrage of sexually provocative literature, he began to inflame the imaginations of his followers with sexual desires, but all in the name of Jesus—in the name of what is "natural, God-given, God-created, and perfectly normal." In a Letter entitled "Come On Ma! Burn Your Bra!" he condemned those within our ranks who continued to hang onto their "misconceived Christian morality." As in days past—when I was classed with the "unspirituals"—the disciples who were dragging their conservative heels were in peril of receiving the same condemnation.

> *A Revolution is a total break with the traditions of man and his churches and his preconceived ideas about God and misconceptions of morality. We have turned completely around and are going a different direction, no longer man's way but God's way, and we are free to enjoy to the full the beauties and wonders of His Creation with all of its pleasures which He Himself created for our enjoyment.[10]*

Mo warned his followers that those who could not handle the Mo Letters already written on sexual freedom "in the Lord" would certainly not be able to handle the "heavier forthcoming Letters." He wrote,

> *So if you think that sex and the human body are something evil and to be hidden instead of the beautiful wonderful creations of God to be revealed and enjoyed to the full, then you are indeed an old bottle and I doubt very much if you will be able to stand the even heavier Letters which are already on the way![11]*

My dad was writing this Letter as preparation for a new wave of perverted doctrine he was about to unleash on the disciples. Breaking down the traditional Christian morality of his followers was a delicate process and needed to be handled in stages. He used effective psychology to keep the disciples eager for the next Letter. Most of the followers were very insecure and didn't want to be "left behind." Playing on their insecurity, feelings of inferiority, and spiritual pride, Mo goaded his followers on, gently pitting one against the other to see who was "more revolutionary." He chided the reluctant: "If you can't receive it, then you're an old bottle. Only the true revolutionaries, the truly liberated, and the truly spiritual can receive God's new wine—God's specially revealed truths for today." The reward was the carrot of sensual pleasure.

> *If you can't take these and understand what is happening you'll certainly never be able to take what is coming, and we're very sorry for you.—Because if you quit now, you'll really miss the main events! We're not out to change the world—we're creating a totally new one! And if you don't fit it, I'm afraid we'll have to leave you behind.[12]*

With exhortations like this Mo fully "primed the pump," preparing the disciples for the "main events," which he was already practicing. By the time "Come On Ma" was published on December 22, 1973, he and Maria were taking the first steps toward instituting what Dad called "the exciting but dangerous new ministry of Flirty Fishing." The movement had reached another turning point.

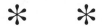

It began in London. Mo and Maria enrolled in an evening dance school. Dad's ploy was to send Maria out on the dance floor as "bait" to lure unsuspecting men into their lair. The very first person caught through Flirty Fishing was an Englishman named Arthur. After numerous evenings on the dance floor, Arthur and Maria began a sexual relationship. After Arthur was thoroughly caught in Moses David's net of immorality, he was passed on to one of Mo's other wives; Maria was commissioned to catch another "fish." If my father's cup of iniquity was not presently full, it would soon be overflowing beyond all imagination.

Maria kept up her new tactic of seducing men into the "kingdom." Each night Dad and his team would get a detailed report, record it, and transcribe and edit it for eventual publication. My father boasted that he had found a new method of ministry, but in reality he had only resurrected the pagan practice of religious prostitution. It was nothing more or less than the kind of worship with which the prophets of Baal led the Israelites astray thousands of years ago.

Along with this, however, I believe the demonic influence in my father's life reached new depths. Sexual perversion is a stock feature of occultic practices. Mo credited his revelations on sex, like his other prophecies, to Abrahim, his spirit guide, of whom he wrote,

> *People do come back [from the dead] and are helpful to someone, like Abrahim is to me. He is with me all the time, virtually incarnated in me! I never go any place without him. He travels with me. In a sense, I'm his Vehicle now just like his body was before.[13]*

❋   ❋

As the Flirty Fishing continued, Dad grew fearful that it could spell trouble for him in sophisticated England. He didn't feel he could promote it on a large scale among the followers there. So in March 1974 he and Maria and a small group of disciples moved to Tenerife in the Canary Islands, near Spain. There, in the freer atmosphere of the tourist resorts, the technique of "FFing," as Mo calls it, was developed and refined practically into an artform.

In Tenerife Mo virtually abandoned the name "Children of God" for his movement. Henceforth he would call it the "Family of Love." He adopted for himself the title "Father David." This reflected the strong impact that certain aspects of the island's Catholic culture made on Moses David. He used the title while he lived there, but abandoned it when he left.

Other changes came in the movement with the advent of Flirty Fishing. Not all the "fish" became Forsake All disciples. Tenerife was a tourist resort and many of the "fish" were interested only in the prostitution. Others were established citizens such as businessmen or civil service workers; they were not interested in giving up homes, families, jobs, or lifestyles to join the movement. Rather, Moses David accommodated them by conducting "Love Church" meetings. These meetings were more or less informal church services conducted by disciples and attended by various "fish" or interested tourists.

This marked a significant change in the movement. No longer was every proselyte to the movement expected to become a Forsake All follower. There were now "closet" followers who indulged in the Children of God as their religion, but kept their established way of life. This pattern has been maintained in the movement ever since Moses David initiated it on Tenerife. For every disciple living full-time in a COG colony somewhere in the world today, there are countless others who align themselves to the movement clandestinely—including government officials, wealthy buisnessmen, and the man on the street.

In the spring of 1975 Moses David interrupted his activities on the island of Tenerife to visit Moammar Gadahfi, the head of state of Libya. Dad had been courting a relationship with the dictatorial colonel from long distance after he began to receive special revelations about Gadahfi from Abrahim in 1971. In June 1973 Mo wrote a special Letter, "Gadahfi—and the Children of God," in which he explained why Gadahfi was someone special.

> *He may either be the Antichrist himself, or he is preparing the way for the Antichrist. But it is God-ordained, and it's obvious God has predicted it: He has prophesied it, He has revealed it through the Bible, Grandmother, Jean Dixon and us!*
>
> *We're to be absolutely friendly toward him. . . . We are to help him, we are to cooperate with him, be friendly toward him, and agree with his Third Alternative. . . .* [14]

According to Mo, Gadahfi would have an intimate relationship with the future Antichrist, and he left open the possibility that Gadahfi was the Antichrist himself. It was our duty to help the Libyan ruler in any way possible. While visiting Gadahfi in May 1975, Dad commented privately to the disciples with him, ". . . according to . . . Bible prophecy and some of the prophecies that God has given us, we're actually going to help the Antichrist to power."[15]

The disciples also were distributing, by the thousands, a particular Mo Letter that was favorable to Gadahfi. Entitled "Gadahfi's Third World," it praised the colonel and his "Third International Theory"—a plea for worldwide "godly socialism." Mo said that the Libyan was "the only world leader I've heard of who is raising his voice against both Capitalism and Communism and offering us the only alternative of a Godly Socialism. . . ."[16]

Impressed by this enthusiasm and the unexpected and unsolicited promotion of his cause, Gadahfi was prompted to invite COG representatives to visit him. After a visit from my brother Hosea and my sister, Gadahfi arranged for Mo to fly to Tripoli, the Libyan capital.

Dad spent about a month in Libya, but things weren't going the way he thought they would. He had taken with him a troupe of girls and started an FF ministry among some military leaders and Gadahfi's personal staff. But Gadahfi was not interested in prostitution—the Koran forbids it—even though his officers were. Rather, the Libyan wanted only to make use of the ten thousand COG disciples who were distributing literature around the world. Certainly we represented an efficient means of promoting Gadahfi's "Third International Theory." But Moses David was not interested—he was in over his head, and he knew it. He realized that Gadahfi could crush him like a bug if he wished.

In the beginning Dad was flattered to receive a personal invitation from a world leader, and he nurtured hopes of somehow using Gadahfi. But Dad soon saw that Gadahfi was out to use "this old man who was running around the world trying to act like a prophet and king." After spending his second month in Libya in a house guarded by armed soldiers, Dad realized that he was virtually a prisoner. He decided it would be better to keep his relationship with Gadahfi at a distance; so he quickly left Libya while he still had the chance.

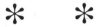

From Libya Dad flew directly to Italy, where he lived in my home for about five months. I was writing childcare and educational material for the Family in that country at the time. Upon leaving Italy, Dad returned to Tenerife and devoted his attention to promoting the still fledgling Flirty Fishing ministry.

Moses David launched a full-scale assault on the bars, discos, and night clubs of the small island. He brought in disciples from many other colonies. In the first of a series of Letters on Flirty Fishing, published in April 1976, Mo announced,

> *These letters together form a very important series of lessons on how to Flirty Fish when literally using sex as your bait. . . .*
> *We have already written a whole series on our FF experiences during the past three years, but which for security reasons we have not felt wise to release until now. We also felt it better to more thoroughly explore this new area of our ministry and pioneer it before revealing it to you. . . .[17]*

In a three-month period Moses David published twenty-three Mo Letters on FFing in a series he called "King Arthur's Knights." One Letter after another bombarded the disciples, and by the end of 1976 the COG became a world-wide prostitution network. (The total number of Mo Letters pertaining to Flirty Fishing has probably reached nearly five hundred to date.) Disciples litnessed during the day and FFed at night.

But success didn't come without a struggle. Flirty Fishing brought Dad unwanted publicity and attention from the law. It eventually spelled the end for his sojourn and prostitution network on Tenerife. It happened this way:

A man I can only describe as "a very good friend" of my father had been with him on Tenerife for some time—whether more or less than a year, I do not recall. He obviously had become a good friend, because Dad allowed the man to photograph him—something Dad had scrupulously forbidden for years in order to maintain his prophetic mystique. Whether the man was "planted" by journalists or was simply a tourist who at some point decided to exploit a ripe situation, I do not know. What is known is that the man left Tenerife in 1977 and published in *Stern*, a prominent West German magazine, a sensational article and the photograph—a picture of Moses David with a bevy of Flirty Fishers, including Maria.

The publicity went world-wide. *Time* magazine published the photograph along with a full-page article entitled "Tracking the Children of God" in its issue of August 22, 1977.* The results were predictable. Moses David described the situation in a subsequent Mo Letter:

> *We came out in the open with a whole army of 70 disciples and made a frontal attack! Then finally after a year's all-out battle we got all that publicity and boom! The island exploded! . . . with Europe-wide coverage!—maybe even the rest of the world. . . ."[18]*

A flock of FFers was arrested and charged with prostitution by Canary Islands authorities. As the leader of the group, Dad was indicted and summoned to court. He appeared for questioning on two occasions, but at the first opportunity he fled from the island and the authorities. He left the women there to stand trial.

Yet Flirty Fishing prospered elsewhere. Moses David's annual statistical newsletter for 1979 reported the growth of his new "ministry":

> *Our dear FF'ers are still going strong, God bless'm, having now witnessed to over a quarter-of-a-million souls, loved over 25,000 of them and won nearly 19,000 to the Lord, along with about 35,000 new friends.[19]*

The organization of David Berg had run an amazing gauntlet since the days of Huntington Beach—from witnessing to litnessing to Flirty Fishing. The evil that was imbedded in my father's heart in 1968 and earlier was now being planted in the hearts of hundreds of thousands of people throughout the world. His personal sin had now become the sin of thousands—and who could

---

*The *Time* report was prompted in part by a tape-recording sent to Time-Life offices the week before by Queen Rachel, who claimed that the voice on the recording was Moses David's. The tape denied the authenticity of a purported "Mo Letter" making the rounds which was entitled "God Bless You—And: Good-Bye!" The apparently fraudulent Letter included a "confession" by Moses David that he was a false prophet and said he was abandoning his movement.

Moses David and a bevy of Flirty Fishers on Tenerife in 1977. The photo, first published in Stern, *also appeared in* Time *and is probably the last published photo of David Berg. Maria is holding Mo's left hand.*

stop him? In a message to his army of FFers on the island of Tenerife in 1977, he said,

> *They will never stop us, because we're going to scatter into so many countries in so many ways that only the world government of the Antichrist could possible really organize a world-wide concerted attack against us. . . .*[20]

Part Two

A page from Mo Letter No. 666 (left) denouncing Bill Davis and portraying him as "Alexander" mesmerizing Deborah. The letter played a key part in Bill and Deborah's decision to forsake the cult. (Right) A Mo Letter depicting Moses David as a leonine prophet. He is usually sketched this way or as a bearded patriarchal figure; often a lion's head is pasted over his face in a photo. This tactic helps to preserve the prophetic mystique.

Chapter 10
"If the Truth Kills, Let It Kill!"

It doesn't matter if it kills Deborah, she'd be better off [dead]. . . one way or the other, God's will be done.

You tell Rachel I sent her there with a message . . . the truth of God.

Rachel is the executioner and I sent her to be the hatchet man, and she's either got to save them or kill them, one or the other! I know this business. . . you run the risk of killing the victim.

You tell her to get busy and kill them! Kill them! The quicker the better! I mean if they can't stand the truth they ought to die and be dead! Let's hope maybe they'll go to Heaven and not to Hell!

My Lord, if people would only receive what I tell them and obey it and do it! It doesn't matter if it kills people!

If the truth kills people, then they need to be killed! And if they won't believe and receive and obey the truth, then God damn them! Let them go to Hell as far as I'm concerned!

This message directed against me and my husband Bill, by my father on February 21, 1978, marked the beginning of the end:

the end of a thirty-one-year relationship of father and daughter, and the end of ten insane years in the Children of God.

Understanding this message and the details surrounding it brings to an end our adventure into the world of the bizarre, the unbelievable, what I call the "insanity of sin." It all seems so vague, so remote, like the fleeting memories of a distant nightmare. Yet it was no dream. It was all very, very real.

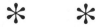

After my Coronation in London in September 1972 and my demotion six weeks later, I stayed in England for about six months. Dad had virtually excluded me from all leadership activities, so I lived in reclusion in a large Colony outside London. However, my seclusion was short-lived. The pressures of the situation, concern over the welfare of my children, and Dad's promptings forced me back into the mainstream of activities.

My brother Aaron had disappeared somewhere in France, and Dad ordered Jethro and me to the Continent to find him. Aaron had been losing touch with reality for some time. Circumstances brought his condition to a point of extreme aggravation when British Immigrations refused to allow his reentry into England. He had been on a short trip to Scandinavia and upon his return was turned away because of his association with the COG and the fact that he was a Berg. We had been receiving bad publicity at the time.

Aaron wanted to return to London to see Dad and resolve their differences. That he couldn't see Dad devastated him. He was forced to live in Paris, where he began to disappear for days at a time, taking long train rides to unknown destinations. He would return from these trips in a daze, as if he didn't know where he had been.

My father—though he will not admit it to himself—is keenly responsible for the death of his son. Aaron could not understand why he was experiencing many doubts, why he was suffering frustration and spiritual torment. He told my mother shortly before his final disappearance that his doubts about Dad were driving him crazy. He felt like a terrible sinner because he kept questioning his father's revelations concerning his role as the Endtime Prophet. Aaron had memorized vast portions of the Bible, and his knowledge of Scripture kept conflicting with the things his father did and said. Aaron's own involvement in sin compounded the weight of guilt and frustration. His self-condemnation weighed so heavily upon him that he could endure it no longer. Because of his intense love and his deep loyalty to his father, Aaron's mind was being torn in two.

Aaron wanted to love and follow his father; but inwardly his conscience was telling him No. The psychological and spiritual torment pushed him beyond the limits of rational thinking. His only alternative: end it all. He found it impossible to turn against his father, yet he could not rid himself of the negative thoughts.

The situation was compounded by my dad's attitude. Dad knew instinctively that Aaron was having serious doubts, and this was an affront to the Prophet. Dad put great pressure on Aaron to yield to his authority and, unsuccessful in that, finally rejected him. And Aaron knew his father didn't want him around. I believe that when Immigrations barred him from the country, Aaron considered it an act of Providence.

Some members of my family do not like to hear Aaron's death called a suicide. I respect their right to hold that opinion. I was not there with Aaron on that mountain in Switzerland. To my knowledge, no one was. So I cannot say with absolute certainty that Aaron took his own life. But I lived through the same hell he did; I know firsthand the struggle that can push a person to the brink of self-destruction.

Aaron's body was found at the base of a large cliff by two mountain climbers. According to the police report, he had been dead about two weeks before his body was discovered. Dad wrote a Mo Letter glorifying Aaron's death, a letter he called "Aaron on the Mountain." It explained to all the disciples that the "Lord took Aaron while he was mountain climbing." Dad tried to make it sound like the story of Enoch: Aaron was so "spiritual" that God finally just took him home. What a lie!

What makes Aaron's death all the more tragic is that he was in a real sense a spiritual catalyst from the early days of the movement. From the time of "Teens for Christ" onward, music played a vital role in our ministry; it was often the point of first contact with potential converts. Aaron—Paul—was our leading lyricist-arranger-composer. Many of his songs became stock in trade for the Jesus People and have nurtured Christians who have no idea of the music's origins. What a legacy!

The circumstances under which we learned of Aaron's mysterious death were themselves unusual.

Jethro and I had searched Paris and Geneva for several weeks and never found any indication of Aaron's whereabouts. We left his photo with the police and filed numerous missing-person reports. Being unsuccessful, we were instructed by Dad to continue south to Italy to help prepare for the wedding of Rachel to a wealthy Italian. Emanuel Canevaro, Duke of Zoagli, had taken an interest in the Family and specifically in Rachel. Dad was willing to give up one of his own wives for the sake of such an important union. It was not every day that an Italian duke married into the Children of God!

So in March 1973 I went to Italy.

Marrying a duke was no small affair. Emanuel and Rachel were married on the steps of a public plaza in Rome on Easter Sunday, April 22.

On the wedding day my mother, who had come to Italy for the ceremony, received a phone call from the Swiss police. It was a notification that a body had been discovered matching the description and photo on our missing-person report. Mother told no one, but went silently to the wedding as if nothing had ever happened. Later she explained, "I didn't want to spoil the wedding."

Dad had actually played a trick on Jethro and me. He fully intended that we move permanently to Italy and had lured us there with his request that we go for just a few weeks to "help out with the wedding." I spent ten months in Italy altogether, living with Rachel and Emanuel on one of the duke's large *fattorias* outside Florence.

In December I returned to Bromley, England, to have Christmas with Dad. When I arrived I was in for a big shock. I knew my father was changing and doing things that bothered me—many of which I could not understand or relate to—but despite these changes I still related to him as my father, as the man I knew in my childhood. But the change I saw in my father in December 1973 was incredible. He was no longer "Dad." He was 100 percent "Moses David." He was Maria's puppet.

It was my desire to have a happy Christmas, so I had set myself to buying presents, fixing a Christmas tree, and so on. But when I arrived at Dad's house, I found that access to the Prophet was now screened through Maria. We were no longer permitted to see him whenever we so desired. We had to clear it with Maria. I had come all the way from Italy to celebrate Christmas with my father only to discover that he was "too busy" with more important matters, that he was engaged in a secret mission! Dad and Maria were mysteriously going out every night, and no one knew exactly what was going on. Later we found out he was pioneering his new method of "evangelism" with Maria—involving a man named Arthur. Christmas Day came and Dad was gone. New Year's Eve came and Dad was gone. Dad was gone . . . lost in the world of Flirty Fishing.

Finally I managed to corner Dad so that I could discuss my purpose and future in the Family. My time in Italy had been a nightmare, so Dad gave me permission to work in Paris. Going to Paris permanently separated me from Jethro.

I arrived in Paris in January 1974, stunned over the drastic change in my dad and wondering what would now become of my life. It seemed that things were far beyond my control and even further beyond my understanding. For all practical purposes I was divorced, even though Dad did not allow divorce, just indefinite separations. I wondered how my children would respond to this new situation and what would be the end-result of Dad's change in personality. He was steadily growing more distant from his immediate family.

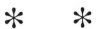

Paris became a place of dramatic change in my life. I had reached another breaking point. Again I faced a crucial decision: Retrace the footsteps of the past and face the truth, or cover it all up and go on. I was a master at masquerading, at hiding my true feelings, at putting up the front required of the Prophet's eldest daughter. I chose to go on—but with a twist. This time I would slowly and systematically starve myself to death. I guess I was an early victim of what was then an uncommon and little-understood disease, anorexia nervosa.

My efforts were nearly successful. At the end of six months I weighed eighty-five pounds, had an infectious blood disease, was hemorrhaging internally, and on the verge of aborting a three-month-old baby.

During this time I had been living with Bill Davis, and it was, in fact, his child I was carrying. He was known in the Family as "Isaiah." He was in charge of the COG's French Publications Department and was one of the key leaders in France.

Bill joined the Children of God on January 1, 1972, in Dallas, Texas. He was a young, idealistic youth—a product of the rebellious and restless counterculture of the late sixties and early seventies. Reared in a moderately wealthy suburb of Columbus, Ohio, Bill was brought up to be a Roman Catholic. But he rejected all notions of church and God when he began to study philosophy intensively at Ohio University. Running the gauntlet of drugs, political protest, existentialism, and depression, Bill experienced a spiritual conversion late in his junior year of college. Ironically, it was a witnessing team of the Children of God who had traveled from Cincinnati to the university in Athens, Ohio, who "led him to the Lord." He was a good student in college, despite his rebellion, and he graduated with honors. However, his discontent led him into an encounter with the COG in Dallas. Believing he had found the Truth, he threw himself—mind, body, and soul—into the cause.

When I met Bill in Paris I latched onto his youthfulness and zeal the way a drowning man grabs a life preserver. Bill and I began living together in January 1974. Yet even though I found great comfort in Bill's presence, I remained determined to continue my methodical starvation. Bill was oblivious to my state of health and was totally unaware of what I was doing. But by July my condition had so deteriorated that during a gala performance of our Parisian Show Group, "Les Enfants de Dieu," in Southern France, Bill felt it necessary to drive me to Geneva to seek medical assistance.

I was too weak to walk when we arrived in Geneva, so Bill took me to the doctor of a friend of ours. He took one look at me and said, "Has she been in a concentration camp?"

The doctor refused to prescribe medical treatment unless I admitted myself to a hospital. I refused. The same friend who had recommended the doctor owned a large hotel and put me in one of the rooms and said, "Please stay here until you are well." My hemorrhaging continued until I began to lapse in and out of consciousness. Bill was at a loss as to what should be done. One morning he was suddenly gripped with a fear that I was on the verge of death. Without telling anyone (which was not the thing to do where the daughter of Moses David was concerned), he wrapped me in a blanket and drove me to the hospital.

In the hospital I was placed in Intensive Care. All night long, according to reports, my life hung in the balance. My body simply did not have the life force to sustain the baby I had been carrying for four-and-a-half months. Between the condition of the blood disease, the baby's drain on my system, my acute loss of blood, and my body's state of malnutrition—something had to give. Apparently my body knew that if the baby wasn't aborted, I would die.

I began to fear for the baby's life and realized the folly of my self-starvation. My mental state was completely confused; having drifted in and out of consciousness for nearly forty-eight hours, I had no real sense of my condition. Doctors, needles, nurses, and medical objects kept appearing and disappearing along with my consciousness. I started to cry, pleading with God not to take the baby. I was delirious all night. I remember that the nurses were very kind; they kept trying to calm me down. "Don't worry, everything will be fine. Everything will be all right."

Early in the morning God took the baby. It would have been Bill's firstborn. Again, things had not worked out the way I had planned. Instead of my life ending, an innocent child died. Now I had to live with this trauma instead of being rid of all my problems. In my confusion I sobbed, "I didn't mean to do it. I didn't want it to happen like this." The nurses didn't really understand my situation.

My condition stabilized after the miscarriage and several blood transfusions. I was removed from Intensive Care, but stayed in the hospital for more than two weeks. It was another month before I was able to get around without a wheelchair.

At the doctor's suggestion my father ordered me into temporary retirement, so in September 1974 I moved to Cannes on the French Riviera. Bill and I lived in seclusion, with instructions that I was to write booklets on childcare and education for the Family. We stayed in Cannes for about five months and then moved to Zoagli, Italy, to live in one of Duke Emanuel's villas.

Zoagli is a very small, picturesque village near Chiavari on the Mediterranean coast. Our villa overlooked the Gulf of Tigullio— perhaps the most beautiful place I have ever lived in. The peaceful surroundings, exquisite Italian food, and rest from the mainstream of COG activities had a wonderful healing effect on me. I think the healthiest factor was that I was living away from Dad and the rest of the Royal Family. Any contact with my immediate family would only bring unspeakable tension and pressure. The Royal Family lived in a world of competition and envy, and their disease infected anyone who was nearby. I knew of several disciples who later told me they would do all they could to leave town when they found out two or more members of the Royal Family would be there together.

In Zoagli Bill and I worked intensely on writing "Deborah Letters" for the Family. We produced a lot of material for Dad to publish. The disciples never knew it, but Bill wrote all the Deborah Letters.

I was beginning to enjoy life once again as I lived alone with Bill in that beautiful villa. I was telling myself, "Perhaps the days of peace have finally come. Perhaps the days of hell are passed."

But in June 1975 I received a disturbing phone call. It was my father announcing that he was coming to live with me. He was returning from his two-month visit with Colonel Moammar Gadahfi and would arrive at the Genova (Genoa) airport with Maria. Bill and I were instructed to meet them alone at the airport. I couldn't believe my ears. Dad, the Endtime Prophet, was coming to my little hideaway on the Côte d'Azur. Bill was shaken. Very few disciples had the privilege of seeing the Prophet face to face—this was Big Time!

Dad arrived and passed several uneventful months with us.

He kept to himself in the upper portion of the villa and left me very much alone. He treated me like a landlord from whom he was renting. The villa was built like a duplex so that the upper portion could be used as a separate dwelling. He had Rachel and Emanuel visit him on numerous occasions for leadership meetings. Rachel was moving up in importance in the family and would soon become the No. 1 leader apart from Mo himself.

Dad finally left in August, on the day after I returned from the hospital from delivering my seventh child—Bill's first—Alexander David.

Dad's leaving was filled with trauma for me. He had kept the fact that he was leaving a secret from me, for some unknown reason. I met him and Maria coming down the stairs and knew instantly that he was leaving for good. I was carrying the new baby in my arms and walked with Dad and Maria along the walkway leading to the iron fence that encompassed our property. I was extremely upset that he was leaving and that he hadn't talked with me. I was crying and asking him to let me go with him to the train station. His secrecy hurt me deeply. I felt betrayed—but most of all rejected. As with Aaron, Dad was rejecting me, the worst form of punishment possible.

Maria kept interrupting, saying it wasn't necessary for me to see them off. When we finally reached the iron gate, Dad stepped through and Maria quickly closed it in my face and locked it. I tried to keep it ajar, but with a baby on one arm and my other hand on the gate, I was unable to win the tug of war.

I looked at Dad, the locked iron gate, and Maria proudly tugging on Dad's arm—and I knew he was gone. Locked into his own world—a world he had created by his own devices. Instinctively I knew I would never see him again.

Unknown to me, Dad was on his way back to Tenerife to continue his full-time pursuit of the Flirty Fishing ministry. While in Zoagli he never made mention of it to me. Before coming to Zoagli, he had spent about one year in the Canaries. He was returning now to shift FFing into high gear.

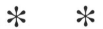

In February 1976 Dad made a deal with Jethro and me. He requested that we go to Latin America to be the leaders of the work on that continent. Jethro had been living in Northern Europe following one of his demotions by Dad, typical of my father's pattern of political Ping-Pong. First a promotion, then a demotion, followed by another promotion. Up, down. Up, down. It was like being on a roller coaster.

We were now on our way back to the top. Latin America was in a mess, and Dad needed our talents. He could always count on Jethro to get things rolling again. But he wanted a Berg along, because he never really trusted Jethro. Dad was always afraid of one leader by himself getting too powerful. My father is deathly afraid of male leadership, consistently cutting them down and putting women (who are loyal only to him) in their place.

Jethro and I agreed to call a truce and work together once again. We both felt that, South America being a long way from Dad, perhaps we could find some peace. Moreover, we could bring the children together so they could be near both Mommy and Daddy. So off we went to South America and settled in Lima, Peru—the new H.Q. of the COG south of the border.

Dad wanted the movement and the public to think that Jethro and I were still married; we kept our private lives hidden and did not let on to anyone that we had both been living with new spouses for several years.

Our time as leaders of South American operations lasted two-and-a-half very long years. In that time COG activities began flourishing and we were able to pull Latin America out of its tailspin.

But trouble was brewing once again. Dad was feverishly pushing Flirty Fishing world-wide, and he was receiving reports that the leadership in South America was dragging its heels in this "ministry."

Dad sent my sister Faithy to Lima to spy on us, and he also planted spies among our personal staff who reported all our activities to him. At the same time, the Mo Letters were getting progressively more bizarre. The only theme of Dad's writings right then was sex, sex, and more sex. It permeated every fiber of his being. Soon, despite our own lethargic attitude, all of South

America was Flirty Fishing. Immorality soared to an all-time high as the Mo Letters insisted that everyone "share" God's love. Things were truly getting wild.

Then Dad began to write publicly in the Mo Letters against Jethro, Isaiah, and me. Isaiah (Bill) had been in charge of publications for Latin America and was editing the Mo Letters for street distribution. Dad accused him of "tampering with the words of the Prophet"—one of the gravest of all crimes. Then we were accused of having withstood Dad by keeping disciples from FFing. My response was to try to regain the Prophet's favor by plunging myself into total obedience to the Mo Letters. To no avail. Dad wasn't the least bit impressed with my outward obedience and my FFing—or with any of the key political figures I had on my "fishing line." The die had been cast. Heads would soon roll. Dad was going to fire every leader in the Revolution, and Jethro and I were first on the list. He had special plans for Bill.

On February 7, 1978, Moses David received a special revelation from his faithful spirit guide, Abrahim, stating that Bill was an evil magician leading me astray from "the Lord and his work"—which is to say, Moses David and the COG. The spirit spoke these words through my dad:

> *May God damn him and give him what he deserves! He led so many astray. This man hath bewitched her, and he re-interprets my Letters. He contradicts them and he defies them, and I want to get rid of him!*

Rachel, who was now the top leader by virtue of earlier prophecies, was given the job of personally delivering the special revelation against Bill. It became Mo Letter 666 and was entitled "Alexander the Evil Magician." Rachel's orders were to fly to Caracas, Venezuela, and read the letter privately to me and then to Bill. She was also instructed to demote Jethro and me from our leadership positions. Bill was to be exiled to one part of the globe and I to another. Yet by this time Bill and I had been together four years and had two children from the union.

It was the intent of this revelation that I be permanently separated from Bill. He was the devil; he had led me astray. I was never to see him again. It was imperative that he be gotten rid of.

He would be banished to Africa. And I would be consigned to Australia—far removed from established Colonies where my influence might not poison the minds of disciples against the Pure Doctrine.

Thus my relationship to the man I loved was to be terminated by order of the Prophet. Once again my father had turned my world upside down. But this time his insanity overreached itself. Ten years of living under the influence of his madness had taken its toll. This would prove to be my final breaking point.

The atmosphere in the COG at this time was weird and foreboding. Everyone had a sense that a tidal wave was about to break over us. Flirty Fishing was flourishing, sexual freedom was commonplace, carnality ran rampant. The fabric of the order of things was coming apart.

In this context Dad fired every leader in the Family, destroying the "chain of command" that had served as our governmental structure for years. The sheep were left to fend for themselves. Within one week there was no leadership, organization, or semblance of order: only utter chaos and anarchy, both moral and physical. There was a spirit of "me first" among the disciples. People became like sharks, ravaging one another to stay alive.

The trauma of that time can hardly be expressed in words. Even as Rachel arrived with Mo's special Letter, she too was an emotional wreck. She had spent the last two years on Dad's personal Flirty Fishing team in the Canaries and was experiencing her own breaking points as a result.

Through the years Rachel and I had grown very close. We loved each other, and I trusted her as my most intimate friend—as much as was possible under the circumstances. It was a very cruel thing for my father to have Rachel deliver such a message to an intimate friend. But that was his way of "proving one's loyalty to the Prophet." Knowing how much I loved Bill, Rachel could not go through with it. She just couldn't read the Letter to me. She felt that on top of all else that I had suffered, it might be the last straw. She reported to Mo by telephone that she had not yet delivered the message, saying, "I'm afraid it might kill Deborah. . . ." My father exploded. He was furious! "How dare you withhold the words of the Prophet or question my decisions!" For thirty minutes he blasted away: "If the truth kills, let it kill her. . . ." This phone call was transcribed and became Mo Letter 678, "If the Truth Kills, Let It Kill!"

Shaken by the phone call, Rachel called me the next day and I was taken to a Colony to hear "Alexander the Evil Magician." Later it was read to Bill. As these scenes were played out, I began to slip into a state of mental shock. They were going to send Bill away! I couldn't believe it! He was my life, my reason for living in an irrational world. I was flooded with new doubt about Dad, the movement, everything—all I could see was Bill. A deathly fear gripped me that indeed they would take him away and I would never see him again.

But Bill wanted to stay faithful, stand strong, and keep believing in Mo. After my father had called him the devil, Bill still wanted to stay faithful to him! It was really unbelievable. He was so dedicated, so loyal, so determined to follow Moses David that nothing would deter him—even when Dad viciously denounced him and took away his wife and children and ordered him banished alone to Africa.

Rachel did not have the heart to send Bill to Africa, but instead arranged that he be sent to Martinique, a small French island in the Caribbean, not far from Venezuela.

The trip to the airport was the longest ride of my life. I felt as if I were accompanying Bill to his execution. When he was finally put on the plane, my world caved in. I wept until the tears could no longer flow, slipping ever deeper into mental shock; I was dangerously close to catatonia.

For four months I lived in a lost, isolated world. The daily activity of caring for the children was the one thing that kept me in touch with reality. Sometimes I would wake up and wonder if I were truly alive, if this was all a dream. I simply lived to get the next letter from Bill. Each one brought me back to a state of half-life. But in spite of it all, I couldn't bring myself to believe the growing perception that we were going to leave Dad and the movement. How could we possibly do that?

Yet the pressures of despair, loneliness, and an indescribable state of "lostness" continued to build. Bill's firstborn child, David, who was three years old, kept asking me, "Mommy, where's my daddy? I want my daddy. I want my daddy. . . ." He was little and innocent, free from all the insanity and cruelty of my father and the wickedness of life in the Children of God. His tender mind could not understand why his father had suddenly disappeared, yet the pain of the madness around me was reaching through and torturing his little world. Each time he asked me about his daddy I would begin to cry in despair. His pitiful pleas for the return of his daddy were like burning irons that pierced my soul, leaving scars I would carry for a lifetime.

My worst experience came one day while I was shopping. Little David suddenly sat down in an aisle in the middle of the store and began to cry his heart out. "I want my daddy! I want my daddy!" He raised questioning eyes, void of understanding, and asked, "Why doesn't my daddy come home?"

A flood of pain and sorrow had been rising inside me for more than ten years and I knew the dam would soon have to break. My pride was the only thing holding back the flood, pride that had forbidden me to say, "My father is wrong. He walks in darkness. I must forsake him." Pride can bring a person to ruin, and mine brought me to the gates of hell. It brought my three-year-old into a world of misery he could not comprehend. How much longer would I go on?

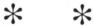

While all this was happening we made our way to the United States as the first step in getting to Australia. As American citizens we could not go directly Down Under from South America. So we came to San Francisco to apply for visas through the Australian consulate in that city.

Our group comprised all my children, their personal teacher and his family, my former husband and his wife and their children, and me—five adults and twelve children.

Returning to the United States after a seven-year absence brought tremendous culture shock. We had left the country when the counterculture and notions of protest were still present though fading; and we had left under the aegis of Mo's endtime warnings to a doomed nation. How were we to survive, let alone "live," even for a while in a society we had so bitterly rejected?

The drastic change of climate was an additional complication. We had left the warm, mild zephyrs of Caracas to encounter the cold and rain of San Francisco in March. We didn't have proper warm clothing, and the children immediately got sick. This complication affected another part of the plans: in keeping with COG custom, we were expected by my father to raise part of our travel fare, through litnessing and the children's public singing.

Given the hardships of our situation, we considered the implications of traveling so far away. We'd be quite stranded with many children to care for once we arrived in Australia. Nevertheless, we endeavored to raise the money necessary for the fare. But after six weeks we decided not to go. We concluded it would be better to stay in the States for a while and "dry out" before making such a drastic move. And I was not resigned to going to Australia without Bill.

We traveled through California living from campground to campground. We had purchased an old twenty-eight-foot motor home and a station wagon. Living like nomads, we'd go from town to town, making a living through the children's singing on the streets and collecting donations. We eventually settled in a dusty, dirty campground in Escondido, where we stayed for six months. I lived with my little year-and-a-half-old daughter, Davida, in a two-man pup tent. Our physical conditions seemed to match perfectly our mental trauma. It's amazing what God has to allow before a person will wake up to reality.

My ex-husband, Jethro, had gone through his share of breaking points and was no longer able to take any more of my father's rebukes, chastisements, and purgings. There comes a time when an individual can no longer submit himself to a man who wields totalitarian power, who can instantaneously take away one's job, home, and family.

Dad had threatened me with excommunication if I contacted Bill—which of course I had been doing. So the question was before me, should I defy my father and ask Bill to come to the States? That would be the final break: No more Dad, no more Moses David, no more Children of God, no more "Family of Love." But the spiritual chains of deception and thirty-two years of living under the influence of my domineering father kept pulling me down, keeping me bound to an irrational loyalty I felt unable to break.

Jethro finally said to me, "Well, Deborah, it's up to you. It's in your hands now. I'm ready to get out if you are. I don't care any more. If you have Bill come back, you know that means we're excommunicated."

I had been hanging on, hoping that Dad would change his mind, hoping against hope that things would return to "normal." In the meantime we received a message from Rachel questioning the "progress you are making on getting to Australia." She stated that Mo had heard a rumor that I had been in contact with Bill, and she reminded me that such an act was strictly forbidden.

At that point I knew the end had come. I had to sever completely my relationship with my father. In His mercy God had allowed me to be driven to a point of choice: either to continue to follow the insanity of Moses David, or to break free to live a life rid of his evil grasp. On the surface I did not see it that way, but rather as a choosing between my father and Bill. Finally I said to myself, "I'm ready, despite the consequences. I want Bill to come home."

For the first time in years I began to look up. I had made a willful decision that I was willing to live with. That moment was the genesis of freedom from a lifetime of bondage.

Throughout my lifetime my father had controlled and manipulated my every action. Any person or thing that had ever been around me, Dad had somehow managed to control or do away with. Bill was the first thing in my life to which Dad was unable to do either. Though Dad tried very hard, he failed to control Bill or get rid of him. This is the irony that surrounds my exodus from the COG movement: I cannot boast that I left the COG voluntarily. In a backhanded way God delivered me: my father turned against us and virtually drove us out.

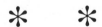

At the same time that God was opening my eyes to the truth, He was working on Bill, to bring him to a position where he too would begin thinking with clarity of mind. But Bill was a fiercely proud person and was determined to follow Moses David to the bitter end. The best thing in the world for Bill was to have been stranded on a tiny island with an abundance of time to think, agonize over the loss of his wife and children, pray, and read his Bible. For four months he clung to his faith in Mo, believing that God would change Dad's mind. Bill could not let go of his belief that Mo was God's Prophet, and since he believed that to be true, logic dictated that all he needed to do was hold on until God revealed the truth to Mo. Bill felt that for some unknown reason God was testing him through this dilemma.

As the months rolled by, Bill faithfully continued to win disciples for the kingdom of Moses David. Their little Colony on Martinique regularly received the latest Mo Letters, and eventually the Letters about Bill were published and received in the mail. The Mo Letter declaring Bill to be an "Evil Magician" came, and the Colony read it—but still Bill believed in Moses David.

Then the Letter "If the Truth Kills, Let It Kill" arrived. "But how," Bill thought, "could a father want his daughter dead? It's not natural, it's not even human. I can understand him wanting to get rid of me, but why his own daughter?"

That Letter left Bill deeply shaken, and through his tears he stumbled out into the night and walked to the top of a deserted hill. Under the strain of it all he broke and wept bitterly. Looking heavenward he was suddenly consumed by a marvelous peace and the profound realization that it was God who loved him, not Moses David. It was Christ who had died for his sins, certainly not Moses David. Yet he had been following the man Moses David, believing in and obeying his teachings as if they were the direct voice of God. In a sudden illumination he became aware that in his zeal he had supplanted his faith in God with faith in a man. The madness he was experiencing was not a testing from God, but the product of the deviousness of a man—David Berg. Indeed, God loved him first and always.

The next day another Mo Letter arrived, "Prayer for the Poor." It proclaimed that all the Israelis deserved to die—men, women, and children—and that God should slaughter them all. That was it. The end had come for Bill. Despite his confused condition, he determined that no one who was a man of God could say such a thing. Something was terribly wrong. He phoned his parents and explained that that he was stranded and needed a plane ticket to San Diego, California. His dad simply asked how much and where the money should be sent.

Thus, through His incredible mercies, in spite of our sins and utter foolishness, God delivered us. The end had finally come. But as one era passes, so a new one begins—with its own new set of difficulties. We were now to begin life as ex-cult members.

Coming out of a cult is more difficult by far than being in. While in, it is a simple matter of keeping one's head in the sand and staying blind to reality. But in emerging from a life of falsehood and sin, it becomes a painfully excruciating experience to face life as it truly is, accepting that you have been wrong, terribly wrong.

In coming out, moreover, we had no foundation of truth on which to stand. We had been programmed to hate and condemn the churches and to stay away from established Christianity. My dad had destroyed faith in the Bible through his perverted interpretations, so I couldn't turn to it for guidance. Each time I tried to read it, I only became more confused because it reminded me of all the twisted doctrines Dad preached. Coming out was hell!

To come out also meant it was time to earn a living. In the movement my dad created a lifestyle that taught the disciples to be professional beggars. He programmed his followers to believe that the world owes them a living because they are "serving God" full-time and no one else is. For men leaving the cult, earning a living can be extremely difficult.

Many men enter a cult in their early twenties or late teens. In normal life this is the age when one begins the pursuit of a career. In ten years time he is usually well-founded in a profession, has bought a house, and is on his way to having an established lifestyle and financial security. But a former cult member emerges from the movement in his early thirties with a wife and children and absolutely no profession or skill that can land him a job with a salary adequate for supporting his family. Not only does he have to start over spiritually, but he is forced to start over socially and financially. It's impossible to support a family on minimum wage.

When a man faces this fact, it triggers deeper depression as he realizes he has foolishly wasted ten of the most important years of his life. He realizes that everything in the system is against him.

This is a time when family support can be very beneficial. If parents can understand how difficult it is to readjust and the despair and discouragement a man or woman faces, they can give them the encouragement and the helping hand that is vitally needed. It will be a tough time for all concerned.

But God is ever faithful, and in His infinite mercy, He pulled us through our situation. I believe the worst thing we experienced was spiritual confusion: not knowing what was right or wrong. The effects of the cult stick with you, like hands dipped in dye; the doctrines become a part of your personality, tainting your mind and character. It is at this point that we encounter once again the power and reality of sin. The devastating effects of the cults are clearly seen to be the consequences of sin. *You can be out of a cult physically, but still be very much "in" the cult, for the cult is part of you.* To find total freedom from a cult, you must find victory over sin. You must come face to face with sin, see it in your own life, identify it, and then seek divine forgiveness. Otherwise you remain a prisoner, ensnared by guilt, fragmented, and forever alienated.

✳   ✳

Our real deliverance came three years after we left the Children of God. For those three years we wandered on the edges of reality, drifting about in a fog of spiritual darkness. Those were dark years, void of peace and clarity of mind. My oldest child, Joyanne, was experiencing as much trauma as we were, and the effects of her life in the cult began to emerge. I had no one to turn to for help, so in desperation I asked the help of a doctor and his wife, Dr. and Mrs. Richard Price, casual acquaintances I had met through the school our children were attending.

The Prices seemed so stable and successful. I hoped they might have some answers on what to do with Joyanne, as they had a son exactly her age—seventeen. We did not tell them who we were or what we had come out of, just that we were having problems with Joyanne. Several days later they put 150 dollars in my hand and sent us—Bill, Joyanne, and me—off to a Christian seminar in Long Beach. We had no idea what it was all about, but they assured us it would be perfect for Joyanne. The fact is, it was precisely what Bill and I desperately needed. We will be eternally grateful to the Prices for the sequence of events triggered by their act of concern and generosity.

We walked into a huge auditorium along with twelve thousand other people. As we sat down, a man in a dark blue suit walked modestly on stage and began talking in a quiet voice. He spoke so softly we couldn't even hear him until the crowd stopped shuffling about. Behind him was a towering fifty-foot screen, and as he talked he placed transparencies on an overhead projector. He began speaking on subjects such as self-acceptance, purpose in life, self-image, peace and harmony at home, moral impurity, responsibility, gaining a clear conscience, moral freedom, incorporating past failures into your life's message, and allowing Jesus Christ to be the center of your life.

For six days we sat in stunned silence. The format of the seminar was very much like a college lecture, but the material went deeper than the intellectual level—it held solutions to the problems of our tormented souls. We felt as if someone had designed the seminar specifically for us. The painful questions and gnawing doubts that had plagued us since the day we had left the cult three years earlier were all being answered one by one.

The most critical day came on Friday when the concept of moral impurity was discussed and the Twelve Steps to Reprobation were presented. At one point Bill turned to me, his eyes wide with astonishment, and said, "My God, that's us! That's the Children of God. That's the story of your father's life in a twelve-point outline."

The seminar is called the Institute in Basic Youth Conflicts, and the man who delivered the lectures is Bill Gothard. Through the biblical principles taught in the six-day seminar, we gained a complete and lasting deliverance from the effects of the cult and the bondage of sin. The Bible was given back to us as the inspired Word of God—something we could trust in, the Light of Truth by which to guide our lives once again.

The movement's headliners in 1970 making music, always a vital factor in David Berg's strategy: (from left) Deborah, Paul, Jonathan, Artie [Joshua], Faith.

Victory did not come overnight; this was only the beginning of a long process that involved putting the principles we learned into practice in our daily living. But April 1981 marked a new beginning for us. We were set on the road of truth, and the Cross of Christ was once again ours to follow. We emerged from the seminar changed people. It was there that Christ met me and showed me the pathway of truth.

When truth is compromised, error and destruction and misery will consistently emerge in one's life. When I chose to follow my father I began compromising the truth; as I have reexamined my life, it has become apparent that one compromise led to another, like the chain reaction of falling dominoes. Freedom involves going back to the beginning—to the sin of rebellion and the desire to be the boss of one's own life, to the disposition of self realization: I am my own god. Freedom lies in making Christ the boss of one's life—going back to the original compromise and repenting, making it right with God. *That point of compromise is different for each person; but I can guarantee that for someone who has been in a cult, compromising the truth usually begins long before he actually gets involved with the cult.*

Chapter 11
"The Lord Will Go On. . .With or Without You!"

In May 1968 I made a decision to join my father and his work among the hippies of Huntington Beach. At the root of that decision was a deep lack of spiritual self-acceptance; my motivation was the result of false standards adopted in an attitude of self-rejection. In my own life I was endeavoring to conform to an outward standard of acceptance, rather than seeking to conform to God's inward standard mirrored in the character of Christ. Unfortunately, outward standards of acceptance rule and govern the lives of many people, Christian and non-Christians alike.

At that time I was terribly unhappy with my state in life. I was twenty-two years old, a mother of two children, and eight months pregnant. My marriage had become a source of sorrow and frustration. There were times when I would lock myself in the bathroom and cry for hours. Boredom and loneliness consumed me. We did not have any "outward" show of religious activity, something I greatly desired, because I had, after all, grown up in a very religious family. So that May we went to visit my family in Huntington Beach to see what "great things God was doing with Teens for Christ." I sat in the car and talked privately with my father in front of my grandmother Berg's house. Dad was offering me a chance to "get busy for God!"

"Take a look at your life, honey," he charged. "What are you really doing for the Lord? You and John [Jethro] have been getting further and further away from the Lord ever since you left me in Texas.

"Even your grandmother died very saddened at your spiritual state, the fact you are doing nothing for God. This is your opportunity to get back to the Lord. Don't worry about losing your husband. You'll lose him anyway if you don't follow God, as high as the divorce rate is."

In my dad's eyes, and in mine as well, following God meant one had to be doing something "for" Him, to be active, performing deeds—as if He needed a helping hand.

"You've been raised on this life of self-sacrifice," he said. "You'll never be happy if you just live for yourself, living in your own selfish little house, with your selfish little family."

He went on to explain the reason why my life was so empty, my marriage on the rocks, and my relationship with God impoverished: I was not following His leadership. Having a relationship with God presupposed doing some ministry for Him. My father had the perfect solution, of course: Follow him and his work among the hippies.

"Honey, we'll go on with or without you; that's what we've always done before. The Lord will go on with or without you. But God is giving you another chance." My dad's offer was nothing glorious at the time, but it was nonetheless a way out, an escape from my present boredom and unhappiness.

People fall prey to the cultic lure for various reasons—perhaps impatience, fear of responsibility, a lust for power or position, a desire to leave home, boredom, or an unhappy marriage. Regardless of the "outward" reason, the cult victim exchanges his present state in life for an alternative lifestyle; he sees in the cult a chance for opportunity, change, relief, or escape. By contrast, a person who lives in a state of contentment realizes that God has given him everything necessary for total happiness. People grow discontented because they begin judging themselves by outward standards.

For me, getting back to God meant sacrificing and ministering—activities that were visible forms of religious work. However, it is now painfully obvious to me that at some point "Christian service" can actually be a form of escape, rebellion, and a rejection of God's will in a person's life.

Consider that all my life I had been raised in the limelight of Christian activities. First I was involved with my grandmother and her work as a famous healing evangelist. Later came my father with his "soul-winning" ministry. As a teenager I worked and sang with Youth for Christ and then sang in the public relations ministry of Miami Christian School. In 1968, to suddenly find myself alone, without a "ministry," a "mere housewife," did not fulfill my image of a Christian winning the world to Jesus. Earlier I believed I had been "called" to the mission field; life had certainly taken a wrong turn. How ironic to think that I wanted to win the world to Jesus when in fact He had yet to win my stubborn will to Himself.

By accepting my dad's invitation to follow him and "do something for God," I was actually rejecting God's highest plan in my life. Being a housewife and the mother of three children was precisely the place He wanted me to be, the perfect situation to make me the kind of Christian He desires. It was the perfect place to learn patience, meekness, unselfish love, faith, and the other fruit of the Spirit.

Well, I did not think it was the perfect place. I knew better, and therefore I began to rebel in my heart against my station in life. Unknowingly I was rebelling against God and the biblical principles governing the family structure. (These many years later I am once again in the situation of a "mere housewife"—but this time thankful to be here and learning these lessons joyfully.)

Trusting God to bring joy and fulfillment into my marriage and life was not at all within my understanding of the will and ways of God. Such simple faith and trust were beyond me. The fact is, commitment to my situation would have involved suffering—truly godly suffering. I was willing to sacrifice—to kill myself, as it were—with religious works, but I was not willing to stay in my situation alone with God and give Him the opportunity to develop a Christ-like character within me. I didn't care to suffer like that. I preferred an outward show of religion as opposed to the reality of Christ within. I have learned the hard way that it is a great deal more difficult to allow Christ to develop character within than it is to work sacrificially "without"; but in the long run any other path will only bring sorrow. There is but one road to follow: to be conformed to the image of God's Son.

David said, "The sacrifices of God are a broken spirit; A broken and a contrite heart, O God, Thou wilt not despise." (Psalm 51:17 NASB). A broken heart and spirit I did not have. I violated one of God's greatest principles, and it led me into a ten-year nightmare of sin and sorrow. I was not willing to accept myself in His plan, to place myself behind His will, to make His will my will. This is the basis of self-acceptance in a divine perspective. The result of such acceptance is a state of personal contentment and peace, and of harmony with the plan of God.

In the years following my departure from the Children of God I began to wonder, What is the specific reason for more than five thousand cults with five to ten million members on the North American continent? That is no small number, and it is growing every day; cults are obviously filling a great need, and people are finding something quite attractive in them. But if the cults are wrong, if they are built upon a lie and the people are flocking to them, then there must be something wrong with the people. What is the weakness of character that renders these people susceptible? Why did *I* join? Why did *I* follow? The obvious or general answer is "sin"; I knew that rebellion is one of the root causes of all sin and that people are drawn into sin by their lusts. Yet I wondered if there was something I was missing, a principle or truth I could teach my children that would strengthen them from falling prey to deception. If the cults are indicative of character weakness in people, what is the cause of that character weakness and, even more important, what is the cure?

I have come to believe that the problem of spiritual self-acceptance is the cause of that character weakness and lies at the root of the cult experience—that is, why people join cults.

Cults offer a counterfeit version of self-acceptance. When an individual fails to realize self-worth through the *inward* qualities that reflect the divine character, he is left to seek a sense of acceptance based upon *outward* qualities and values. Cults are but one of many options available in current society. When I refer to the concept of self-acceptance, I am not speaking of viewing oneself positively as taught by psychologists and motivational speakers. Rather, it is how one views himself before God: Self-acceptance in a divine perspective. Spiritual self-acceptance.

The Institute in Basic Youth Conflicts wisely teaches, "One of the major areas of conflict in both youth and adults is that of having wrong attitudes about ourselves. These attitudes affect every other relationship in our life."[1] God's fundamental reason for creating us is that we might have fellowship with Him through Jesus Christ, and that the full expression of Christ's love might be experienced in our lives.

The key to this objective is the realization that God has created each of us perfectly to fulfill His purpose. Conflict and confusion over this truth arise when we begin to place a value on ourselves according to false standards, when we compare ourselves with the outward standards of those around us (whatever they happen to be) to gain approval. In so doing, we develop inner conflict. Concern over outward appearances or conditions will often bring varying degrees of self-rejection. When we begin to reject ourselves, it will manifest itself in our actions and attitudes. Evidences of self-rejection are seen in the values and priorities people set for themselves: trying to "impress" others; being highly competitive; selfishness; abnormal love of self; bitterness, inability to face the truth about ourselves; moral impurity; love of money; and the like.

There are many indications of self-rejection, but the end-result is the adoption of false values. When we examine ourselves against the false standards society has erected, we always feel inferior. Who can measure up to them? Even those who have seemingly attained, when questioned, feel as if they have failed in a multitude of ways. Society teaches us that there is a universal standard by which social position, financial status, and physical appearance can be measured. This is entirely false. Living by such standards always causes us to reject ourselves. At that point we can see why self-rejection is a sin. When we reject ourselves, we are ultimately rejecting God. He is the One responsible for our physical appearance, our parents, our race, and our nationality—all the unchangeable features are His responsibility. Hence, if through comparison we fall short of our desired self-image and develop subsequent feelings of inferiority, we must either consciously or unconsciously blame the One responsible; a rejection of self and all that "self" represents is a rejection of God.

True spiritual self-acceptance is the kind demonstrated and experienced by a young missionary martyred in Vietnam. She was a person who radiated the love of God, and during her time in Vietnam she became known as the "Belle of Da Nang." She had such a beautiful spirit that before long she was the sought-after prize of the American soldiers. However, she felt her duty to God and the people of Vietnam came before her personal life; she graciously declined the romantic gesturing of her many suitors, chose to date no one, and dedicated her time fully to God.

She was captured by the Viet Cong. With another prisoner she was forced to march a great distance. They were given little food for the journey. Toward the end she gave her small portion to her fellow captive that he might live. Soon she died, but he lived to tell the story. What a marvelous person she was—bringing life and joy to many and finally giving her life completely to the cause of Christ and the glory of God. Ironically, her background was the antithesis of her virtuous end.

Before the war and before coming to faith in Christ she had two great weaknesses that led her to the brink of destruction. She was deeply involved in immorality, and she had never found true self-acceptance. She had never accepted herself for what she was, a person created in the image of God. This caused her to rebel against life, against God, against His moral standards. She rejected herself as a young girl and threw her life into a downward spiral of physical and spiritual destruction. She filled her life with false values, wrong priorities, evil passions, and bitterness.

When this young woman finally came to Christ, a new world opened up within her—the world of inward beauty and truth. Her life took on new meaning, new perspective, new truth. It was a natural step to accept herself as a wonderful creation of God, with an unlimited potential for knowing and fellowshiping with an eternal God and sharing that love and truth with others, even to the point of death. Consequently she turned from her immorality and self-rejection.

When, amid self-rejection, we come to see ourselves from God's perspective, life changes drastically. The key is the awareness that nothing we achieve outwardly has significance if we haven't developed the character of the Lord Jesus Christ inwardly. God's ideal is a person empowered by the qualities of humility, meekness, piety, mercy, purity, peace, and spiritual hunger.

In the book *All God's Children,* Carroll Stoner and Jo Anne Parke analyze the cultic phenomenon and survey the kinds of people who join a cult. Are they rich or poor? Talented or inferior? Religious or irreligious? Their basic finding is that there is no stereotype, no predictable category. I agree. Cults fill an inward need, and this cannot be detected readily by outward characteristics. A person who has rejected himself inwardly may keep it very well hidden until the day he finds an avenue that will lead to acceptance and fulfillment. Then he surprises everyone and joins a cult.

Yet Stoner and Parke did find a common denominator, and it is related to self-acceptance. This common characteristic was perceived by a psychiatric social worker, as related by Stoner and Parke.

> *A young psychiatric social worker from Boston who has worked with scores of ex-cult members and their families, helping to put lives back together after a cult experience, says that the whole generation is afflicted with copious narcissism, but that those who are lured into the cults seem even more narcissistic than their peers. The cults appeal to inflated egos with their recruiting techniques: "Gee, you are wonderful. We need someone with your special talent to help us change the world." Cult recruiters are trained to flatter, to give false confidence to those without confidence.*[2]

This observation seems to me to be very significant. *Narcissism* is "excessive love or admiration of oneself." *Copious* implies abundance. The result is an abnormal love of self that in cult members exceeds that of their peers.

How does this abnormal condition occur? As I began to look at myself and at people I know in the COG, the pieces of the puzzle fell into place. The problem of copious narcissism is really a problem of inferiority and points directly to self-rejection and broken fellowship with God. This condition follows a predictable sequence:

An individual, for various specific reasons, becomes a victim of self-rejection. Perhaps he rejects his position in life, his alcoholic father, or his physical appearance. This state of self-rejection will cause bitterness. The self-rejection and bitterness will eventually lead to a rejection of God, his Creator, the One ultimately responsible for his state in life. When a person rejects God inwardly he places himself in a position of rebellion to God and God's Spirit. Consequently one cannot take pleasure in the things of God and must therefore seek things contrary to Truth. Self-acceptance will be sought apart from the standards of God, and this condition will ultimately lead to a false sense of acceptance and a fallen ego. Rebellion—the devil's sin—forces the person into spiritual pride to support this fallen ego.

Spiritual pride is a lie, a false perspective of reality, and will therefore lead a person into worshiping something other than the "Truth," which has long since been rejected. Hence, a cult offers the person the perfect solution to his dilemma. A cult is full of counterfeit truths—self-righteous, world-saving, outward manifestations of religion. A cult, like any false religion, masks the real problem of rebellion, self-rejection, and spiritual pride. The mask is the carefully adorned counterfeit of religious works.

What the Boston psychiatrist had encountered over and over again were those people who had not found their self-acceptance in God, consequently rejected themselves and, instead of developing a healthy love of God and others, turned this void into an unnatural and abnormal love and concern for self. It seems that rebellion causes one to love self and desire the worship of others. That need to be accepted is basic and demanding. Yet if we know that God has accepted us, "self"-acceptance falls naturally into place.

The Bible demonstrates that happiness and self-acceptance are not found in outward appearances or conditions, but in a personal relationship with God. Scripture records that Lucifer was not satisfied or content with his place. He didn't care to be just the "bearer of the Light"; he wanted to be the Light itself. He desired to be like the Most High; he desired to be something he was not. Yet Lucifer was the most beautiful of all the angels.

This is an amazing truth. Even with the angelic beings of heaven we see that happiness and peace have nothing to do with outward appearance, but only with a personal relationship with God and the humility to accept ourselves the way God created us—be it beautiful or ugly. Hence, the ugliest person in the world, or a person without legs, or a person whose father is a false prophet and sexual deviant, or a person born blind—each possesses as great a potential for joy and happiness as the most beautiful angel in heaven. If a person, or even an angel, rejects what God has done or allowed in his life, he places himself out of harmony with God's sovereign purpose and cannot find true peace and fulfillment. When we fall prey to self-rejection and rebellion against God's purpose for life, we are left with seeking a counterfeit. And cults offer that counterfeit.

When I came out of the Children of God, I was confronted with a double measure of self-rejection because of my father. To come to accept myself before God was a tremendous struggle and required a calculated, terrifying leap of faith. Three years had passed and my life still lay in fragments. I bore the guilt of helping to found the cult, of immorality, of a divorce and a broken home.

I thought back to 1968 when I was faced with accepting an unhappy marriage and a little boredom. It seemed like nothing in comparison to what I was now facing. After thirteen years things were fifty times as bad. God had brought me back to point zero; I was once again in the very same place facing the very same choice. Would I cop out this time as I did when I chose to run with my father in Huntington Beach? No, I would not do that again.

This time I threw myself, my life, and all my unbearable circumstances on God's altar and said, "Please, Lord, use my circumstances to build Christ's character within me." It was a prayer of hope. My situation was so desperate that I knew only God could

The Berg family singers around a portable organ during the days of mobile ministry about 1953: (from left) Paul [Aaron], Faith, Jane Berg, Linda [Deborah], and Jonathan [Hosea].

mend it. So I gave Him the bits and pieces of my life and heart, knowing it was up to Him to bring meaning out of my failures.

That is the way it has to be with God. A person who sets about to find acceptance in Him must put "all" of self on the altar. It is then God's business to purify the sacrifice. The key to virtue lies not in the purity of one's past, but in the present direction of life—that is, the influence God is having on others through one's life regardless of past failures. Given my past and my parentage, only God could purify the sacrifice and bring peace and harmony.

I can now say that He has made me a whole person inside. I no longer feel fragmented, torn in pieces. I still live with the consequences of my mistakes—divorce, the effects of the cult on some of my children, and the pain of a divided home. I cannot change these outward circumstances. My responsibility now is to respond to them with the proper attitude.

God is showing me the inward beauty and peace of Christian character. Certainly the mercies of God endure forever.

Chapter 12
"If We Have An Order To Believe . . . We Will Believe!"

During my first three years outside the Children of God I did not understand either my role in the cult or my responsibility for it. Then a story told by Richard Wurmbrand opened up the truth to me.

My husband and I were studying the tapes and writings of this Christian pastor who had suffered at the hands of the Communists. Wurmbrand was a Christian pastor at the time of the Russian invasion of his Rumanian homeland in 1948. During a national convention of the leading clergy, sponsored by the newly imposed totalitarian government, Wurmbrand was the only one out of the four thousand priests and pastors to speak out publicly against the Communists. He was imprisoned and tortured for fourteen years. Hundreds of thousands died in Communist prisons of Eastern Europe during the years after World War II, but Wurmbrand miraculously survived.*

---

*Many Americans are familiar with Wurmbrand's exposure of the barbarity of the Communist regime in Russia and its brutal treatment of both Christians and

This is the story: Wurmbrand was talking one day with one of the Russian soldiers who had invaded his country—identified as an intellectual by nature of his rank. Wurmbrand asked him, "Do you believe in God?"

Wurmbrand explained that if the man had answered No, it would have been understandable—there are many who don't believe in God. "But," he recalled, "when I asked him, 'Do you believe in God?' he lifted toward me eyes without understanding and gave me an answer which rent my heart in pieces. He said, 'We have no order to believe; if we have an order from Stalin, we will believe.'"

Wurmbrand continued, "I am a man who has passed through Nazi prisons and through Communist prisons. We have known what it means to lose six children in one day. But if you were to ask me what has been the most dramatic moment in my life, I would say this.

"Tears ran down my cheeks. I had seen for the first time a man who was no more man. He was a brainwashed tool in the hands of the Communists. He had lost the greatest gift which God has given to a man: To be a personality of his own, who can say yes or no to his fellowman, who can say yes or no, even to God! This Russian soldier could say neither yes nor no. He expected from Stalin his order to believe."

There stood before Wurmbrand a man who had forfeited his right to be an individual. Communism seeks to destroy the possibility of fellowship with God by destroying the personality. The Russian soldier was not a man; he was an empty shell, a living corpse, because the cord that connects humanity with the Godhead had been severed: he had no mind to make moral decisions.

When an individual is destroyed like that Russian soldier, he loses his moral character and the ability to know God. He becomes capable of the most heinous crimes and sins. People are shocked

---

non-Christians behind the Iron Curtain. In May 1966 he testified in Washington, D.C., before a Congressional Internal Security Subcommittee, stripping to the waist to reveal eighteen deep torture wounds covering his body. His story is told most completely in his book *In God's Underground,* formerly entitled *Christ in the Communist Prison* published by Diana Books.

at Hitler's crimes. Yet Stalin was responsible for killing five times the number of people killed by Hitler's regime. Stalin had more than thirty million people put to death in Russia alone. How did he do it? Not with his own hands. No, the lone Russian soldier, waiting for his order to believe, did it.

In the Children of God I became like that lone Russian soldier. Our Stalin had a different name; we did not wear uniforms or carry guns; we did not use violence or force to enslave. Yet our movement rested on the same evil. Each disciple of the COG waits daily for "his order to believe" from Moses David. Throughout the world thousands of COG disciples anxiously await their orders to believe in the form of the latest Mo Letter.

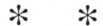

Three years after I had left the movement I clearly saw that I was ultimately responsible for joining the COG, for choosing to follow my father, for choosing to believe that Moses David was God's Endtime Prophet. I could so easily blame my father—after all, he had influenced and dominated me since birth. It would be only natural that I follow in his footsteps. However, to place the blame on him would be to deny my individuality. Have I been all my life a robot incapable of making moral choices?

A man who forfeits or will not accept the responsibility of his moral decisions is no longer a man. In seeing myself as that Russian soldier I painfully realized that to know God I must be an individual, and to be an individual I must be willing to accept the responsibility for my actions.

I thought long and hard about why the soldier's answer had such an intense effect on Richard Wurmbrand. Stating that Communism's aim is the destruction of the individual, the dissolution of the personality for the sake of the state, Wurmbrand continued by recalling the relationship of God and Moses in the Old Testament. In the Bible it is written that "God spoke to Moses face to face" (Exodus 33:11). Wurmbrand, being of Jewish origin and fluent in Hebrew, explained that the phrase "face to face" is an old Hebraic expression meaning that God spoke to Moses "as a person to a person."

"Suppose for an instant," Wurmbrand explained, "that Moses did not have a face. Suppose that Moses did not have a personality of his own. God could not have spoken to him anymore."

Moses was an individual and consequently was able to have an individual, personal relationship with God. God can no more have fellowship with us if we are not individuals than we can have a personal relationship with a stone.

There is a platform of evil from which Communism derives its power. A cult derives its power from the same source. There is an evil inherent in both Communism and cults that renders them synonomous: they seek to destroy our individuality before God.

This truth can be seen in the story of David and Bathsheba. King David of Israel was an individual. He was also a man who made mistakes. He committed adultery with Bathsheba and then had her husband murdered to cover up the sin. When Nathan the prophet confronted the king with his crimes, the only words out of David's mouth were: "I have sinned." That is all he said. There was no making excuses, no attempt to justify himself, no explaining away the sin or the guilt or the responsibility. In a dramatically profound admission of responsibility he stated, "I have sinned against the Lord" (2 Samuel 12:13). This rings loudly of individuality. The "I" says, "No one else made me sin. It is true that Bathsheba was a beautiful woman and I was tempted. But I, and only I, allowed my lusts to conceive in my mind and bring forth sin within me. That sin overpowered me and I sent for her and carried it to its logical conclusion. Yes, I have sinned. Therefore I am responsible. I am subject to the consequences of my sin."

David accepted his guilt, his responsibility—and he remained an individual. What if he had said, "I am not responsible—I was tempted and lured by that woman; after all, it was she that consented"? In doing so he would have surrendered a moral choice. In refusing to accept his responsibility and guilt he would have rendered himself a nonindividual, just like the Russian soldier—a person incapable of knowing God. But the Bible records that David was "a man after God's own heart," a truly remarkable characteristic. David understood something keenly important in the mystery of life; he was aware of the relationship of God to man, of judgment to mercy. In accepting his responsibility he walked boldly to the throne of judgment, knowing full well that he was guilty and deserving of death. What was the source of his confidence? He believed in the mercy of God and cast himself upon it.

In Psalm 51 David prays for the remission of his sins after being confronted by Nathan the prophet. This prayer reveals the depth of David's understanding of the nature of God. By confessing and acknowledging his terrible sin David voluntarily faced the imminent wrath of God; but instead of judgment he experienced an amazing outpouring of God's mercy. Through it all David came to a realization of what God truly wants from us. He writes,

> *Have mercy upon me, O God, according to thy loving kindness: according unto the multitude of thy tender mercies blot out my transgressions. . . .*
>
> *For I acknowledge my transgressions: and my sin is ever before me. . . .*
>
> *Behold, thou desirest truth in the inward parts: and in the hidden parts thou shalt make me to know wisdom. . . .*
>
> *For thou desirest not sacrifice; else would I give it: thou delightest not in burnt offering.*
>
> *The sacrifices of God are a broken spirit: a broken and a contrite heart, O God, thou wilt not despise* (Psalm 51).

David knew what God wanted. He knew that the God of judgment is also the God of mercy.

I began to see an important principle at work here. It is the same principle that Wurmbrand perceived and the same one that established God's personal relationship with Moses: If I accept the guilt of my sin, I acknowledge God's sovereign right of judgment, which in turn frees Him to reveal and extend His mercy to me. Expressed negatively the statement reads: If I attempt to cover or hide my sin, if I refuse to acknowledge my responsibility and guilt, I am foolishly denying the omnipotence of God and His obligation to pass judgment; this nullifies God's ability to reveal mercy. To cover my guilt is to despise, to spit upon, the very mercy God would so willingly extend.

At this point in my life the message of the Gospel was revealed in a manner I had never known. God wants and expects us to be honest with ourselves, to accept our guilt; it is our link with humanity, the anchor of individuality. It keeps us from becoming heinous killers like Stalin; through it we remain individual personalities; and ultimately it is our link with God. It is confessed guilt that opens our eyes to the reality of judgment and mercy.

> *To know God I must be an individual. . . .*
> *To be an individual I must be willing to accept the responsibility of my actions. . . .*
> *In accepting the responsibility of my actions I must be willing to admit my guilt.*

Human nature is ever intent upon avoiding guilt, yet *the greatest tormentor of ex-cult victims is guilt.* Its weight can drive a person to the doorstep of insanity, and sometimes beyond. My guilt seemed overwhelming. To consider the thousands of lives that have been ruined by my father's doctrines, the spiritual and moral atrocities that have been and are still being committed in the name of Jesus, and the physical deaths and suicides that have occurred as a result of the ministry of Moses David is more than one can bear. The realization that I helped to found that movement led me into mental states of isolation. Seeing the effects of the Children of God on my own children often pushed me into unbearable states of depression. Then a marvelous illumination occurred. The very guilt that was pushing me ever closer to the brink of destruction became my most wonderful ally, bringing me to a place of hitherto unreachable joy and peace.

In looking at the Children of God and my father and my relationship to them, I realized that a cult could not exist but for the cult in my heart.

Many parents and well-meaning friends have viewed my situation and lovingly tried to vindicate me, saying "It never would have happened—it was your father's fault." I am grateful for their kindness and concern. But unknowingly they are denying my right to be a responsible individual as acutely as the cult denied it. To become a whole person I had to see and accept my personal responsibility and guilt in joining and living in the COG. In ac-

cepting this fact I was no longer that Russian soldier. I had regained my individuality, that priceless gift I forfeited when I
chose to follow Moses David.

✳ ✳

In taking this moral step I faced a new question and another
trauma. The subconscious guilt that haunted me and nearly drove
me insane was now visibly before me. The weight was unbearable;
I could not live with it. I had regained my individuality, but unless
I were healed from the burden of guilt I would not be able to go
on living. The question was, What do I do with my guilt? Where
do I go from here?

At this point a wonderful experience occurred, one that I had
never known in a conscious, real way. I had nowhere to go, no one
to turn to. I had painfully regained my individuality but was a
miserably guilty individual. I saw no purpose in living. My life had
been ruined, shattered. Moreover, *I was responsible!* Then God
revealed the meaning of Grace in a most unimaginable way.

Through His grace I recalled all my childhood training and
experiences in Christianity and what they meant to me—the different stories, the parables, the birth of Christ, His healing ministry—
and finally I arrived at the foot of the Cross. As I lifted my eyes
slowly to Him I perceived for the first time a Man suffering and
bleeding, in an agony of unparalleled love, dying on the Cross *for
me.* In my hands I held the very sins which had placed Him there.
It was not the sins of my father, of Moses David, or of anyone else.
I had crucified my Lord. For an instance—yet an eternity—there
existed no one else in the world but Christ and me. It was for me
that He suffered and died, for it was I who had placed Him there.
I had heard countless stories and sermons about Jesus dying for
the sins of the world, but never had the reality of Calvary become
so personal. Clearly, it was I who had caused this horrible event.

The sins and the guilt that I held before me began to tear my
heart in pieces. I hated myself and my sins: how could I have been
so wicked?

And then the mystery unfolded. Those very sins had
brought me to Him. My sins—so horrible, so painful—had led me

to Him. That which had threatened my sanity, which drove me to the depths of depression and nearly to the point of ending it all, had brought me to Christ. There was nowhere else to go. The mystery was clear: Christ died for *guilty* individuals.

This is why the cults struggle so earnestly to justify sin, to rationalize guilt, to destroy the individual through benign deception. If I try to remove the burden of guilt artificially, I will not need my Savior. But one does not remove guilt by any means. Guilt becomes a part of us and there is no separating it from our being. One deceives himself to think that it can be reasoned away.

Guilt had become my ally, my link with reality—the Divine Reality. It was indeed the anchor of my soul, for it brought me face to face with God. To sever that cord through false reasoning sets one adrift upon the sea of eternal frustration and alienation.

As I stood quietly at the foot of the Cross, the words that will echo throughout eternity fell on my soul, filling it with joy and peace: "Father, forgive. . . ." I laid my guilt, my sins, my responsibility at His feet. I became a *forgiven* individual.

Christ restored my fellowship with God. Like David of old I glimpsed for the first time the relationship of God to man, of judgment to mercy. I cried for a long, long while. Tears of sorrow turned to tears of thankfulness, a thankfulness I had never known or experienced, for which I was altogether unworthy. I was beginning to see through my tears what David was referring to when he wrote, "God desires a broken and a contrite heart." The lone Russian soldier could not have a broken heart. A nonindividual cannot have a broken heart. One who refuses to accept guilt and responsibility will never know truth in the inward parts; to him the mystery of the Cross will remain hidden.

Because the pain and the shame of facing my guilt and admitting my responsibility were incredibly intense, I was afraid to face that. I did not know then that God's comfort—His grace—was waiting to come crashing down like a mountain of snow to encompass and strengthen my soul. Confession was the key that triggered the avalanche.

By accepting my own guilt and responsibility I unknowingly set myself free from the snares of bitterness, resentment, and alienation. There exist many unforeseen blessings in obeying

God's principles. If I had been intent on blaming my father or anyone else for my involvement in the COG in order to *reason away my guilt,* resentment would have permeated my mind; the destructive seeds of bitterness would have grown deep within me.

A response of bitterness is an instinctive means of revenge toward the one whom we feel has wronged us. Only God has the right to punish. "Vengeance is mine; I will repay, saith the Lord." Man's attitude is expressed in bitterness; God's, in mercy. Bitterness is a strong sign that a person is harboring unconfessed guilt. A person who has not yet received divine forgiveness finds it difficult to show mercy to anyone else. A bitter person tries to relieve the pain of unconfessed guilt by focusing resentment against the person or object that offended him. The tragedy is that it is forgiveness, not vengeance, that sets a person free. Indeed, forgiveness is the most divine quality known to man. It sets one free to love.

In studying Richard Wurmbrand's writings I found that I had a great deal in common with him. In what way? How can that be when he was suffering torment and deprivation in a Communist prison while I was enjoying much physical freedom and pleasure in the Children of God. Our common experience is this: we were both prisoners. He was a prisoner of Communist tyrants for fourteen years; I was a prisoner of a cult for thirteen years.

Richard Wurmbrand was arrested, tortured, and imprisoned because he was a Christian and lived by his Christian principles in the face of opposition. He was in prison because he knew God, had courage, and believed that suffering and loving God are synonymous. I was in prison because I did not truly know God, was filled with fear and self, and followed my own image of Christ. A common captivity, for opposite reasons.

Guilt. Responsibility. Individuality. The principle linking the relationship of these three words is ultimately responsible for my total deliverence from the cultic phenomenon. It broke the invisible chains that kept me bound to a life of frustration, mental torment, and spiritual confusion for a period of three years after I had physically left the cult.

Chapter 13
"Brainwashing?
That's Ridiculous!"

Two years after my husband and I left the Children of God, his mother asked him, "Bill, do you think you were brainwashed?"

"Brainwashed?" he quickly answered. "Why that's ridiculous, Mom! I wasn't brainwashed! There was no one telling me what to do, or forcing me. I did it of my own free will, because I wanted to. Brainwashing? That's ridiculous!"

Bill was offended at his mother's suggestion that he had been made to act according to someone else's will. He was vehement in his argument. However, one year later he told his mother, "You know, Mom, you were right. I *was* brainwashed."

Was Bill right the first time or the second? And if he was brainwashed, is he responsible for his actions in the COG?

Bill's mother raised the question naturally, because while he was in the Children of God she saw a 180-degree transformation in him. She knew her son inside-out—his personality, his temperament, his disposition—and she could say with complete accuracy, "Something is wrong with Bill. Something's not right. He's got blinders on. He's brainwashed."

The word *brainwashed* in the context of a religious cult conjures up thoughts of an evil force, a sinister plot designed to make zombies of respectable, middle-class youth. Our minds flash back to POWs emerging from Communist prison camps with gaunt faces and blank stares, parroting Marxist philosophy and condemning "American imperialism." The brainwashed POW appears to us a rather miserable creature, the victim of intense propaganda, mind-control techniques, and great physical abuse—his change of mind the result of a coercive environment. We can all understand this kind of experience—a clear-cut case of brainwashing.

But what about members of the Children of God and other cults? No one is kept forcibly against his will. Members are not captured by Viet Cong guerrillas and marched at gunpoint to the "Hanoi Hilton." Cult members join willingly, like Bill, drawn by something they see and like and desire.

It is important to note that physical coercion is not necessary for cultic brainwashing to occur. In fact, the use of force is a rather primitive method of thought reform. The kind of brainwashing we see in the religious cults is far superior to anything the Communists have devised. We need to abandon our stereotypes of brainwashing to understand the plight of people like Bill in cults like the Children of God.

The term *brainwash* comes from a literal translation of the Chinese phrase "thought reform." Thought-brain; reform-wash. Hence, "brainwash."

An encyclopedia defines brainwashing as "a method of forcing people to change their beliefs and accept as true what they previously had considered false."[1] It further says, "Most victims regain their original beliefs soon after returning to their own environment." The latter comment applies to victims of Communist thought-reform programs and implies the use of force as an ingredient in the process. A person forced into something can revert to his former state if the coercion is removed. Research shows that most victims of the Communists return to "normal" after being placed in a free environment. This indicates the limited effects of their program and suggests why it is inferior to cultic mind-control. Whether or not cult victims revert to their earlier mind-sets readily after coming into a free environment is clearly a matter of debate.

A remarkable aspect of brainwashing is that the victim doesn't know he is brainwashed. It is like a man who is color-blind. You might say to him, "Excuse me, sir, but I just want you to know that you are color-blind."

"Color blind?" he responds. "I beg your pardon! What are you talking about? There is no such thing; I can see just fine!"

"But sir," you persist, "it's quite obvious you can't tell the difference between green and blue."

Our color-blind friend promptly ends the conversation. "Oh! Now I see! You're one of those unenlightened devils who believe the green-and-blue lie!"

The color-blind man, unless shown pragmatically, is unaware of his own blindness, because he has lost or has never known a perspective by which to judge his error. Truth is ultimate perspective. But the man does not have the truth.

This is why Bill argued with his mother. He could not see the reality of his own condition. Not until the perspective of truth and reality were restored did he recognize it. The brainwashed person will believe strongly that it is everyone else who is distorted in the view of reality. My husband thought his mother was confused.

Cultic brainwashing is primarily internal. There is nothing in the appearance of a person on the street to characterize him as a cult member—red robes notwithstanding. The distinguishing marks go below the surface into the mental distortion of reality.

The complexity of the problem is demonstrated when two parties enter into litigation. If a parent accuses his offspring of being brainwashed, the youth responds by accusing the parent of being a selfish and narrow-minded individual, an avid bigot, and the victim of alcohol abuse. The child will say, "Whose reality is distorted? It is you who are brainwashed." The pot is calling the kettle black. Both parties assume that there is a standard of truth and that the other has strayed from it and adopted a false standard.

If the youth has joined a cult and sincerely believes a lie, then he is in fact a victim of brainwashing. The question then arises, when does the turning point occur? What makes a person susceptible to mind control? How does it happen that a young, highly intelligent, affluent youth becomes brainwashed—or for that matter, a not-so-intelligent, economically deprived loner?

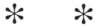

The process begins when a person opens his mind to an outside influence he views with favor. There must be a voluntary suspension of the will.

This process is quite similar to something that occurs everyday. It happens when we go to see an exciting space movie, watch a suspense thriller on TV, or read a good novel. The writer of a good novel must be able to weave his words and create images in such a way as to allow the reader to voluntarily suspend his disbelief. In short, the reader must forget that he is reading a book or the author has failed.

The same is true of a good movie. *Star Wars* is a fantasy, a futuristic space adventure that has thrilled millions around the world. To really enjoy the movie the viewer must willingly trip a switch in his mind that allows his consciousness to change tracks and say, "Forget about the movie theater. Pretend you are in outer space. Forget about the exhorbitant price you paid to get in here. Disregard the fact that the people you are seeing are just actors who don't live in the year 3000, but actually live in Beverly Hills, California. Pay no attention to the fact that the people dying are not really dying." The viewer must suspend the real facts that his mind is telling him with computerlike accuracy. His conscious disbelief must be suspended to thoroughly "enjoy" the movie. This is done willingly. Hence the willing suspension of disbelief is a common experience of most *Star Wars* moviegoers.

For the children in the audience this is a much more serious matter than for adults. Han Solo and Chewbaca are not mere fictional characters in children's minds; they are as real as Santa Claus, and this reality is reinforced by the Han Solo doll and toy spacecraft at home in the bedroom. Are these little ones brainwashed? It sounds harsh, but to a limited degree they are. Reality for them has been distorted. "Oh, but that's harmless. They'll grow out of it." Perhaps. But the child remains in the world of *Star*

Wars longer than his mother or father. An adult suspends his disbelief only as long as the projector is running or until little Johnny has to go to the bathroom. As adults we remain in a state of suspended reality only as long as our disbelief is unaltered. Then reality jumps back like the snapping of a rubber band.

Brainwashing as experienced in the COG and other cults results from a voluntary suspension of disbelief. A clue to the phenomenon is found in the word *enjoy*. To "enjoy" a movie we must flip the switch. It is a voluntary mental action. In the realm of movie-making, our willing suspension of disbelief is facilitated by the excellent technique of the producer and director, the skill of the photographer, the intensity of the acting, the genius of special effects, and so on. A high-quality film makes it easier for us to believe, and consequently we fall into place and vicariously take a trip into the adventures of *Star Wars*. With the cult recruit, a very similar process takes place.

Unlike the moviegoer, however, a cult victim who suspends his disbelief doesn't necessarily come out of it. He stays in that state. The cult and its doctrine become his reality. It is significant that when we go to a movie theater we are already prepared to suspend our disbelief. We fully intend to enjoy the movie. So it is with the cult victim. In many cases he is ready to suspend whatever mental reservations he has in order to "enjoy" life. Stoner and Parke, the authors of *All God's Children*, write, "These young people are idealistic and are frequently searching for a goal, a purpose, and a sense of community, so the promises of the cults appeal strongly to them. Many are willing, even anxious, to be persuaded."[2]

This enjoyment principle is a key factor and motivating force. The enjoyment a prospective cult member seeks lies on a deeper level than mere entertainment; he is hoping to find fulfillment, purpose, and direction for life. But like the movie goer who attends *Star Wars* seeking enjoyment, an individual joins a cult because he wants to enjoy the movie of life. A lack of spiritual truth and fulfillment prepares the youth for the cultic lure. He is ready to accept the beautifully clothed lie of benign deception.

Living in a society that is corrupt, tense, disappointing, and lacking the foundation of scriptural principles will produce the same yearning as the physical and mental deprivation employed by the Communists in their thought-reform programs. Through years of carefully designed imprisonment encompassing mental and physical manipulation, the Communists wear out their victim's minds and generally make life as miserable as humanly possible, bringing them to a point where they will be happy to adopt new truths and new philosophies to gain relief. It's a simple process, totally inhuman, but not at all difficult to understand.

When a cult recruit crosses the invisible barrier in his mind—when he enters the world of the cult and its doctrine at some point during his flirtatious sampling of the cult—he is tripping the switch of his voluntary suspension of disbelief. Brainwashing or mind control then occurs naturally, sometimes effortlessly. In many cases the new cult member will struggle hard to brainwash himself. He must do this in order to balance out the guilt he feels. When doubts rush in like a flood, he tells himself, "I am following the truth. The rest of the world may be going to hell, but I am following the truth!"

Other brothers and sisters are there to encourage the new recruit. He either accepts their help and counsel, or he rejects it. If he rejects it, he doesn't stay around long. If he receives their help, he goes deeper into the cultic doctrine. He will sell flowers, chant, memorize, litness, or read Mo Letters, whatever it takes, to the utmost of his ability to prove to himself and others that he is right. The brainwashing that occurs in the cults is the finest, purest, and most effective around. The Communists have something to learn from Moses David.

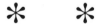

Another part of the cultic brainwashing process involves certain social and spiritual conditions.

Cults are a manifestation of social evil and personal character weaknesses. Cults are a social statement. Stoner and Parke affirm with poignant accuracy and candor,

> *Religious cults, whether we are willing to face it or not, are frightening manifestations of deficiencies in our culture.*[3]

This is an unsettling observation. If social conditions are contributing to the problem of cults, does it make sense to talk about brainwashing? Do counselors, psychologists, and deprogrammers achieve their desired ends if they return cult victims to a social environment that bred them in the first place?

In many cases the emphasis on mind-control and deprogramming results from society's attempt to escape the guilt it feels. It places the blame on a cult's use of mind-control techniques rather than blaming the character deficiencies of youth resulting from an imbalanced social environment. By the same token, many parents want to blame cultic manipulation instead of themselves or their children.

The root of the problem is that society is moving collectively toward denying moral absolutes. Christ gave us a very strong absolute, namely, the world lies in sin and He died for the remission of sin. We are absolutely instructed to "love not the world, neither the things that are in the world. . . . For all that is in the world, the lust of the flesh, and the lust of the eyes, and the pride of life, is not of the Father, but is of the world. And the world is passing away, and the lust of it; but he who does the will of God abides forever" (1 John 2:15–16). Christ gave us absolutes to deal with our problems, but no shortcuts or easy answers.

Christ prayed in the garden of Gethsemane that His cup might pass. It did not, and He drank it. He set the example that the road to righteousness is absolute, but there are no shortcuts from suffering. The way of the Cross can cost a man his life. God's absolutes are anything but easy.

Stoner and Parke make a statement that troubles me greatly. They write,

> There are no shortcuts or easy answers in a world with no absolutes. There is no question that life is simpler with a set of unbreakable rules. It is this simple, no-option world that religious cults offer young people.[4]

The authors are partly right in what they have written, but they have missed the vital moral issue. They imply that living by a set of unbreakable rules is a copout, a neglect of responsibility. They overlook the fact that cults offer youth only a counterfeit solution to their tensions. They have replaced those given by God with a false set of human design. Having unbreakable rules is not inherently the problem; having the wrong set of rules is.

The Apostles certainly testified with their lives that true Christianity isn't easy. It makes demands on the individual. One must resist evil within and without. Living the absolutes they learned from their Master resulted in a martyr's death for all but one of the Apostles. More than simplistic, Christianity offers us a clear understanding of life. The fact that cults offer their members a life with a set of absolutes offsets the failure of a society that, in adopting secular humanism, has left its youth without foundation and without security.* Stoner and Parke recognize this problem.

> *Today's youth is living in the midst of a day-to-day future shock. They are about to inherit a world with no clear-cut rights and wrongs. No one can tell them how to make life work for them. Old formulas are not always valid. Even the ethics of today's culture are relative, rather than static. To be sexually curious or totally chaste; to marry or to live together; to have a child or an abortion; to grow long hair or to cut it short; to smoke marijuana or not to smoke are viewed by many as relative choices.*[5]

In this, parents and society have failed their children and made them fair game for the cultic lure which is, in the final analysis, the lure of sin. Society and parents must face the unwelcome fact that they will be held accountable, both by God and by life itself, for their failures. In short, cults are a present judgment of God. But there will be more to come.

---

*Secular humanism excludes God. It makes man his own highest authority. Moral standards are relative in humanism and give way to situational ethics.

The philosophy of humanism began with Satan, who said in his heart, ". . . I will be like the most High." It was the philosophy that Satan used to trick Eve: ". . . And ye shall be as Gods. . . ." "Humanists" are defined by Paul as those "who changed the truth of God into a lie, and worshipped and served the creature more than the Creator. . . ." Humanism is being promoted in our day through false religions, cults, and godless philosophies.

Magazines that encourage sexual freedom without the responsibility of marriage are promoting humanism. Advertising that encourages people to live only for the present is built on humanistic philosophy. Government programs that promise to solve social evils without God are humanistic (*Men's Manual*, Institute in Basic Youth Conflicts, vol. 1, p. 32).

Cults are a clear sign of the sins of society, the result of society's boastful assertion that there are no absolutes and man is his own god. Oswald Chambers writes,

> *When our Lord faced men with all the forces of evil in them, and men who were clean living and moral and upright, He did not pay any attention to the moral degradation of the one or to the moral attainment of the other; He looked at something we do not see, namely, the disposition.*
>
> *The disposition of sin is not immorality and wrong doing, but the disposition of self-realization—I am my own god.*[6]

Throughout this book I have stressed the responsibility of the individual who joins the cult. This is the ultimate conclusion: When I stand before God, I will not be able to blame anyone else for my sins. However, I do believe that the degenerate condition of society is largely responsible for the cultic phenomenon, and I would be foolish to deny that the social condition is a major factor in many going astray.

E. Stanley Jones clearly defines the power of the social condition: ". . . If I had to choose . . . I think I should have to conclude that an unchristian social order produces more thwarted and disrupted lives than any other single cause."[7] Nevertheless, a decadent social condition begins with decadent individuals, and for this reason every member of society (like every cult victim) will be responsible before God for his individual part in allowing our social order to become apostate. The moral deterioration of individuals leads to a condition which becomes self-perpetuating, and we soon see the sins of the parents manifested in the lives of the children.

As individuals and as a society we need absolutes. The absolutes revealed in Scripture go far beyond making life manageable; they give us truth and understanding. But there are no shortcuts.

Stoner and Parke finally address the need of the youth face to face. But they only define the need in its specifics; they offer no solution.

> *The young people who are drawn to these new religions . . . need to belong, to have friends, to be secure, and to feel impor-*

tant. Their energy and enthusiasm need constructive channeling. They need direction and discipline and a clearly defined purpose in life. They need to be taught how to think for themselves and to develop their own systems of self-discipline.[8]

I hold suspect anyone who says that a cult member was "hypnotized" into joining, that he was sucked up by the giant vacuum cleaner of cultic hocus-pocus against his will. This appears to be as big a lie as the cult itself. People join cults voluntarily; of their own free will they suspend their minds to cultic doctrine, and then the brainwashing process occurs. Spiritual brainwashing—the kind we see in the cults—is the result of a person's own sin. Cults are an offense against God, not a crime against innocent victims. How can a person be innocent of sin?

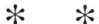

This is what makes cultic brainwashing so effective. Dogmatic belief in doctrine justifies and supports deep-rooted sin in a cult member's life. Sin has distorted the reality of that person's life before God, and the doctrines ameliorate this distortion.

Cultic doctrine neutralizes sin, making it seem permissible, normal, and necessary. The more a person embraces a cult and its beliefs, the greater comfort and security he feels. The more he embraces it, the deeper this security grows; but at the same time the deeper his sin grows. As he enters further into the sin habits of the cult, the more intense becomes his weight of guilt and his subconscious awareness of this sin. Hence, a stronger embracing of the cult doctrine is needed to make his position secure. The cycle continues and deepens. It is a spiritual "China syndrome" which, like a nuclear chain reaction, ends in destruction.

Society's common interpretation of cultic indoctrination is summed up in the following illustration by Richard Delgado, a colleague of Robert J. Lifton:

The surgeon first asks his patient if he can examine her leg. The patient consents. Then the surgeon says there seems to be slight infection and tells her he wants to apply an antiseptic. Then, since the leg is clean, he decides to examine it further and asks if he can anesthetize the wound area, and she consents. Now he tells the patient that the wound needs to be probed. Again, she consents. The surgeon finds cancerous tissue and suggests that since the leg is already anesthetized and germ-free, he should remove the malignant growth. The patient is frightened, but she gives further consent. Ultimately in this obviously exaggerated sequence of events, the patient consents to having her leg amputated.[9]

To Delgado, this illustration typifies the deception of the cults. Like the patient, the unwitting cult victim gets himself in over his head and ends up losing more than he bargained for. The analogy is quite fitting and rational. Delgado has perceived the subtle deceit of the cultic lure.

However, from the cult's perspective this deceit is merely part of the "training process" of a new convert. The mature cult member doesn't feel he is being the least bit deceptive. He is simply presenting truth in doses suitable for a "babe," or new member. The salvation of the new convert is at stake, and the disciple has a divine responsibility to assist the convert into the cult 100 percent. Delgado acknowledges the fact that the convert does "consent to each step" of the conversion process—that is, there is a voluntary choice. But the wrongdoing, as Delgado sees it, is that the cults misrepresent themselves; they don't honestly display themselves for what they truly are. Delgado is more right than he realizes. Evil never is honest in its looks.

Yet, are cult victims truly innocent? Delgado's analogy overlooks the most vital issue of life. Cults are evil, and men and women are victimized by evil because they fall prey to temptation. Here is another illustration, much like Delgado's. However, this one is a true story:

It involves two marvelous people, a beautiful garden, and a very crafty snake, and it's told in Genesis 3. Were Adam and Eve informed by the snake of the consequences that would follow their decision to eat of the Tree of the Knowledge of Good and Evil? Were they informed of the final outcome of their decision? On the contrary, they were led to believe that it would greatly benefit them. They were tempted and deceived, step by step, and they lost a lot more than a leg. They lost their righteous standing before God and were banished from His presence.

The Delgado mentality overlooks an important reality, namely, that the universe is in a conflict between good and evil, wherein evil will ultimately be judged. Moreover, while the universe is in a continuous struggle, so is each person in his own battle between good and evil within.

Delgado's conclusion, shared by others, is that society should enact laws which would somehow make these cults transparent. If this were done, they argue, people would see them for what they are, and we would stand a chance of curtailing the evil effects of the cults and could protect "innocent victims." It would become society's responsibility to police religions, and decide what is bad, and pass laws accordingly. Most people fear this kind of legislation because it contains elements of totalitarian rule and denies religious liberty.

Legislation against wrongdoing is necessary, and in matters where cults are breaking the law, they should be prosecuted. But legislation against evil must by nature of the case be generalized, allowing exceptions only with assumed risks; and even then, its effectiveness in preventing evil and administering justice is limited. Passing laws against cults will in no wise stop them. Delgado is striking out at the extension of evil and not at the evil itself, which he cannot destroy.

I admire Delgado's courage and conviction in wanting to do something to stop the damage the cults are doing, but passing laws will never totally solve the problem. It is the evil within us, from which the cults emanate, that must be conquered, and there is only One who has overcome evil.

I have learned firsthand that the painful consequences of sin are not only part of God's judgments, but also helpful teaching aids that substantiate the truth of God's principles in the order of the universe.

Therefore, it is dangerous to apply to cult victims the statement "the patient would not have consented to all the surgeon's steps had she known the outcome of his process." There are two reasons why. First, it threatens the individual's God-given right to make a moral decision in any given situation and be held responsible for the consequences. Second, it overlooks the reality of evil in a morally charged universe and the workings of Satan in cultic organizations; it falsely presupposes the cults are independent agents disassociated from satanic influence. The statement renders the patient neither innocent nor holy nor guilty—simply a factor in a circumstance.

I ask myself how many things I would not have done had I known the outcome. How many times have any of us said, "If only I had . . ."? Mistakes are important steps to growth; through them we learn a framework of right behavior. We never know beforehand the final outcome of a moral decision. We only presuppose the outcome based on our previous experience or moral ideologies. And as Christians we don't necessarily make decisions based on the final outcome, because making the right decision often spells out suffering. The saints who died a martyr's death because of their stand of faith looked far beyond the temporal results of their decision.

To stress the point that the patient would not have consented had she known the outcome is wrong from a Christian perspective. It avoids the most basic issue of life. It places blame on the surgeon's deceit and subtleties. Granted, the surgeon was wrong. He is deserving of punishment. However, positioned morally before God, each person must answer directly to God for his actions, regardless of the deceit of surgeons, cults, Hitlers, Stalins, David Bergs, or even Satan himself.

The true and ultimate purpose of cultic brainwashing is to deaden the voice of conscience so that a person can adopt a philosophy or theology that is morally wrong. The people most susceptible to mind manipulation are those who are sensitive and sincere, who cannot accept committing a blatant wrong. They need justification or a rationale for committing sin. They need to believe that "wrong" is right—otherwise they cannot do it.

One truth remains, even through the manipulative techniques of mind control: No one ever joins a cult against his will; no one ever commits sin against his will; no one becomes a victim of mind control against his will; likewise, no one commits himself to a true faith in the Lord Jesus Christ against his will.

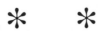

Justifying sin and the resulting guilt through mind control will not give a person rest and peace of mind. A conscience laden with sin and guilt will torture a person forever. Why? Because the conscience is the law of God within us demanding justice for our sins.

I believe one reason why many psychologists and counselors meet only partial success in helping cult victims back to normalcy is that they are not separating the two guilt factors. There is a guilt born of personal failure, the result of human pride. For example, an ex-cult victim will experience guilt because he has failed the cult, failed his prophet, and become a Judas, a backslider. The "guilt trips" placed on cult members by cult doctrine produce a form of human guilt, what I would term "unrighteous guilt." This kind of guilt can be singled out and eliminated in counseling.

But there is another form of guilt, proceeding from a man's conscience. This is the guilt of sin, what I call "righteous guilt." It cannot be counseled away. To eliminate this kind of guilt a man must seek and find divine forgiveness. The guilt of sin is a spiritual matter. Non-Christian psychiatrists, psychologists, and counselors do not recognize the reality of sin or the guilt that accompanies it. Consequently they lump all guilt into one category and view it as "unrighteous guilt." They talk of "false guilt."

If these two guilt factors are unknowingly lumped together and justified, the victim will continue to feel the pain of guilt, the result of sin. He will remain fragmented and alienated. Counselors are baffled as to why so many ex-cult victims are not healed and continue to suffer severe depression, anxiety, and emotional trauma. They don't understand why they cannot seem to "break away" from their experience in the cult. The reason is that they are still carrying the guilt of sin.

I find it impossible to look at cultic brainwashing and mind control strictly from a human point of view. It must be viewed in a spiritual perspective—that is, from the standpoint of sin. Oswald Chambers writes,

> *At the beginning of life we do not reconcile ourselves to the fact of sin. We take a rational view of life and say that a man by controlling his instincts, and by educating himself, can produce*

"Brainwashing? That's Ridiculous!"

a life which will slowly evolve into the life of God. But as we go on, we find the presence of something which we have not taken into consideration, namely, sin, and it upsets all our calculations. Sin has made the basis of things wild and not rational. We have to recognize that sin is a fact, not a defect; sin is redhanded mutiny against God. Either God or sin must die in my life. The New Testament brings us right down to this one issue. If sin rules in me, God's life in me will be killed; if God rules in me, sin in me will be killed. There is no possible ultimate but that. The climax of sin is that it crucified Jesus Christ, and what was true in the history of God on earth will be true in your history and in mine. In our mental outlook we have to reconcile ourselves to the fact of sin as the only explanation as to why Jesus Christ came, and as the explanation of the grief and sorrow in life.[10]

Society in subtle ways—as well as unsubtle—is trying to do away with the need for a Savior. It is becoming a common belief that a thorough understanding of the dynamics of mind-control techniques will free a person from cultic bondage and ease the burden of an ex-cult member's guilty conscience. No, it won't.

If guilt and sin can be explained away, there exists no need for a Savior. The apostle John wrote,

If we confess our sin, he is faithful and just to forgive us our sins, and to cleanse us from all unrighteousness (1 John 1:19).

Sin denies us our righteous standing before God. But to push sin under the rug (such as by justifying mind control), thereby denying its reality, is to obscure the one pathway to finding a personal relationship with God.

For millions of cult members, brainwashing is a reality. It is a deadly snare that blinds them from the truth they so desperately need to see. To step through the twilight zone of mind manipulation into the light of reality, rediscovering the truth about life and about self, is often a slow and painful process. It takes time, perhaps years.

The friends and relatives of ex-cult victims should remember three things: Be compassionate, be patient, be sensitive. It is a difficult thing to admit mistakes, to face sins. This process re-

181

awakens all the deep-seated guilt. It must be a voluntary experience. We cannot force any to examine themselves. They must do it as the grace of God is revealed in their lives. They need understanding; they need our love. They must accept their responsibility by their own choice. But when they do, they will experience a spiritual awakening. And it is most exciting.

Sin lies at the root of cultic brainwashing. To explain away sin and guilt through the dynamics of mind control is an attack against Jesus as the Savior. Guilt, the result of sin, cannot be removed psychologically. It is Christ who removes the weight of guilt. It is Christ who died and rose from the dead for our sins. The cults will ultimately prove His lordship. True mental health and peace of mind lie in the remission of sin, and that gift is open to every individual.

In the end, the world will see that the cultic phenomenon only proves the unseen reality of the remission of sin.

Chapter 14
"All Things Are Lawful"

The husbands practically have to be pimps for their own wives!
God bless them! They've got to help manage them and protect
them and guide them. They need the fisherman to help them fish.
Oodles of men do it for money in the World! Why not for God?[1]

How many ways can we explain the phenomenon of Moses David—his character, his personality, his movement, his perversion?

How could David Berg, once kind and tender as a father, become so perverted and base, leading thousands of people into sinful darkness?

Is his mind diseased? Is he mentally deranged? Is he a psychopath?

In that I am neither a psychiatrist nor a psychologist nor a sociologist, I am forced to see my father through the eyes of a daughter—through the relationship of flesh and blood, through emotion and filial love. He is my father, and I cannot alter the fact. In viewing him as such, I have a perspective no one else has.

However, human weakness can cause that perspective to be distorted and consequently dull the sense of vision. Because I am his daughter, there exists the temptation not to see him as he really is.

My father is a man of exceptional intelligence. He is a most charming man, highly mannered and quite gracious to those he meets in public places. I often tell people that a child could not have had a more concerned and loving father. I remember vividly the day I graduated from eighth grade. My father had been traveling in another state on business, but he flew hundreds of miles just to be there. He came late to the graduation ceremony, marched right down the main aisle, and pinned a beautiful corsage on my dress just as I was walking up to receive my diploma. There wasn't a sacrifice he wouldn't make for his children. Yet, like a psychopathic killer, Moses David calculates with an uncanny genius the realization of his desires.

A psychopath, according to medical definition, is a person with a constitutional lack of moral sensibility although possessing normal intelligence. This definition fits my father's character acutely.

What causes psychopathy? Psychologists or psychiatrists would most likely interpret Moses David according to the dynamics of the mind. They would cite the behavioral patterns developed as a result of his personality, social environment, parentage, and so on. Through inductive reasoning they would establish why "he is what he is" by looking back on his life and piecing together past actions and circumstances that resulted in his present condition.

Thus the phenomenon of "Moses David" can be explained in many ways in the social sciences. Yet none of these explanations deal with the vital issue. They do not confront the moral problem, namely, the presence of evil. Given that others were exposed to the same circumstances of life as he, the question persists, Why did my father become psychopathic? Secular psychology doesn't have all the answers.

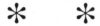

To answer the question we must view David Berg from a greater perspective than mind science or even filial bonds. I began to understand my father's condition when I was able to see him through the eyes of a repentant sinner.

There is but one way to view my father honestly. There is only one way to account for what he is and why he has become Moses David. It is to recognize the overpowering and consuming consequences of sin. Lewis Sperry Chafer wrote,

> *Moral evil is an ultimate fact in the universe which can neither be explained nor explained away. When traced to its inception as committed by the first fallen angel, the truth is developed which estimates sin to be a mystery, irrational, and exceeding sinful.*[2]

The personality of David Berg is the epitome of self-centeredness. Once a warm and loving father, he is now a man consumed with fulfilling his desires, promoting his ideas, advancing his own form of morality, and satisfying himself in every way. He is a man consumed by the forces of lust whose heart continually screams, "I want it, and I want it now!"

This self-centered personality reflects the very nature of sin. Chafer writes,

> *The creature—whether angel or human—is created to be God-centered. To become self-centered is a contradiction of the basic law of creature existence. The falsification of God's moral order, is, when self-centered, complete.*[3]

I have seen through the years that the character of Moses David has become a mirror-perfect image of the sin of Satan.

Satan, through whom sin entered the universe, has a distinct and predictable nature because his being is wholly evil and self-centered. Chafer explains,

> *The fall of this mighty angel was not a compromise between good and evil. He became the embodiment of evil and wholly void of good. The essential wickedness of this being could not be estimated by the finite mind. His wickedness, however, is constructive and in line with vast undertakings and ideals which are evil because of their opposition to God. . . . Satan is a living personification of deception.*[4]

How much like Satan is Moses David, who has systematically constructed, since his days at Huntington Beach, a network of deceptive doctrine designed to fulfill the lusts of his heart and bringing moral, spiritual, and physical destruction on the lives of thousands! What a master deceiver he is, promoting all manner of sexual sin in the name of Christ!

Does David Berg consciously know that he is an unrestrained tool in the hands of the devil? No, I am sure he does not. Do his followers know that their works are evil and that their Prophet walks in darkness? No, I am sure they do not. Satan is the deceiver of the whole world, and, Chafer reminds us, "few indeed would knowingly march under his banner. Yet, it will be seen that there are but few who do not to some degree give allegiance to him."[5]

How else can we explain why husbands in the Children of God would continually give their wives to other men? It is unnatural. Why would thousands of youths throw their lives away following a sex-mad old man? It is not normal. Why would people, infected with herpes and other venereal diseases, knowingly pass these afflictions to other people and call it "the love of God"? Why would men feel no obligation to the children they have fathered, walking off at a second's notice and abandoning wife and child so that they might be free to "serve God"?

These questions can be answered only by understanding sin. I cannot look at my father in any other way. Scripture teaches us that "sin is any want of conformity to the character of God, whether it be an act, disposition, or state."[6]

There is abundant evidence in my father's writings of the self-centered life and its destructive consequences. Mo Letters expound the "All Things" doctrine, perverting the words of the apostle Paul and becoming Moses David's license for immorality.*

---

*In 1 Corinthians 6:12 Paul writes, "All things are lawful unto me, but all things are not expedient: all things are lawful for me, but I will not be brought under the power of any." Moses David exploits the first four words, ignoring the rest and ignoring the context.

For example, Mo berates a husband who worked on his personal staff during the FF revolution in Tenerife, because the young man had countermanded his orders. It seems the husband was reluctant to let his wife commit adultery. Mo wrote,

> *Our wives are not our own!—They belong first to the Lord and then to me as their commander-in-chief.*[7]

Like cattle, Mo claimed a right to all the wives and girls in his movement. He backed this husband into a corner, forcing him to give up his wife to FFing. Mo relates the discussion this way:

> *They're my soldiers, and it is not up to you to give her contrary orders just as she's about to carry out my counsel.*
>
> *If you flatly refuse to let her follow the Lord, and you start giving her orders contradictory to my counsel, then what's going to happen? (Hubby: I'll have to go.) If she wants to stay and continue but you don't, yes!*
>
> *But the choice is yours. What do you want to do? (Hubby: I want her to be bait.) Why? (Hubby: Because I know it's the Lord's will.) For whom? (Hubby: For both of us.) For whom? (Hubby: For Jesus!) Right!*[8]

By coercing, intimidating, and playing on a person's sense of pride—not wanting to be the one left out or the one who failed the Lord—Moses David brought his disciples into line. As for leaders who were dragging their heels and not following Mo's dictates, he said, "You don't deserve to be a leader if you're not leading. . . . Report to us any leader who's not doing it [FFing] and not enthusiastically supporting and encouraging it!"[9]

I could easily fill this book with examples of his depraved mind and how he treats both adults and children like objects on a game board, to be moved around, used, abused, and exploited for the sake of his personal pleasure and the "cause."

He revels in the sexual immorality of his followers throughout the world. Through video cassettes he has begun to circulate pornographic films among the Colonies. Yet he calls it just "seeing the beauty of God's creation." Disciples are required to participate in these videos to prove their "spiritual freedom."

This is not the man I once knew as my father. Moses David is not my father; Moses David is a man consumed by sin. I still love David Berg and pray for his soul.

But I came to a point in my life when I decided I must be honest with myself and others: David Berg is a man given over to evil. The Scripture has been fulfilled in his life: "Wherefore God also gave them up to uncleanness through the lusts of their own hearts. . . . For this cause God gave them up unto vile affections! . . . As they did not like to retain God in their knowledge, God gave them over to a reprobate mind . . ." (Romans 1:24, 26, 28). Three times in Romans 1, the apostle Paul declares, "God gave them up!"

Paul deals with the condition of reprobation in Romans 1. Reprobates are people who see this world through the tainted glass of wickedness. In verse 28 Paul writes,

> *And even as they did not like to retain God in their knowledge, God gave them over to a reprobate mind to do those things which are not convenient [proper].*

The frightening truth affirmed in this verse is that God will not always strive with the wickedness of man, but will "give him over" to a mind intent upon doing evil. Being programmed by divine decree to live a life of evil is a terrifying judgment. I believe that Moses David has been given over to a reprobate, or depraved, mind to do things that are not proper. Paul describes the consequences of reprobation in verse 29–32.

> *They have become filled with every kind of wickedness, evil, greed and depravity. They are full of envy, murder, strife, deceit, and malice. They are gossips, slanderers, God-haters, insolent, arrogant and boastful; they invent ways of doing evil; they disobey their parents; they are senseless, faithless, heartless, ruthless. Although they know God's righteous decree that those who do such things deserve death, they not only continue to do these very things but also approve of those who practice them (NIV).*

The King James Version of the Bible says in conclusion, ". . . but have pleasure in them that do them." I can easily see how my father has fulfilled this catalog of sins. He has become filled with greed and depravity of mind. He is jealous of anyone or anything that threatens his position. His heart is full of murder. In a tirade against the Jews in April 1978 he wrote,

> *May God damn the Jews! My God, I think if I could get over there and had a gun I think I'd shoot 'em myself!*
> *. . . God damn them! O God, if I had a gun I'd shoot them myself.*
> *Lord . . . do something to annihilate them! There's not one of those civilians that's innocent! May God damn every Israeli! They're all guilty. They all deserve slaughter.[10]*

He culminated his denunciation by threatening God:

> *If He's going to allow the anti-Christ oppressors to oppress the poor this way, I'm through! And all hail the oppressor, all hail the Anti-Christ, all hail the God damned Jews, all hail the rich, all hail iniquity, all hail evil, all hail the Devil.[11]*

My father is arrogant, continually inventing new ways to commit evil. He is heartless, having lost all natural affection. He no longer loves those he should. He is motivated by a lust for power and sensual pleasure; to him, love is lust. He states that "God is sex!" He thinks nothing of taking wives from their husbands, or sending fathers away from their children, never to see them again. He has proudly proclaimed, "I don't like that word 'married' anymore either!"[12] People in the movement are now "mated" for convenience' sake. When one tires of another, move on. And as for the children? God will take care of them.

Scripture says that God has no alternative but to give up a person to be totally consumed by his lusts. I am shocked at what my father has become.

There is a definable path to reprobation. Individuals and societies alike follow this route. It begins with natural curiosity, the temptations common to all people: the lust of the eyes, the lust of the flesh, the pride of life. Drawn by lust, we fall into sin. Once drawn into evil, our conscience—the awakening of guilt and the law of God within us—sounds an alarm. As the conscience amplifies the guilt, we feel frustration, spiritual irritation, and a sense of alienation. These are God's warning signs, His method of drawing us to Him. The pain of guilt can be relieved only by the remission of sin. But rather than turning to God, confronting our sin and confessing it, our tendency is to deny its reality and our accountability to God.

My father's involvement in sexual immorality, incest, and adultery (beginning when he was a boy) caused him to reexamine the laws of God as revealed in Scripture and twist and interpret them to satisfy his moral condition. In 1980 he wrote, "No, I don't have to keep the ten commandments! All I have to do is love and do whatever I do in love! Nothing else, no more! That's all there is to it, thank God!"[13]

More recently he wrote,

> *I almost laughed in my father's face when I was twelve years of age and he set me down in his office to tell me about sex!*
>
> *By the time I was twelve I knew about all there was to know about sex.*
>
> *I can remember at the age of four I was very interested in little girls and what they. . . (Sara: That proves how sexy the Holy Spirit really is! Because you were filled with the Holy Spirit from your mother's womb, yet as far back as you can remember you were always interested in girls and sex—and Davidito has your spirit and he's the same way!) Fascinated!*
>
> *So I started at an early age and engaged in sex all my life, but I don't think it's hurt me, thank the Lord! Maybe it was good for me.*
>
> *After age seven, when I finally learned how to do it with my little cousin, I was a confirmed addict!*[14]

As a young man, having been unable to free himself from sensual lusts, he threw himself into religious works. But this gave him neither peace nor freedom. When a person never fully repents of his sin, the first reaction is usually an attempt to counterbalance guilt with religious works; but this provides no lasting satisfaction.

My father eventually reached a state of total frustration. He was bound in sin and he knew it. Pride and rebellion hindered him from seeking true forgiveness in Christ, and consequently he was unable to "let go" of those sins. Unable to find freedom, only one alternative remained for my father: Define Scripture in such a manner as to make room for sin. Hence, the "All Things" doctrine was promulgated.

Bill Gothard wisely observes, "There is a continuous mental effort to justify personal moral behavior on the basis of the existing moral code [in my father's case, biblical morality]. Thus, if that code can be 'reinterpreted' to include as 'moral' what was previously immoral, the mind is eager to accept this and to reject previous codes as 'straight-laced,' 'mid-Victorian,' etc."[15] This is precisely what my father did at some point in his life. I can't specify exactly when, but I believe at some point in his marriage, perhaps during the time he worked for Fred Jordan, he consciously rejected scriptural morality and redefined God's laws to suit his lustful passions.

Reprobation is seen in its final, completed stage when a person begins to argue and teach others his redefined morality. A reprobate will attempt to bring others into his perversion, because sin loves company. The apostle Paul states, "They perish because they refused to love the truth and so be saved. For this reason God sends them a powerful delusion so that they will believe the lie and so that all will be condemned who have not believed the truth but have delighted in wickedness" (2 Thessalonians 2:10–11 NIV). Moses David has steadfastly taught thousands of people a corrupt moral code based on his weakness and inability to conquer moral impurity.

Perhaps the cruelest thing the Prophet has done is to set thousands of people on a sexual rampage without any thought for its results. Specifically, what will happen to the children? Mo casts the future well-being of thousands of children to the wind and says, "Oh, just let the Colonies take care of them. Everyone can be a mommy and daddy!" In July 1976 he announced,

Pregnancies from sex of FF'ing need no longer be considered as obligations to marry as before. Some have not felt free to help each other for fear it might require marriage if pregnancy occurs. That's optional.[16]

In other words, sex is no different than eating and carries as little obligation as having dinner. In one quick word from the Prophet, all personal responsibility surrounding sex was dismissed. Children born through adultery and FFing would be collectively cared for in his marvelous family of love! He arrogantly proclaimed,

> *Our children belong to the Family and all of us, and we are all their parents and they are all our children, so no "unwed" mother need fear for herself nor her children. Several of our children call every adult in the Home "Mommy" or "Daddy," and that's as it should be!*
>
> *Marriage in the Family is to Jesus and they are all "Jesus Babies!"—And we are all married to each other in His love. Read "One Wife," "Law of Love," "All Things Tree" etc.[17]*

But Mo's "heavenly ideals" were as foolish as his morals were perverted. To command that the disciples "treat all as one" does not work when people's lives are ablaze with lust. There is but one thought: Me. Me First! One disciple tells how Moses David's edict of "universal love" worked out in her life:

"In November 1977 I fell in love with a brother named Elkanah. He was already married when I met him. (It was his third wife and she was pregnant with his baby—his fourth child by three different women.) Having two wives is not uncommon in the Family, and at first things seemed to work out quite well in our threesome. In fact, things were going so good that Elkanah and I prayed for a son. Shortly thereafter I left our Colony in Naples for Malta to begin an FF ministry among the Libyans that frequent that island. I was pregnant with Elkanah's baby when I left. Visa restrictions to Malta are strictly limited to three months, and although I would be gone just a short time, Elkanah encouraged me to go, as he strongly believed it was the Lord's will to FF the Arabs.

"I returned to Naples several months later, but the tables had turned. I was no longer wanted in his Colony. At that point Elkanah decided to move from Naples to Sicily, and so the Colony packed up and headed South. About two weeks after we arrived, things went from bad to worse. He literally threw me and my two children out on the streets. At the time I was four-and-a-half months pregnant and of no apparent value to him. I was in a terrible predicament, as I couldn't speak enough Italian to get by. My five-year-old son translated for me.

"We returned to Naples and squatted a deserted villa. Each day I went litnessing with my two children (aged five and one-and-a-half) in order to survive. It was the rainy season in Naples, and for two months we were forced to go out in the freezing rain and distribute Mo Letters. I'd have to say it was one of the most depressing periods of my life. For four months we lived like that. Due to the stress and difficult living conditions, I started premature labor. I sent word to Elkanah informing him of my condition and the potential threat to the baby's life—the danger of death was imminent. I asked him to pray for the baby, but the only reply I received was, 'Work out your own salvation.'

"At that point I contacted all the Colonies in Southern Italy, and none of them would help. No one wanted the extra responsibility of a pregnant mother with children. No Colonies would take me in. It was a time in my life when I felt it was not worth it to go on living. Little did I know worse things were to happen yet."

In the experience of just this one disciple we see the reality of my father's All Things doctrine. Sin has caused this man, Elkanah, to become a self-centered, insensitive, product of Moses David's teachings, and, like my father, devoid of natural affection.

The abominations of Moses David are thus being passed on to his followers. We cannot look at what he is doing as anything but sin. There are many people who have in their minds a knowledge of God, but as the Scripture says, "they do not retain Him there" (Romans 1:28). The knowledge of God is cast aside because it inhibits the full expression of lust. What does God do in such a case? He patiently endures for a season.

When I was seven, Dad's lusts burned within him and drove him to desire incest. When I was twelve, he attempted it once again. When my sister reached the age of ten, he burned with lust toward her. Now he teaches his followers that incest is not forbidden by God. God's patience can endure only so long. There comes a point of rejection. Consequently, because of Dad's stubborn willfulness, God gave him over to unrestrained desires to commit the grossest of sins as a reprobate. My father is chained in sin, his conscience is seared, he is beyond the point of feeling. I have witnessed, in the life of my father, one of the most frightening punishments of God—to be cut loose from restraining forces and set adrift in the boundless sea of sin.

Matthew Henry writes, "It is a great aggravation of sin when it is committed against knowledge. It is daring presumption to run upon the sword's point. They 'not only do the same, but have pleasure in those that do them.' To be pleased with other people's sins is to love sin for sin's sake: it is joining in a confederacy for the devil's kingdom. Our own sins are much aggravated by our concurrence with the sins of others."[18]

How painfully the words struck me: "to love sin for sin's sake." I see the thousands upon thousands of people following Moses David in his insanity, "running upon the sword's point," as if in gleeful madness impaling themselves upon the deadly sword of sin—and my father praising it, glorifying it, reveling in it. He has joined "a confederacy with the devil's kingdom." Abrahim. Goddesses. Flirty Fishing. Jesus Babies.

To varying degrees, COG disciples are taking on the nature of Moses David. Sin never sits still. With our finite minds we cannot begin to estimate the essential wickedness of Satan or the unbelievable horror of sin. The apostle Paul writes, ". . . that sin by the commandment might become exceeding sinful" (Romans 7:13). So too, it is beyond my finite mind to fathom the wickedness flourishing under my own father.

Moses David is indeed a psychopath. But he is far, far more: he is reprobate. In consequence to the unrestrained lusts of his unregenerate heart, God has given him over to a mind of reprobation to do those things which are purely wicked. He has created for himself a world of unmitigated evil.

Chapter 15
A Wonderful Servant,
A Terrible Master!

There are many people in contemporary society, hungry for "freedom," who argue that those who adhere to Christian morality are "misguided old prudes" inhibited by enormous complexes. "Sex is great," the critics say. "A person should have the freedom to express himself fully in this area. The old puritanical taboos and phobias that have been placed on sex are wrong, limiting, and narrow-minded. Total freedom of sexual expression is 'natural' and, of course, anything natural could never cause problems or be wrong."

Some who say these things could not condone my father's actions, yet his life illustrates absolute sexual freedom. What my father and others in society consider natural is actually perverted and quite unnatural. There is written within the nature of sex itself a law; and that law determines what is moral and immoral, natural and unnatural. Moses David is working against that law and living in conflict with it. Consequently, sex has turned against him and is destroying him.

Even many who would shrink from my father's lawlessness

do not fully understand the nature of sex. What is it? What are the laws that govern it and keep it honorable?

The nature of sex has as its ultimate fulfillment new life. Creation. The sex drive is the urge to create. E. Stanley Jones writes, "The primary end of sex is the procreation of children and their nurture in an atmosphere of love."[1]

Sex is, indeed, a marvelous God-given urge. It is a wonderful privilege to be a part of the creation process. We learn from history, however, that procreation is not the only purpose for sex. A baby is not the only commendable expression of the sex drive. Jones says further concerning sex,

> *The sex urge can be sublimated . . . physical creation is not its only creative area. It can function as creation on other levels of life. It can become creative in the realm of the mind—creating new thoughts, new systems of thought, new mental attitudes both in ourselves and others. It can be creative in the realm of the social—it can give birth to new movements for social justice, for social betterment. It can be creative in the realm of the moral and spiritual—it can create newborn lives, new hopes, new moral and spiritual movements. . . .*
>
> *Some of the greatest work in the world is done by those who, when denied, voluntarily or otherwise, the normal outlets for sex, turn the tides of this strange power into creative activity in other ways. Their sex life is not suppressed, but expressed in other channels. Abstinence then can be health, provided the abstinence of sex on one level is practiced in order to loose it on another level. If sex is just dammed up with no outlet on any level, then it may prove a source of conflict and frustration. The way is always open in some direction for sex expression; so conflict is not necessary.*[2]

In light of this statement, let us consider what Moses David has done to tens of thousands of people around the world. In stark contrast we will see that immorality subverts the God-given creative urge, and that the perverted sex doctrines of Moses David are having far-reaching effects on the lives of COG members, the consequences of which we may never fully comprehend. Bear in mind that today's sexually liberated society often mirrors, in thought if not in practice, the sex doctrines of the COG.

At about the age when youth are most likely to join a cult (seventeen to twenty-five), the sex urge is in fact at its height. The desire to create, to build, to reform, to improve society is very strong. At the same time, most of these youths find themselves in college or the beginning stages of a career. When the sexual drive is high, what direction should it take?

It seems likely that God has designed this creative urge to heighten precisely at the time a person is preparing the foundation of his life's vocation. To direct these youthful desires and passions into the energy of becoming a doctor, a salesman, a craftsman, or a teacher would seem not only logical, but extremely powerful. Yet look what my father has created: an organization that vehemently directs its youthful members to release their creative energies in immoral and perverted practices.

The concept of sex sublimation is not at all new, nor is it restricted to Christian morality and teaching. Napoleon Hill, a famous contemporary writer, speaks of the mysterious power and importance of sex sublimation in his best-selling book, *Think and Grow Rich.* Hill is not writing from a Christian perspective, but from the platform of "success principles." Concerning the development of genius he writes,

> *Man attains the status of genius only when, and if, he stimulates his mind so that it draws upon the forces available, through the creative faculty of the imagination. Chief among the stimuli with which this "stepping up" may be produced is sex energy. The mere possession of this energy is not sufficient to produce a genius. The energy must be transmuted from desire for physical contact into some other form of desire and action, before it will lift one to the status of a genius.*
>
> *Far from becoming geniuses because of great sex desires, the majority of men lower themselves, through misunderstanding and misuse of this great force, to the status of the lower animals.[3]*

Certainly Moses David, apart from wasting his positive creative powers, has succeeded in arriving at "the status of the lower animals." Hill explains that the reason the majority of men who succeed in life do so after the age of forty is that prior to this age they have a "tendency to dissipate their energies through over-indulgence in physical expression of the emotion of sex. The majority of men never learn that the urge of sex has other possibilities, which far transcend in importance that of mere physical expression." He further states,

> *The finer and more powerful emotions are sown wildly to the four winds. Out of this habit of the male grew the term, "sowing his wild oats."*[4]

Hill believes that the master salesman attains the heights of greatness because "he either consciously or unconsciously transmutes the energy of sex into sales enthusiasm."[5]

Reading Hill's book, I was amazed by his insight into certain spiritual laws. He recognized quite clearly that sex has written into it a moral code, even though he doesn't call it by name. He recognizes that within the nature of sex there exists a certain cause-and-effect principle and specific negative effects result when sex is pushed beyond its natural boundaries.

> *Every intelligent person knows that stimulation in excess, through alcoholic drink and narcotics, is a destructive form of intemperance. Not every person knows, however, that overindulgence in sex expression may become a habit as destructive and as detrimental to creative effort as narcotics or liquor.*
>
> *A sex-mad man is not essentially different from a dope-mad man! Both have lost control over their faculties of reason and will-power.*[6]

Hill once again pinpoints the character of Moses David in his observations. My sex-mad father not only has lost control of his faculties of reason and willpower, but has succeeded in destroying his positive creative powers. He lives in a world of negative forces and passions and self-destruction, and he desires to drag along as many as will follow him.

Note that Hill draws a parallel between sex and drugs. What

accompanied the free-love era of the late sixties and early seventies in the counterculture? An abundant use of narcotics and alcohol, which destroy a person's natural drives and motivation. Drugs and immorality—common bedfellows—destroy the positive, natural, creative forces God has placed within us. They form a losing combination.

E. Stanley Jones writes,

> *The battle of life as a whole will probably not rise above the sex battle. Lose the sex battle and defeat spreads into every portion of your being; win the sex battle and all life is uplifted by that victory.*[7]

It is plain to see that my dad has miserably lost the sex battle. According to his own writings, he started to lose it before the age of twelve.

Where do we wage the battle? Where do our problems with sex begin? E. Stanley Jones suggests that problems begin when the natural pleasure surrounding procreation becomes detached from its ultimate purpose and becomes an end in itself. Pleasure for pleasure's sake is self-serving. Once a man starts down the road to selfish sensual fulfillment, there can be no positive end. What began as pleasure will become precisely the opposite. Jones writes,

> *The pleasure must be the by-product of the will to create, or it will cease to be. The sex urge is first of all a creative urge, and not a pleasure principle.*[8]

My father has made pleasure the purpose. So have those in our society who advocate unlimited sexual freedom.

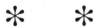

Has there ever been a society more liberated than ours? Perhaps Sodom and Gomorrah or ancient Corinth. But today's freedom of expression rivals theirs. Sex is practiced even in the elementary grades by a significant percentage of children. One young girl told me, "If you haven't done it by the time you are thirteen, then there is something wrong with you, you're weird."

Yet people are becoming more and more empty of joy. They continually seek new thrills and new relationships. But as the search intensifies, the pleasure decreases. People quickly become burned out, frustrated, or begin seeking "strange flesh." Many direct their energies along the path of perversion. Why? Because, as Jones puts it, "there is an immoral way to use sex, and there is a moral way. And that way of moral use is written into the constitution of sex!" He adds, "The very nature or reality of sex is Christian, and this nature is working against society's un-Christian sex attitudes."[9]

I had never looked at sex from this perspective. I had always understood that immorality was a matter of breaking one of God's laws. But the truth goes deeper than that. Immorality violates the nature of sex itself. Indeed, the moral code written into the nature of sex is the same moral code we find in Scripture.

This concept of the nature of sex is not widely understood and accepted in society and it is even misunderstood in traditional Christianity. The prevailing view is that sex existed in an amoral way since the beginning of life. Then, at a certain point in history, we received the Ten Commandments and the laws of Moses, and later we received the four Gospels and the Epistles. The impression is that sex came first and then a moral code; the Scriptures and Christian morality were placed over sex like a straitjacket, confining its natural purposes and limiting its potential to the narrow-minded views of Purtian morality. In other words, sex had absolute freedom until scriptural morality came along and stifled it.

But this view is wrong, as E. Stanley Jones explains. The same Being who wrote the Scriptures created sex. Logic tells us that it is improbable that God first created sex and then later on realized that He needed some rules to govern its use. Sex and its moral code were created simultaneously. The moral codes we see in Scripture are not an outer covering for sex but rather mirror what has always been there. To contradict scriptural morality is to transgress the very reality and nature of sex. So sex dually issues a

warning: "Stop using me in ways I was not designed to be used."
Jones writes,

> *Men thought that, if they could only get rid of puritanical taboos*
> *and of moral codes written in the Scriptures, they could be free to*
> *do as they liked with sex. But they now find that the moral law is*
> *written in sex itself. Keep that moral law, and there is heaven;*
> *break it, and there is hell—here and now.*[10]

Both my husband and I have lived in that hell; by the mercy of
God we were delivered from it. My father still lives in it; in January
1980 he wrote,

> . . . *The Devil terrifies me sometimes at night! And I'm getting*
> *worse, not better. Sometimes I'm so terrified I could sit up and*
> *scream.*
> . . . *Sometimes I almost go crazy in the night, I get so*
> *terrified and so paranoid! It doesn't really seem to matter how*
> *much I pray and cry to the Lord and agonize and fight and*
> *battle, or even try to drink to drown my fears . . . .*
> *My God what horrors and nightmares I have!*[11]

It is indeed a nightmare. My father, at one time in his life, possessed the ability of true genius, but he lost the battle of self-
discipline. It seems that society desires the same freedom that my
dad has sacrificed all to achieve. Yet in sacrificing all, he committed spiritual suicide. My father sought freedom through lawlessness; sin deceived him and led him to believe that happiness
would be found in doing whatever he pleased. Instead of finding
freedom, he found only bondage.

There is a formula that states that true freedom comes
through power, and power through discipline. Society, like my
dad, is drastically losing sight of this formula. Power comes by
discipline alone. It is the type of power that grants an individual the
freedom to do what is right. Christian discipline brings an individual into a sphere of existence that greatly enlarges the positive
potential of life. Moses David has led his disciples in precisely the
opposite direction. Instead of learning power and discipline over

sin, they have been systematically taught to respond instantly to whatever lustful desire arises. Consider this illustration:

> . . . *When a dam is thrown across a river—the even flow of the river is interrupted and restrained, but only in order that a power house might be installed to create power and light. The disciplined you is not free to do as others do, but free to do what others cannot do—to be a contributive soul, full of light and power. Some will say, "I am free to do as I like" but you will say, "I am free to do as I ought." You are dammed up on one level, but only in order to raise the level of life, so that you can function on a higher level.*[12]

When Moses David first began his full-scale push into "Flirty Fishing" on Tenerife, many girls were required to participate on a regular basis from two-to-five nights a week. They were to engage in immoral sex in order to be "a living sample of the love of Jesus." Mo teaches, "Just as Jesus laid down His life, so you must lay down your life (or wife) for these men."[13] For most of the girls it was not an enjoyable experience, unless the girl had reached a point of total insensitivity. But in time even the most liberated "burned out."

A Peruvian girl told me of her experiences in Caracas as an "FFer": "It was so bad just going out every night and going to bed that I had to drink at least a half a bottle of bourbon in order to go out there; most of the time they carried me out of the clubs." This girl eventually burned out and left the Family. One year later she rejoined and is now "serving Jesus full-time" and Flirty Fishing.

Why did she go back? To answer that question is to understand the consequences of immorality and the evil power of Moses David's doctrines.

Cults seek to destroy the individual, as we have already seen. Moses David has used a two-pronged approach to accomplish this goal within the Children of God.

The first means he has used is the Mo Letters. By declaring these the Word of God he has stifled the creative mental powers of his followers. They no longer have to think for themselves, read the Bible and apply it dynamically to their personal lives, or do any form of creative prayer. Their only function is to read the Mo Letters, let Mo do all the communicating with God, and follow what Mo writes. It is simply a question of obedience. Their minds are to be like computers, and he's the programmer. Any new data and information will enter their minds only through his work. They are little more than uncreative robots.

What, then, is happening to all their creative energies and urges? Certainly they have them? Indeed, they do. Many of the COG disciples joined at a time when they were quite eager to change the world, to enact social and spiritual reform. In the beginning of the movement these energies were sublimated into the practice of witnessing. That was the chief activity of most disciples until 1974. In the early spring of '74 the disciples began practicing litnessing—selling literature on the streets. One disciple told me that for two and a half years after he joined the COG in January 1972, he never touched a girl; moreover, he never desired to do so. He and many like him were directing their creative energies into Bible study, witnessing, and litnessing. This was the case for many members until Mo began to stage his sexual revolution. Then things began to change.

What became of the disciples' creative energies then? This is the second prong of Moses David's attack. Mo gradually introduced more and more sex material into his letters. Since Mo Letters did all the thinking for the disciples, they naturally began to think more on sex. Their thoughts increasingly turned from activities of the mind and spirit toward sensuality.

It was a Mo Letter that lit the spark, and each new Mo Letter fanned the fire. The youths were set up! Instead of spending eight or ten or twelve hours a day witnessing to lost hippies, they began Flirty Fishing. All with the same self-sacrificing spirit, and all in the name of Christ.

The process by which Mo's revolution became full-blown is instructive, for it is the same kind of evolutionary process that we can see in contemporary American society. Television is doing to today's youth what the Mo Letters did to the disciples of the COG. A steady diet of sexual themes saturates the mind until one doesn't realize how far he's come.

As the first step my father introduced the concept of "sharing," that is, helping out brothers or sisters in need. If they needed sex, go ahead and share with them. This was only right, seeing as how it would be an "unselfish" act. Anything unselfish would be a loving act and therefore pleasing to God.

Next came sharing with those outside the Family in special circumstances. This was done in order to make them disciples—to bring them into the Family. Maria pioneered this with Arthur. That led to the development of Flirty Fishing as doctrine—a special "truth" revealed to Moses David as a means of "winning souls to Christ."

As time went on, the question of lesbianism arose. "There is nothing in Scripture that forbids it," Mo explained. "If it is done in love it's okay, although it is not God's highest order."[14] Then came the concept of child sex: let children do whatever they want. Masturbation was greatly encouraged and considered a healthful practice.

Then child-adult sexual activities were introduced: child molesting. This was pioneered by Maria's illegitimate son, Davidito. Letters were published picturing him engaging in sex acts with his adult childcare worker, Prisca (Sara).[15] Eventually homosexuality was brought into question. Mo said go ahead, but only do it in love; it wasn't God's highest order.[16] (There was such an outbreak of homosexuality that he later had to counter that order with a reprimand.)

Then came group sex. Mo encourages communion services to be followed by group sex.[17] It is fine to involve the children. Many members of the cult will write home to their parents telling of their work in winning souls and other traditional practices such as, "We had a communion service"—which really means they had an orgy.

Next came incest. Mo revealed publicly his long incestuous relationship with Faithy. The directive followed that families should practice incest with their children, just like Mo.[18]

Is there a limit? One can see from this progression, occurring in less than a decade in a closed society, that immorality just doesn't stand still. Nor does it satisfy or bring lasting pleasure. It grows and steadily becomes more perverse and wicked. Sex most certainly contains within it a moral code and a self-destruct principle. What form of sensual pleasure lies beyond what the COG are now doing? What form of perversion lies beyond incest, sodomy, and child abuse? I do not care to put that answer in print.

One mother, an ex-disciple of the COG, explained to me that she believes it will be the children born into the movement who will become the real Frankenstein's monsters. Those children raised in the COG will have nothing to fall back on, having never known any other morality. She says, "They'll grow up believing you can do anything in the name of Jesus!"

Just as Mo is denying his followers the power to create, to sublimate their creative urges into useful, positive activities, so too our society, with its drive for sexual freedom, is diverting and subverting the positive creative urges of our youth through the print and broadcast media. We are raising a generation of people intent upon seeking only a pleasure principle. This desire is self-destructive. The God-given creative urges are being drained from our youth through the bowels of sensuality. Society is following too closely in the footsteps of the COG.

Indeed, sex is a wonderful servant, but a terrible master!

Chapter 16
"God, How Could You Do This to Me?"

Bill and I had been out of the movement about three years, desperately trying to restructure our lives and forget the past. But the past refused to remain silent, because the "past" was very much a part of our present lives and the lives of my children—especially Joyanne, my firstborn, who had been influenced the most.

As we endeavored to change our lifestyle and shed the habits of the COG, Joyanne did not at all wish to do so. She saw no need to change: life in the COG was all she had ever known. I was insensitive to this fact and did not understand her reasoning; since I was rejecting the standards of the COG I felt that she should automatically follow my leading and change with us. Joyanne's rejection of my authority as her mother and her disrespect infuriated me. Her defiance became the cause of intense frustration. Inwardly I became very angry. I wanted to lash out at her violently.

I remember one incident specifically. I was putting away clothes in her bedroom and discovered in the bottom of her dresser a collection of over one hundred empty cigarette boxes. She had been secretly collecting them to make a pyramid in her room. I had strictly forbidden her to smoke cigarettes, yet she was smoking in deliberate defiance of me, while to my face denying all association with smoking. It was ever so clear that she had been lying to me for a long time. Although I did not smoke, I was unaware that other aspects of my personal life were giving her license to smoke and do as she pleased, what parents allow in moderation, children excuse in excess.

On my birthday I decided to make a stand. I was going to "let her have it" and get things straightened out once and for all. "How dare you do such a thing in my house! I'll have none of it! and what's more you'd better never do it again, or you'll be sorry! And as far as the way you dress, it is nothing less than disgusting! How could you be so disrespectful to me! What do others think?. . . "

I pulled out all the stops. Oh, it was horrible! It was the worst thing I could have ever done. But why did I do that? Why did I react that way? In the following six months the answer came—painfully slow, yet painfully clear.

Through her rebellious behavior, Joyanne was illuminating my failure as a mother. She was like a neon light walking around my home, flashing in bright colors, "Look at what a failure you are. See the result of your mistakes! See the consequence of your sin.. You have failed as a mother!" My guilt over the past was already at flood level, but this was more than I could bear. My one desire in life had been to be the "perfect mother," and instead I had succeeded in being the worst.

In the COG I created my own schools for my children wherever we went. I always tried to give them the best education available. I even followed "God's Prophet" in order to give them the best spiritual training. But it had all been in vain. Consequently, I wanted to wipe away the past and immediately start over again and begin doing things right. Then the frightening reality began to sink in: all those years of exposure to the sin and error of the cult was not going to be wiped away like chalk from a blackboard. The effects of sin had become visible marks on the character of my children. *How could I live with the horror of that?* So I panicked.

Life had been one nightmare after another, but this was too much.

What could I do? Watching Joyanne everyday was like having alcohol poured into an open wound; the pain of guilt was so intense that I experienced an agony of soul I never dreamed possible. How could I be such a failure? Then pride came to my rescue. Pride has an inherent ability to cover over sin and guilt. Pride gives way to bitterness, which is the opposite of mercy. *A response of bitterness is an instinctive means of revenge toward the one we feel has wronged us.* And that is precisely what my attitude toward Joyanne reflected. I began to react to her, to lash out, criticize, scorn, and reject. She had become an object of my guilt. The more I reacted, the deeper grew her own resentment—instinctively she knew I was rejecting her. The more I rejected her, the more she rebelled. It was a vicious circle to which I was totally oblivious. Thus an incredible tension formed within me.

I deeply loved Joyanne. Yet my sense of guilt was driving me from her, and her from me. On the one hand I desperately wanted to help her and love her; on the other, my guilt and pride led me to reject her. Beneath it all, my guilt was causing me to reject myself. What a mess! The greatest need of teenagers is acceptance and unconditional love, and that is precisely what I was *not* giving. When her frustration became too great, she began to reject me as well.

One morning I found a note on her door. It was the saddest day of my life. At age seventeen, she had moved out.

My desire to be the perfect mother had ended in a nightmare. Instead of seeing perfection, my oldest child had rejected me. No doubt my other children would do likewise. And rightly so. I was the problem, not my daughter. I had a responsibility to love her no matter what she did, what she said, or what type of clothes she wore or didn't wear. I was incapable of showing love and compassion because I was not showing mercy. And I was incapable of showing mercy because I had not yet experienced the mercy of God.

An enigma surrounds human love. We possess an inability to act out fully what we know is right. Even as parents we are often unable to love our children as we know we should. Sin inhibits the full expression of our love. My sin and guilt had created an impenetrable wall between Joyanne and me. What would tear down that wall?

God had to take me beyond my sense of guilt and bring me face to face with my sin. For me to be a whole person capable of loving my own daughter, God had to remove my guilt; otherwise pride would keep me a prisoner indefinitely. As best as I can explain it, I came to a deeper understanding of what Christ had done for me in dying for my sins. The reality of salvation in Jesus Christ took hold in my life in a way I had never known. There was no possible way for me to hold onto my guilt. Christ in His mercy had borne my sin on Calvary, including my incredible failure as a mother. It was mercy in incredible magnitude.

It was realizing God's mercy in my life that freed me to love. That was what destroyed the wall between Joyanne and me. I had been judging my daughter because of my sin. Therefore I couldn't forgive her or love her or show mercy to her. I myself had been resisting the mercy of God. But when I accepted His mercy, the guilt, fear, depression, anxiety, and bitterness went away. Mercy is the gateway to peace and love and harmony. This truth brought a peace and rest in my soul that has never left; it has carried me through many trials.

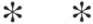

Things began to change in me from that time. I had experienced a kind of emotional death, but also a new birth. Yet much suffering still awaited me. My wrong attitudes and rejection of Joyanne had taken their toll. She had been deeply wounded, and she completely shut me out of her life as a result. Although this was very painful and sad for me, it was a new kind of suffering; it had a purpose that made it bearable. The Bible records that Jesus learned obedience through the things that He suffered (Hebrews 5:8–9). I too began to learn through suffering. I was at peace with my daughter in my heart. There was no hindrance to the love I now felt. I was no longer hurt by the wrong things she did or the offensive things she said. The hurt caused by pride and my embarrassment over my failings was altogether gone. God had indeed set me free to love her.

It was a joyous experience. I believe I began to regard her as God does—with love and compassion. God is deeply wounded by our sin, but that in no wise affects His love toward us. For the very first time in my life I began to love my daughter as God loves her.

An important step for me at this time, was to ask Joyanne's forgiveness. I asked her to forgive me for the ways I had failed her as a mother and for the times I had offended her by wrong and bitter attitudes. I also asked her forgiveness for the divorce from Jethro, her father, and confessed it as sin. I explained that though I could do nothing to change the past, I was aware of how much pain it had brought her. It is hard to ask your child for forgiveness, but it reaps great dividends. I had quite a long list of things to be forgiven; I don't suppose most parents would have such a long list as mine.

Nevertheless, as parents we need to be aware that just because we undergo a big change, it doesn't necessarily mean that a son or daughter will follow suit. I thought everyone else would change because I did. Not so. It may be a long time before my daughter feels the way I do. But that is not the most important thing. The relationship may be a one-way street for a while—perhaps years—but even that has hidden blessings. God will build character in a parent during those years; it takes a teenager a long time to overcome those hurts. I don't know when Joyanne will ever fully forgive me; but I must not get discouraged over time. The manifestation of the answer to prayer and the restoration of fellowship must be placed in the hands of a sovereign God.

On March 23, 1982, I confronted a new crisis. Joyanne left the United States to live with the Children of God in San Juan, Puerto Rico.

Having viewed the reactions of parents from inside the cult for ten years, I was now to experience the agony of a parent whose child is lured into cultic oblivion. For many days I was in a state of shock. I couldn't believe what was happening to me. It had been more than four years since I had left the movement, and I thought I would be able to cover up my entire past, bury all my previous experiences in the sands of history, and go about my own private, personal life. Not so.

Of all my nine children, Joyanne has been the most cruelly injured by the Children of God experience. She was only four years old when I decided to follow my dad in Huntington Beach; she was fourteen when we left the COG behind in Caracas. The COG was the only life she had ever known.

When we suddenly left and were labeled enemies and misfits by those still in the cult, Joyanne just couldn't understand. Life quickly became a matter of survival, as opposed to the glorious, excitement-filled days when we were the "big leaders" in God's Endtime Movement! In a blitzkrieg of experiences we went from a thirteen-bedroom house in Lima, Peru, to a dirty campground in Southern California where we lived in tents for six months. Joyanne lost everything she held dear: her friends, her school, her singing career, and her position as "Princess," the grand-daughter of the King. Her view of reality was shattered.

During the next four years, Joyanne never quite came to grips with the past. Then on March 7, 1982, she turned eighteen—a day she had been waiting for. She determined to strike out on her own and see for herself what the COG was really like. She felt she had been forced to leave the movement; it had not been her choice. Two weeks after her birthday she took a flight to Miami en route to Puerto Rico. A man from Peru—a friend of hers and a casual member of the COG—bought Joyanne's plane ticket. I suddenly found myself going through the same trauma that thousands of other parents have experienced.

I was angry. *Haven't I suffered enough?* I fumed. *Me of all people! Wasn't I doing my best to come out of the COG? Haven't we wasted enough of our lives in that movement without Joyanne throwing her life away as well? How dare she! How can God allow this? How can He do this to me?*

With my anger I felt resentment and hurt. I was hurt because it seemed God wasn't being fair. I said to myself, *It was too good to be true. I knew we would never get out of that cult. We will suffer for the rest of our lives. First it will be Joyanne, then John, then the next one, and so on.*

Looking back on this now, I'm almost amused at my train of

thought. It's ironic. God always gets the blame. Everything is His fault. Bitterness and blaming God usually go underground after a while and bury themselves somewhere in the subconscious. Then come guilt, feelings of failure and discouragement, and depression. What a parent does at this point varies. There exists an infinite spectrum of reactions. In many cases, the experience short-circuits the person, and life becomes one big question mark. *What is happening? Why did she leave? Doesn't she know it's wrong? Where's God?*

My ex-husband and I talked about the situation, and we decided we should go to Puerto Rico to talk to Joyanne. I felt it was worth a try; perhaps there was something to be achieved by it. Yet I knew there was nothing I could do one way or the other to prevent her from doing what she wanted.

I felt extremely guilty that I hadn't shared with her the truth about the Family. We had been out four years, and I had never explained to her the evil things that were happening. As a Princess, she was sheltered even within the cult and did not live as ordinary disciples did.

In the back of my mind I believed the COG would not be able to get her to kowtow to their totalitarian way of life. But I also recognized that the cult is full of once strong-willed youth who fell prey to the lure of sin. Despite Joyanne's independent spirit, I feared the power of the COG's subtle indoctrination. If she were around it long enough, the possibility existed that she might surrender her will to it. I sensed we didn't have much time, whatever we were going to do.

So we flew to Puerto Rico.

Before we left, Jethro contacted a private detective in San Juan through the Yellow Pages and gave him all the information we had gathered about COG activities in Puerto Rico. He proved to be perfect for the task of finding Joyanne. By the time we arrived there, the detective agency was able to ascertain the addresses of several COG Colonies. Within three hours we were peering through binoculars at their main leadership Colony. (In spite of myself I felt as if we were playing out scenes from a James

Bond thriller—it was most exciting.) As we studied the Colony under cover of darkness, I could see through the windows many faces I had known and loved for many years. But no Joyanne.

The next day we followed a lead to find another Colony located far out in the countryside, seventy miles from San Juan. After a great deal of inquiry we found out from the only gas station in that small town the name of a person who was a personal friend of "those nice people who are always singing and playing guitars and have lots of children." He offered to lead us to the Colony. We suspected it might be a wild goose chase, but he was true to his word. Just before we reached the Colony we told him to go on without us; we dared not be seen by any Family members, or our mission would fail. We spied on this Colony all day long, but still we saw no sign of Joyanne.

Predictably, our guide betrayed us. When he reached the Colony ahead of us he mentioned the "two Americans." He described us to the members of the Family, and immediately the phones started ringing from one end of the island to the other. Word got back to the top leadership that someone fitting Deborah and Jethro's description was snooping around the COG.

Joyanne was instructed to phone home and ask for her mom and dad. When she did, of course we were not available. She called my husband, Bill, and asked him directly, "Are mom and dad here looking for me?" The irony grew, for even while she was talking to Bill I was calling home on our two-party line—so Bill had Joyanne on one line and me on the other. In other circumstances, it would have been quite humorous. Confirming that we were indeed looking for her, Joyanne agreed to meet us the next day at a donut shop in a large shopping center. That night I prayed for guidance as to what to say, how to react, and what to do. During our flight to San Juan I was filled with trauma and suspense. I didn't know whether we would find her or whether she would even speak to us if we did—perhaps we were simply wasting thousands of dollars on a lark. I also had no idea what COG members might do, for we were regarded as enemies of the Prophet. Jethro cautioned me never to go anywhere alone.

Our rendezvous with Joyanne was set for early Sunday morning. Our detective had three cars posted with walkie-talkies in the

parking lot and on the street. Just a few minutes before rendezvous time, three carloads of security police pulled into the
parking lot to buy their traditional Sunday morning coffee and
donuts. Since Sunday mornings are usually a very quiet time in
Puerto Rico, the sight of the security police in the nearly deserted
shopping mall was outrageous. Just then we heard over the walk-
ie-talkie that three vehicles bearing COG members were approaching and Joyanne was riding in a van. The vehicles drove
slowly past the donut shop and kept on going. My heart sank as I
feared the sight of all the police might have frightened them off.
But they circled back and pulled into the parking lot.

I was sitting in the shop with the key detective when Joyanne
walked in. She looked around at all the police and said, "Good
grief, Dad, did you have to bring an army with you?" We laughed
and exchanged rather stiff greetings and agreed to move to a
comfortable hotel lobby to talk.

Neither Joyanne nor the COG trusted us, and the disciples
refused to leave her alone with us, fearing we would try to kidnap
her. That night she returned to her Colony and promised to meet
with us again the next day. We met early in the morning again,
and by the end of the day enough mutual trust had been established that she agreed to spend the night with me.

I had no intention of bringing her back against her will. On
the contrary, I simply wanted to talk to her and tell her that she
was getting into a lot more than she realized. I wanted to let her
know that we loved her and that she was always welcome home
regardless of her decisions and actions.

I was armed with all the recent Mo Letters in order to present
as convincing an argument as possible. I marked the passages that
talked about evil things I knew she would find disgusting. I concentrated on the sexual abuse of children. My strategy was to sow
as many doubts about the COG as I could. I would pinpoint every
flaw I could think of. Then, I felt, after we were gone she would
see the evidence of these things back in the Colonies.

We had to treat her as an individual free to make her own
choices. I knew it would be a very critical time in her life—one of
choosing—and as parents we had to play our part and respect her
sense of individuality. We had to respect her rights and opinions.

I was careful to show how the COG deprives people of their individuality, seeks to control their lives, confines them to a set of restrictive rules, and programs them to be mindless robots. She had left home to find her individuality, so I did my best to show her that the Children of God is the antithesis of it.

The thought that Joyanne might choose to stay with the cult never left my mind; I was frightened beyond measure. If she chose to stay, it could be five or even ten years until time and circumstances forced her to leave. There would follow the painful years of recovery and depression such as I had felt, and frustration over having been so foolish as to waste her life in a cult.

As we sat together in a hotel room in San Juan, I studied her face and saw clearly her pain and confusion—her desire to know herself and find meaning in life and reconciliation with the past. Suddenly I felt abandoned and helpless. There was nothing more I could do for her. She was totally beyond my reach as a parent. There was every chance she would plunge headlong into the nightmare of perversion, deceit, futility, and suffering, and I was helpless to stop her. The frightening thought haunted me: *It's all my fault.*

I had read many stories about Christians who suffered under the Communists, and I was reminded of one in particular about a boy who was tortured to death in front of his father. Years after the incident, it was said, the look of horror was still on that poor father's face. The father had been powerless to help his son. I now felt that same sense of lostness and lack of power.

God, I thought, *are You really going to allow this? After all that I have gone through, are You going to let Joyanne throw her life away in this godforsaken movement? Even if my life has been ruined, why hers? Couldn't you save her? Won't you save her?*

At that point my relationship with God took a critical turn. There were several truths I had to face if I were to continue to live as a Christian. First, the time had come to stop blaming God and to start trusting in Him. Second, I had to acknowledge that Joyanne's situation was a consequence of my own sin. Third, my selfish concern over Joyanne and my disinterest toward the thousands of youths still in the COG was very displeasing in God's sight.

I realized that God is not a Being whose arm can be twisted by prayer—even cries of desperation. He was infinitely more aware of the evil that awaited Joyanne in the cult than I was. God's concern for Joyanne was righteous, but what about mine? Was my concern based on right motives? Was I motivated by guilt, embarrassment, or pride? Before I could even begin to petition God in her behalf, there were several accounts that had to be settled between Him and me.

During my four years outside the cult, very few people in my community knew who I was. I simply wanted to forget the Children of God and everything they represented. But Joyanne wouldn't allow that. I became concerned only when she ran away to live with the COG—a selfish motive indeed. I was unwilling to face the fact that I had helped to bring the movement into being. I wanted God's help now with Joyanne, but was I willing to help all the others trapped in the cult? Was I praying for the state of their souls? The answer was a cold No.

The thought came to me that perhaps I could strike a bargain with God. But I realized how foolish that was. What did I have to bargain with? By her actions Joyanne was saying, "Mom, it's over. I'm no longer your child. Your responsibility as my mother, to bring me up right, to tell me what to do, and all the other things a mom does for her child is finished. Those years were spent following God's Prophet, Mom. It's over." Joyanne had severed the cord six months earlier when she ran away from home.

In my heart I wanted desperately to turn back the clock, to erase the failures, the wasted years. I was the mother of a child who was no longer a child. She was a person groping, searching for the key that would set her free from the misery life had become. Yet I believe Joyanne didn't really want to join the Children of God anymore than I did. She was there because she wanted answers. She wanted peace. And amid all the confusion that started for us four years earlier, she thought that perhaps there she would find the missing key.

I wept that night in Puerto Rico. For Joyanne, for Jethro, for my other children who couldn't understand why Joyanne had run away. For the thousands of youth both in and out of the COG who were as lost and confused as my own daughter. I no longer feared for Joyanne's welfare or whether she would leave or join. That night I sensed in a special way the presence of a living Savior who knows our need and feels our pain. Something very powerful was beginning to move in my understanding of God and life. It was awareness that *God is very much in control.*

In an hour of trial, Jesus revealed the peace and confidence that God gives in times like this. When the chief priests, elders, and captains of the temple came to take Him in the Garden of Gethsemane, Jesus said to them, "Have you come out as against a robber, with swords and clubs? . . . but this is your hour, and the power of darkness" (Luke 22:52–53 RSV). This "hour" was part of His destiny. Though they took Him away to be crucified, He was the victor. Though Satan and the powers of darkness seemed to be in control, God was in command.

The cultic experience is no different. When a person joins a cult, it appears that the cult is all-powerful. It is not; it is only "their hour, and the power of darkness." It is important that, at the same time we recognize the evil of the cults, we realize that, as did Christ, we have access to a much greater power. A parent must keep in mind the Eternal, the overall plan of God, which will see the ultimate triumph over evil. Satan is allowed a free hand in certain situations, but only for a season. I am a living testimony to the power of God. I am proof that it is possible for anyone, no matter how deeply they are involved in evil, to walk again as a whole person perfectly free in mind, body, and soul.

Satan is allowed a free hand in certain situations—we see his power in the cults. Yet it is only for an hour, a season. Evil has ultimately been defeated.

When a son or daughter joins a cult, parents must recognize that they themselves are in a conflict with evil, they too will pass through their Garden of Gethsemane, and the victorious are those who share in the victory of Christ. Jesus knew the true reality of His situation; He called it "their hour and the power of darkness." He did not call down legions of angels to defend Him; His power was in a totally different sphere. He went silently, meekly, and—most important—alone to His death. Consequently He went to His crucifixion a conqueror.

There, alone in my room, I felt the presence of a Savior who understood my agony, who was trying to say to me, "But this is their hour. Do not look at the outward appearance of evil; look upon the eternal plan of God." Christ had indeed triumphed at Calvary despite the power of darkness, and He was trying to assure me that He was most capable of triumphing in the life of my own daughter despite my failures.

As I thought about these things and wept, my prayer for Joyanne changed. I prayed not so much for her deliverance from the COG as for her salvation. I prayed that God would become her Reality.

I began to thank God for what was happening. I had learned much about Joyanne and about myself, about her real needs and my real failings. By the time I returned home from Puerto Rico I had decided to write this book regardless of what Joyanne did. I had a duty to fulfill and a debt to pay. My children and society in general would learn the truth about the Children of God and Moses David. I could no longer bury my head in the sand and hide behind pride and guilt and fear, knowing that to expose the cult would expose me.

My ex-husband and I boarded the plane for Miami, leaving Joyanne there in Puerto Rico with the Children of God. It was one of the hardest things I have ever had to do; I did not know whether I would ever see her again.

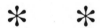

It was a beautiful, sunny day. A gentle breeze lifted the waves in the California surf to just the right size for summer fun. Then, as the sun-tanned bathers laughed and splashed in careless joy, everyone was stunned to a chilling silence by the desperate cries of a drowning youth. He appeared from the shore to be about eighteen or nineteen years old. His father and mother rushed to the water's edge. The mother began to scream frantically for the lifeguard to help. He was at her side in minutes. But instead of plunging into the water, he simply folded his arms and watched the helpless boy. Everyone was amazed. The father cried in a pathetic voice, "Aren't you going to save my son?"

We watched the boy flailing at the water. The father, a man in his late fifties or early sixties, was in no shape to attempt a rescue himself. The lifeguard finally replied, "You can't save a man who is trying to save himself. When he stops trying, I'll save him."

The parents looked horrified. Their sense of helpless agony permeated the entire crowd. But the drowning youth eventually grew exhausted, and when he stopped his thrashing about, the lifeguard rushed in to save him.

Most parents view a son or daughter in the cult just like that drowning boy. They suddenly see their child in a disastrous situation and run to God in panic, crying, "Save my child!" And like the lifeguard, God doesn't seem to respond. Bewildered, they begin to question God. "Why aren't You doing anything? Why have You allowed this! How can You be so unloving as to let my child drown in the sea of cultic sin?"

From the shoreline it is clear that the child is in desperate trouble. But the parents cannot save him. Moreover, neither they nor the child can be rescued unless—like the drowning boy—they stop trying to save themselves.

The feeling of desire *to do something* is understandable. The cultic phenomenon lies beyond the boundaries of traditional religious experience. There is no analogy in ordinary religion for the child who joins a cult. Catholics, Jews, and Protestants all come to understand that tragedy is a part of life. We are taught that death and other traumatic experiences such as marital infidelity can be dealt with in terms of one's religious doctrines. Even the child who is involved with drugs, crime, or an unwanted pregnancy can be accepted and understood. But when a child joins a cult, it is a totally different matter; in many cases it is like a living death.

Almost overnight the parents experience a loss of control. The child is suddenly living in a different world that they cannot reach. They can perhaps visit and talk with their child, but they cannot touch him emotionally. The parent-child bond nurtured for eighteen or twenty years has been suddenly cut, mysteriously severed. At first there is loneliness and confusion. Then there may come bitterness, resentment, hatred, and cynicism. Parents often find already existing family problems aggravated as tensions mount, leading to divorce, alcoholism, depression, or serious illness. Many families break under the pressure of the cult problem.

Sometimes the pain becomes so overwhelming that parents take desperate measures to save themselves and their child. They may decide to "play God" and take matters into their own hands. It becomes more than a question of just getting him out. They pursue the course of Kidnap and Deprogram.

✳   ✳

The question of kidnapping and deprogramming is fraught with controversy. I have spent hours discussing it with parents who still have children in the COG or other cults; I've listened to the testimonies of many members who have been kidnapped and deprogrammed. I always approach the subject with great sensitivity and concern. In some cases the decision to kidnap and deprogram has ended in disaster. Some parties boast great success. But through my own sufferings I have stumbled onto an important truth—namely, whether or not to kidnap and deprogram is not the bottom-line question.

There are issues far deeper, far more important, that must be confronted first. The question I put foremost is, Why do parents want to take that course of action?

If the child went off the track, there was a reason. The desire to quickly get the child home and reestablished in the normal family routine may in fact be a way of avoiding some real-life issues. Such desires may be motivated by pride, selfishness, and a fear of facing one's failings as a parent.

So when parents raise the issue of kidnapping and deprogramming, I immediately ask myself, "Why?" What are their true motives? Are they being driven to action through guilt? A sense of failure as a parent? Or embarrassment because of social pressure and criticism? If so, they are victims of wrong and dangerous motives. Much harm has been done as a result of panic-stricken parents acting from an attitude of "Let's hurry-up-quick get our son back on the track where he suddenly jumped off! We must maintain the status quo at all costs!" Is the parents' primary motivation the child's spiritual welfare or their own self-image? If the status quo was so great, why did the child leave? What was missing from the home?

Consider two typical reactions of parents with questionable motives. I call them the "reactionary parent" and the "indifferent parent." I believe we can see, in many cases, that *the reaction of a parent whose child joins a cult serves as a window into the root problems of the child and his family.*

First we look at the parent who chooses a reactionary course of action—the anti-cult crusader. This kind of parent dramatically casts all the blame for his dilemma on the cult. "They deceived my son! He would never have joined something like that in his right mind! He's been deceived, hypnotized, brainwashed!"

Why is this parent reacting so violently? Could it be that this parent is fighting a tremendous battle with self-rejection and cannot face up to his failures realistically? Is he seeking to cover his feelings of guilt and failure by finding a scapegoat? Is he avoiding responsibility for his actions by putting all the blame on the cult?

This parent, in his inability to face up to guilt and responsibility, is sidestepping the real issues. Moreover, he does not want to acknowledge his son's rebellion. "My son didn't join out of rebellion. He was deceived!" Pride has hindered this parent from seeing the truth about himself; he has adopted a false belief: "It's all the cult's fault."

In many ways, a parent's weaknesses are manifest in a child's behavior. Many youth join cults because they are unwilling to face certain issues, certain realities, certain responsibilities. As a parent may refuse to accept responsibility by blaming a cult, so his child may seek to evade responsibility by joining one.

At the opposite end of the spectrum is the parent who responds with complete indifference. This is the "who cares?" attitude: "It's his life, he can do with it what he wants."

What are the similarities between parent and child in this case? If the parent reacts with indifference, no doubt he has had that attitude for a long time and has left his child drifting without direction or purpose in his spiritual life. A father who does not take the role as spiritual head of the family will leave his child prey to many temptations. It is small wonder that this child will fill his spiritual void with a lie. As long as it "feels good and he's getting out of it what he wants, who cares?" is the attitude of indifference.

Indifference breeds apathy, and apathy leads to selfishness. Cults are the epitome of selfishness. Hence, the indifference of the parent and the child have taken their logical course. After all, who cares what you do as long as it feels good and you are getting what you want out of life?

✷   ✷

How does a parent react constructively to a son or daughter joining a cult?

The parent has before him a great opportunity for self-examination. This is a time of crisis in which to purify motives and establish a relationship with God based on the confidence that He will supply both strength and answers. When we ask God the question, "Should we kidnap? Should we deprogram?" we may receive in reply the questions, "Why? What do you seek to accomplish?" These questions open the door to self-examination and permit us to put the issue of deprogramming and kidnapping in proper perspective.

Self-examination is painful, but properly accomplished it removes confusion, strengthens our character, and allows us to make good decisions to the benefit of all concerned. Self-examination reveals the blind spots in our lives, perhaps weaknesses that God has been seeking for us to deal with for years. Life is not a collection of unrelated incidents without rhyme or reason. A child's joining a cult is no mere accident or coincidence. Nor is God arbitrary in dealing with His children. There is meaning and purpose to every event of our lives, and we must seek to find it. "God reigns, not chance."[1]

The path of self-examination can take three directions. First, a parent may see ways in which he has failed his child and feel pangs of guilt. If these are too painful, pride may cause him to deny responsibility for his child's failure, and consequently he may become reactionary. He will become bitter, resentful, and hateful. He will seek to blame and judge others. The consequences can be tragic. This person could turn to alcohol to avoid accepting reality; family problems can arise that will doom a marriage.

A crisis does not create problems, it reveals them. A child's joining a cult is often cited as the cause of his parent's divorce. But a close examination of the situation will reveal that the cult merely aggravated a condition that already existed. One mother told me, "Our child's joining the cult did not cause the divorce. The problem was already there, but we kept it hidden. The cult experience simply brought to the surface a problem that had been growing between my husband and me for a long time."

The second path of self-examination is similar to the first. Rather than trying to cover over his guilt and avoiding responsibility, the parent of a cult victim may choose self-condemnation, which leads to self-pity. He may escape into despair, depression, alcoholism or drug abuse, or serious illness. The self-condemning person may become reclusive—physically or spiritually or both.

The third route will lead the parent to the foot of the Cross. It will result in the realization of forgiveness and mercy, which will yield great spiritual growth, inner peace, victory, strength, and ultimately joy in the life of the parent.

This third path is the way of peace and joy. It is not the easiest in the beginning, but it bears the fruit of righteousness in the long run.

The key to gaining victory in the crisis is this: *Discern to restore: do not judge to place blame.* The story of Job in the Bible illustrates this truth. Job's counselors erred in regarding his affliction as a sign of God's wrath and conversely regarding prosperity as a sign of God's blessing. They did not see the picture from God's perspective, and they were clearly wrong. They condemned Job falsely and concluded that God was fighting against Job as against an enemy, when in reality God was only trying him as a friend. In the end it was Job who had to pray for their souls, not they for his. God often works in a sphere beyond our human reasoning. Likewise, if a parent turns to God in honesty and sincerity, only good can result. God is greater than any cult.

Self-examination is God's way of strengthening us in crisis. The ultimate purpose of life's experiences is to bring us to an ever-closer relationship with God. Suffering, affliction, and trial have a special place in the life of one who desires to walk close with God. The parent has but two options when faced with a cult crisis: He can respond according to his human feelings and reasoning; or he can turn to God and seek to view the situation from His perspective. Once beyond the motivation of guilt and fear, a parent can begin to see a clear course of action that will have positive results in the lives of all concerned. The answer to the question "Shall we kidnap? Shall we deprogram?" will become strikingly clear.

∗   ∗

When God delivers your child from the cult, will you be ready to receive and help him?

Parents must be aware of the cults' strongest lure: unconditional acceptance. As a result of the fall of Adam and Eve, all people are born into a state of spiritual alienation and self-rejection. We are born into sin and are not acceptable to God. Yet we have an innate desire to be accepted. Acceptance and reconciliation with God come only through Jesus Christ; through Him we gain access to the throne of God and come into a position of fellowship with Him. Parents should be models of God's unconditional acceptance; they should mirror what Christ does for us. Jesus says, "Come unto me, all ye that labour and are heavy laden . . ." (Matthew 11:28). He takes us with our sins, our faults, our fears—everything. Cults counterfeit this kind of unconditional acceptance; they offer a false model of the gospel and divine grace.

Cult recruits are accepted totally on the basis that they are fellow human beings, no questions asked. The relationship changes once they are fully involved in the cult, but this is how they are initially received. This contrasts with the conditional acceptance we experience in society and often in our own homes. Many parents have high expectations for their child in this competitive world, and the child will often feel rejected if he fails to perform according to these hopes. Society, or more specifically the community in which we find ourselves, may accept us only according to certain standards of achievements or wealth or beauty or vocation and so on.

But what do the cults do? They say, "We love you just because you are you! You are valuable, and you want to love and be loved just like us. Come and be with brothers and sisters like yourself. There's nothing to prove. We love and accept you just as you are."

Encountering a cult, a youth perhaps for the first time feels as if he is accepted and appreciated for himself—something he may have been waiting for all his life. This has a drastic effect. The youth will most likely want to give himself totally to the group, and he may in fact be disappointed if anything blocks total commitment. He is home. He is secure. He is finally accepted.

Having embraced the group with open arms, he will come to accept doctrine as a matter of course. Some of the teaching may be difficult to accept at first, but he will embrace it eventually because of his total commitment to the group and the mutual exchange of love among the members. And when he discovers he is following God's Endtime Prophet or the Messiah himself, then he's sure he's on the right track. Brainwashing? Yes—masterfully achieved. In a short time the youth will have accepted new standards and values contrary to those of his parents and his former community.

But the unconditional acceptance offered by a cult is counterfeit. It is a lie. The child is recruited only to serve the aims of the cult and will be exploited, despite the initial appearances. Cultic acceptance does not model Christ's; there is no deception in God's invitation to reconciliation.

As parents we may have failed to follow the example of acceptance that Christ sets for us. *To the degree that children feel rejected by parents they will feel rejected by God.* Having failed once, the parents must not fail again if their child comes out of a cult. Mistakes have been made; the child is gone and in a cult; the parents can't change that fact or undo their mistakes. But God is not finished. He can still give beauty for ashes, joy in place of sorrow. There is the opportunity for parents to establish a new or deeper relationship with God, to learn the reality of divine mercy, to learn the meaning of forgiveness, to learn the meaning of patience and real joy in allowing God to work according to His timetable, to learn trust.

I began to learn these truths myself through a story told by Richard Wurmbrand.[2]

In the hinterlands of the USSR, there may exist no church building for hundreds of miles, so Christians meet in secret to avoid persecution by the government. One Christmas Eve in a certain village, a group of Christians gathered in a stable to celebrate the birth of Christ. An elderly woman had been assigned to stand some distance from the stable to keep a watch for government agents. She had been given a piece of iron to throw against the gate of the stable as a signal for those inside to flee should police arrive.

As this woman stood watch in the snow and cold, she prayed. It seems that her only son had been tortured and killed by the Communists sometime earlier. When his battered body was brought to her door she heard two voices in her heart. One said, "Curse these damned Communists!" The other said, "Forgive them, for they don't know what they are doing. They don't know the love of God." She chose to forgive. As she was an elderly woman and had nothing to do, she passed her time praying for those who had tortured and killed her son. So there she stood that Christmas Eve, with the snow falling gently around her.

Suddenly she was kicked into the snow from behind. She looked up to find an officer standing over her.

"What are you doing here?" he demanded.

"Why, I am praying for you," she replied.

The officer began to laugh. "I don't think you consider me a very lovable being. Why should you be praying for me? You Christians think that we Communists are monsters."

"That is how we consider you," the woman said. "But for criminals, for monsters, Jesus came to die on the cross. For those who whipped Him, for those who nailed Him to the cross, He prayed while He was dying, 'Forgive them.'"

At that moment she looked into his eyes and had an illumination. "It is you!" she cried. "You are the one who tortured and killed my son! If only you knew how I love you! For years I have prayed for you. You have taken in my heart the place of my son, whom you tortured to death. Christ loves you, and I love you. He has placed His love for you in my heart. I love you as I loved my own son."

Tears ran down the officer's cheeks. When the woman saw

his tears, she said, "Now I can tell you what I am doing here. Come, the Christians are gathered over in that stable."

When she brought the officer into the stable, the Christians were frightened. But she told them, "Don't be afraid! His uniform is that of a Communist officer, but his heart is that of a repenting sinner. Receive him as your brother."

Don't parents of cult victims share a common sorrow with this old woman who lost her son? Haven't they also heard a voice saying, "Cursed be that damned cult?" How do they respond to the conflicting voices that would evoke curses on the one hand and forgiveness on the other?

What was the greatest miracle of Richard Wurmbrand's story? I believe it was not the fact that the Russian officer was converted. Rather, his conversion was secondary to the transposed love of that woman. The greatest miracle took place within her heart. Instead of being consumed by hatred, she modeled God's love. It was a power greater than Communist terror.

To hate our enemies is natural. But this woman yielded to Christ's command to "love your enemies." I am sure that she did not yield to this command overnight; it did not come without struggle. But she chose to obey the command, and God brought out of it beauty for ashes. It brought a communist officer to his knees. It is with this kind of love that parents can conquer the cults.

For the parent whose child is in a cult, it is not a time to despair. It is a time to learn, to pray, and to wait on God. It is a time to love one's spouse rather than yield to pressure and frustration, taking out inner tensions on our spouse. It is a time to gain victory over faults in order to be ready to help the child when he returns. It is a time to learn that sometimes God will say Yes to our prayers immediately, but sometimes He will remain silent, even for years.

The time that passes between a child's entering a cult and his coming out of it is crucial for a parent. If it is spent in depression, discouragement, and bitterness, what has been accomplished? If depression leads to self-pity and an obsession with "getting him out," how can there be growth of character? Spiritual maturity and character development are as important for the parent as it is for the child to get out. If the pressure becomes unbearable, parents do well to recall the words of missionary Hudson Taylor:

> *It doesn't matter, really, how great the pressure is. It only matters where the pressure lies. See that it never comes between you and the Lord—then, the greater the pressure, the more it presses you to His breast.*[3]

Parents of cult victims must be willing to endure this time of suffering. Enduring suffering will produce character and will prepare the parents for the day when their child returns home. *And he will return home.*

The Bible speaks of two kinds of suffering. One is godly, the other human. And a parent's response determines which kind his suffering will be.

> *I now rejoice, not that you were made sorrowful, but that you were made sorrowful to the point of repentance; for you were made sorrowful according to the will of God, in order that you might not suffer loss in anything . . . .*
> *For the sorrow that is according to the will of God produces a repentance without regret, leading to salvation; but the sorrow of the world produces death (2 Corinthians 7:9–10 NASB).*

What kind of parent will a child returning from a cult encounter?

The ex-cult member will be faced with trauma and confusion, just as his parents were when he first joined. Parents must be prepared to teach him how to triumph over his struggles: how to overcome guilt, to cope with depression, to gain joy amid suffering, to start life anew without fear, to pray to a God who seems altogether distant and silent, to remain unanxious over unanswered prayer. He must find parents filled with compassion and overflowing with the mercies of God.

Will he find this kind of parent, or one broken and in poor health, divorced, and despairing? Surely at this he will despair of any hope in God.

For years I thought God had abandoned me, but now I know that was only the beginning. For years I looked around me and saw only sorrow and the tragic consequences of sin. I wanted to see things change, but could only despair at the stark realities of life. Then I saw that it was God, much more than myself, who wanted to turn my life around. I had to conform my will to His. My prayer is that parents of cult victims would allow God to turn their world of sorrow and pain into joy and gladness.

✱   ✱

Joyanne returned home on May 22, two months after she left. She had experienced many things in those two long months, most of them harmful to her. Even the thought of what she encountered while living with the COG is painful to me; nevertheless, she came home because she chose to do so.

For the most part Joyanne defended the Children of God on her return from Puerto Rico, standing up for their right to do as they please. It hurt me deeply to hear her say that, for I know that their practices are an abomination to God. Her defensive stance was a covering for the decision she had made to visit them, for by defending them she was defending herself. She was not concerned with their immoral practices; she felt that the COG are no different than 95 percent of contemporary society.

I believe Joyanne began to perceive, perhaps unconsciously, that the members of the Family are mere puppets, nonindividuals incapable of thinking for themselves. She was confronted with what I know to be the frightening reality of sin, the consequences of which turn people into mindless, faceless, desensitized pawns. They have not the slightest notion of God who believe about God only what they are told to believe. They have become gods unto themselves.

Joyanne had to face many more perplexing situations on her return home. Life for my oldest daughter has been very difficult and will continue to be so. Her former reality has been shattered, and she will wander painfully until she arrives at Reality. She is a tender and loving person, but she trusts no one.

This is my most painful wound, to see Joyanne so alone. My heart longs to reach out and tell her to believe, to trust, to love the One who first loved us. My mistakes have broken that bridge of confidence. Joyanne is a wonderful child who is no longer a child—I have to keep reminding myself of that. Her search for answers goes on, and so does my prayer. And each day, I believe, she comes one step closer to finding Him.

Chapter 17
Alive at Any Cost

On coming out of the Children of God I, like all ex-cult members, was face to face with the question of survival. Since coming into a new Reality I have thought about survival, and specifically, What is the sustaining factor that keeps people from breaking under duress? What enables people to withstand torture or imprisonment or even the daily pressures of life?

We don't ordinarily regard alcoholism, depression, or drug dependency as a form of breaking under torture. But in reality they are much the same. The man or woman who can't "cope" with the pressures of life—marital, social, financial, or job-related—and turns to an artificial release such as drinking is running from the problem, breaking, and escaping into an illusion.

I found many insights and parallels to my own situation in *Every Secret Thing*, Patty Hearst's story of her kidnapping and ordeal with the small revolutionary group known as the Symbionese Liberation Army.[1] To some degree, all of us have been in Patty's position. There is a lot to learn from her story.

Through no choice of her own, Patty was kidnapped, abused,

and forced to follow the SLA in 1974. She lived under an ever-present threat of death. Patty decided that in order to survive, to stay alive, she would say and do whatever her captors demanded.

Patty recalls a turning point in her captivity that occurred during a thirty-day confinement in a small closet. She came to the point of having to decide whether to live or die.

> *Under all that stress, my body was surrendering its life force, giving up. I was so tired, so tired; all I wanted to do was to sleep. And I knew that was dangerous, fatal, like the man lost in the Arctic snow, who, having laid his head down for that delicious nap, never woke up again. My mind, suddenly, was alive and alert to all this. I could see what was happening to me, as if I were outside myself.*
>
> *A silent battle was waged there in the closet, and my mind won. Deliberately and clearly, I decided I would not die of my own accord. I would fight with everything in my power to survive; to see this through I would concentrate on staying alive one day at a time.*[2]

Patty's one goal, was to stay alive at any cost. The SLA began to confront her continually with the option "Fight or Die!"

> *I thought about it all the time. It seemed like a hideous offer. . . . Day after day I worried that I would be asked to make a choice, and I did not know what I would say. I did not know what to believe.*[3]

As Patty groped her way down this trail of survival, agreeing with everything they wanted, an interesting phenomenon occurred. She says, "They accepted me. I knew them and thought I understood them, even their foolish quest as revolutionaries to overthrow the entire United States. In trying to convince them I convinced myself."[4]

As she yielded her will to theirs, consciously agreeing and accepting, she opened herself to the effects of brainwashing and mind control. What happened to her parallels exactly the pattern of the voluntary suspension of disbelief. To stay alive, Patty came to accept as reality what she knew to be false.

I experienced the same thing in my life, even though my circumstances were different in detail.

The fear of death triggered in Patty Hearst's mind a well-defined course of action, to which she responded. She would do anything to stay alive. However, throughout her captivity and involvement with the SLA, the underlying fears, resentment, and ambiguities gnawed at her conscience and never gave her peace. She was a woman convinced against her will. She was forced to live with a violated conscience. I experienced this same condition in the COG. Beneath all the thoughts lies a tormenting confusion that does not allow for peace or happiness.

Patty did what was necessary to accomplish her goal of staying alive. In regard to the famous bank robbery in which she was forced to take part, she says,

> *I wanted the SLA to believe in me completely, and to that end I told myself I would accept whatever they told me, and do whatever I had to do to survive. In any event, I had my assignment. I would go into the bank with the others.*[5]

But the decision was taking its toll on Patty's conscious and subconscious. Reality became distorted. She writes, "I never ceased to be surprised when he [Donald DeFreeze, the top leader] accosted me with that question 'Who are you?' and I would retort smartly, 'I'm a soldier in the Symbionese Liberation Army.' I learned by rote, as soldiers do in every army, and, despite myself, I found that I would obey."[6]

As Patty's ordeal of physical captivity continued, she eventually became a prisoner to her fears. I can understand exactly this mental polarity, this conflict of conscience, the melting of right and wrong into an amorphous mess. It is like mixing sugar and salt: to look at it, no one can tell the difference, yet to taste it causes the palate to explode in contradiction. The physical response to the taste is nausea and vomiting. A similar response takes place morally and psychologically in a situation like Patty's.

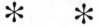

When I returned to my father and his movement after running away in London, I felt as if my mind had been split with an ax. On the one hand I knew how diseased Dad was morally; on the other I wanted to serve God. There was no peace—only confusion and a spiritual and psychological nausea. To try to live in perversion and for the glory of God at the same time was insanity.

Fear is a powerful, though vile motivation. Where conscience is involved, fear creates a moral polarity that tears the soul apart. One lives continually with the question, "What is more acceptable, to bypass one's conscience because of fear and knowingly do what is wrong, or to yield to the demands of conscience and do what it tells you is right regardless of the consequences?"

I will not judge Patty Hearst. That is not my place, but God's. Yet I was faced with the very same kind of choice that she was when I was face to face with my father. So many times I was faced with the choice of living for the Cause of David Berg or resisting him at risk of suffering. I failed. Repeatedly I buckled under to fear. I repressed my guilt, violated my conscience, and did things I knew were immoral and wrong, justifying them through religious reasoning, through the "good works" we were doing.

I judge myself now on the basis of truths I learned the hard way—through failure, agony, and seeing the consequences of my sin in the lives of my children and others whom I love. I think about Patty Hearst and wonder, "What if she had resisted her captors?" According to the conditions of her captivity and the fanatical zeal of the SLA, she would have been shot. What would have happened had I withstood my father? Only God knows. My brother fought the same spiritual battle I did. He could not follow Dad with a clear conscience, yet he would not face him and call him wrong. The confusion overwhelmed him, so he ended it all. I too lived with a haunting desire for suicide.

Until I left the Children of God, I never withstood my father, and no one else in my family has. Why? Because of fear. It is not for fear of physical harm, for as I have said, my dad has never exhibited a violent nature. He was a loving and gentle father as I was growing up. Rather, his power comes from intimidating people through a subtle blend of sin and pride, using their own guilty conscience as a lever against them.

One can become free of my father only through conquering the fear of accepting mistakes and facing one's sin. Conquer this fear, and David Berg loses the power to intimidate. But it is perhaps the greatest of all fears. To expose my dad was to expose myself; so for a long time I decided instead to follow him and sin after him.

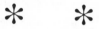

I see that people in a situation like Patty Hearst's or like mine have a great need. That need is for strength of character founded on godly principles. The sixties were an era of great rebellion; but rebellion does not build character. Rebellion is the result of a soul suffering the burden of sin and guilt. And immorality does not build character. Greed and the love of money do not build character. The power that will destroy cults and destructive groups such as the SLA is the strength of character grounded in the power and authority of scriptural principles.

Great men of God in history have not been ruled by fear. Neither fear of death, nor of torture, nor failure, nor social rejection. Rather, they have been governed by divine standards. These standards keep us strong, free from mental polarity, and free from the torment of soul wrought by a fear of conscience.

In contrast to Patty Hearst's decision, consider the ordeal of Richard Wurmbrand. He was face to face with unmitigated evil and abuse for fourteen years, yet he did not break. He did not bend to the will of his captors. He is a living example of his own statement that persecution and suffering reveal strength of personal character or the lack of it.

Many Christians have asked Wurmbrand, "Which Scriptures helped you endure your torture?" His response is intriguing.

"Christians," Wurmbrand wrote, "were tied to crosses for three days and three nights. The crosses were laid on the floor at different times of the day, and the other prisoners were tortured in such a way as to force them to relieve their bodily necessities on the faces of these men. Then the crosses were erected again.

"One does not 'hang' upon a cross," he said. "Your body cries out in agony at the torment of the pain, so you twist and turn to find a more comfortable position, only to find that the new one is more painful than the last. You do not hang upon a cross, you writhe in endless agony.

"In such conditions we knew the verse. 'My grace is sufficient for thee.' But the verse 'My grace is sufficient' was not sufficient. We also knew the Twenty-third Psalm, 'The Lord is my Shepherd, I shall not want.' But the psalm about the Shepherd did not help us. A verse about grace was not sufficient; we needed grace. A psalm about the Shepherd was not sufficient; we needed the Shepherd Himself. No verse on earth could enable us to endure such torture."

The Communists also put Wurmbrand's wife in prison, and his only son was left to himself, without mother or father to care for him, at the age of ten. When the interrogators were not torturing Richard Wurmbrand, then his mind and heart were torturing him as to what had become of his family. Only the person of Jesus Christ, he explains, can sustain a person in such circumstances.

"In the West," Wurmbrand writes, "I see a danger of Christians worshipping the Bible." He makes a statement that puzzled me at first, but when I considered it in light of the confusion and suffering I had experienced because of the Children of God, its meaning became clear.

"The Bible is not 'the Truth,'" Wurmbrand writes. "God is 'the Truth.' The Bible is 'the truth about the Truth.' Theology, if it is the right theology, is 'the truth about the truth about the Truth.' And a good sermon is 'the truth about the truth about the truth about the Truth.' And Christian people live in these many truths about the Truth, and, because of them, have not 'the Truth.'"[7]

Wurmbrand further explains that people must strip away the scaffolding of words that surrounds "the Truth." We must penetrate through everything that is "words" and be bound up with the reality of God Himself. This is the secret that enabled him to endure fourteen years of suffering under the Communists.

Under constant threat of death, innumerable tortures, near-starvation, and bitter cold, Wurmbrand would not recant his faith in Christ, betray his fellow Christians (even though he was sent to prison as a result of another's betrayal), or swear allegiance to his captors' regime. Miraculously he survived. His wife also survived six years in prison. And their son lived to see them both freed.

There are countless thousands of Christians who have not

escaped death—the martyrs of the Underground Church. But more miraculous than the fact of Richard Wurmbrand's survival is the power that enabled him to resist the fear of death.

Because his life was founded on divine principles, because he was bound up with the Reality of God, he was motivated by love and not by hate. The power of his resistance was love. He professed as much love for his tormentors as for his brothers in Christ. The power of the love of God enabled him with strength and clarity of mind to live in forgiveness instead of becoming a twisted, embittered, foul, and hateful man.

Unlike me, Wurmbrand did not choose to stay alive "at any cost." He conquered his fear. He was not intimidated by it or ruled by evil as a consequence. He was in prison, but not a prisoner. Fear is the real prison. Ironically, Wurmbrand found eternal freedom in the cold, dark prison cells of Rumania.

Great men are ruled by divine principles. This is what we must teach our children. This is the one true power against cults or any outside forces that would dominate us. And more than that, through Christ it is the power over evil itself.

✳   ✳

We see a tree, yet we cannot touch its beauty with our hearts because our hearts are bound with fear and sin. We see our children, yet our emotions are not at liberty to open the floodgates of love with which we would engulf them. We see, but we cannot touch. We feel, yet our hearts are bound. How many live in prison? In varying degrees we are all in the prisons of our sinful selves, of wrong and limited ideas. But Jesus can free us of these.

We must teach our children by our own example to understand, believe in, and live by divine standards revealed to us in Scripture. Otherwise they will not have sufficient strength of character to recognize and resist evil. Ultimately, fear will rule their hearts and consequently rule the world.

As I scan the panorama of my past, it is hard to see anything but the mountains of failures and mistakes. But God has set before me a new pathway. God has put to me the question, "Despite your past failures, can you purpose in your heart never again to be ruled by fear?" I have accepted that challenge.

Chapter 18
Where Is God?

As time and the grace of God separate me further and further from the Children of God and its evil world, I sometimes find myself standing in wonder as I experience the unseen hand of God working miracle after miracle in my life. It is something awesome to see the depth of God's involvement in the affairs of mankind. But there have been times also when I was overwhelmed with the ambiguities of life, when all I could see was suffering and injustice. At those times, the question would spring from my doubting heart, "Where is God in all this?"

Many times I have asked, "Why, God? How could it be that You allowed my father to mingle the gospel of Jesus Christ with sexual perversion and occultism? Why didn't You stop him, Lord?" In searching for answers I began to see in my mind's eye a picture that has opened the doors of my understanding.

The history of man's relationship with God demonstrates that mankind is often unaware of the plane on which He operates. After the fall of man, creation grew increasingly wicked. Evil abounded to such a degree that God sent a flood to destroy every living creature, except for Noah and his family and the animals in the ark. Afterward, life began anew. But the fallen human heart continued to sin. In response, God raised up Abraham to be the father of His chosen people, Israel, through whom all the world would be blessed. Through Abraham God promised the Messiah: a King over kings, the Prince of Peace, the Savior of the world who would take away and forgive sin.

Thus Jesus was born. God incarnate. He healed the lame, fed the hungry, and opened the eyes of the blind. He commanded the people to love their enemies; He exposed self-righteousness as the most heinous of all spiritual crimes. He raised the dead. And He Himself was rejected and put to death by His own people. As the Scriptures promised, He was raised from the dead. Appearing to His disciples, He commanded them to go into all the world and preach the Good News. All but one of His chosen twelve were martyred.

The followers of Christ grew and multiplied. Saul of Tarsus, one of the most avid persecutors of Christians, was converted and became the most important leader of the early church. Yet persecution of the church continued. Centuries later, the emperor Constantine was converted, and the persecution of Christians was ended. Rome, the onetime scourge of Christianity, now earned a place in church history as the seat of organized Christianity. Yet peace continued to elude the life of the church.

Eventually a new word crept into the vocabulary of Christendom like a malignancy: Inquisition. Saints of God were butchered under the auspices of the organized church, Christ's representative body on earth. But how could the Body of Christ destroy its own?

Soon came a man named Luther, and with him a reformation. Calvin, Knox, and Wesley followed. Cromwell and Puritans. Catholics and Protestants. Belfast, IRA, and death. The New World and freedom of religion. Denominationalism and Fundamentalism. Pentecostals, Dispensationalists, Charismatics, and Evangelicals. The Moral Majority and Right to Life. Stalin, Hitler, Pol Pot, and holocaust. Israel, the PLO, and more death. Cults. Jim Jones and 912 dead. David Berg, the Children of God, Flirty Fish, Jesus Babies, incest, Moses David, my father.

Where is God in all this? How could He allow these inconsistencies, these atrocities, these injustices? Was God unaware that the murders of the Inquisition were carried out in the name of Jesus? Where was He, and on what plane does He operate?

Amid my confusion I began to see that because of sin, God was forced to reveal Himself to mankind through the intimacy of His suffering. When we come face to face with all the world's suffering and pain, God's position becomes strikingly clear: He is under it all, bearing every sin. As the world suffers, so does God. He is not apart from it. He is not aloof. When sin entered the universe, God's response was to bear the sin Himself. As the Scriptures reveal, "We implore you on Christ's behalf: Be reconciled to God. God made him who had no sin to be sin for us, so that in him we might become the righteousness of God" (2 Corinthians 5:21).

Oswald Chambers writes,

> *The revelation of the Bible is not that Jesus Christ took upon Himself our fleshly sins, but that He took upon Himself the heredity of sin which no man can touch. God made His own Son to be sin that He might make the sinner a saint. He deliberately took upon His own shoulders, and bore in His own Person, the whole massed sin of the human race. . . .* [1]

And the intimacy of His suffering continues to be revealed as we witness the persecution of His Body, the church. Even though Christ died two thousand years ago, His suffering was not limited to Calvary. The truth emerges that He still suffers.

When a voice thundered from the heavens, "Saul, Saul, why do you persecute me?" Saul responded, "Who are you, Lord?" The divine reply was, "I am Jesus, whom you are persecuting" (Acts 9:4). Through this encounter the mystery of the suffering Body of Christ is revealed to us in marvelous clarity. Indeed, Christ continues to suffer.

So where is God in all this—in the perversion of the Children of God, the blasphemies of Moses David, the thousands of Jesus Babies who will never know their fathers? I think I am now coming to understand, in small measure, where He is. He is suffering.

With each sin, with each injustice, with each persecuted member of His Body, Christ suffers. This is the intimacy of His suffering that reveals to us God's relationship to mankind because of sin.

I used to ponder, Who's side is God on—Russia or America, Catholic or Protestant, Arab or Jew? I think now it is not so much a matter of God's choosing which side He is on, but it is man's place to choose to be on the side of God. Each man has to take up his cross personally, individually.

Having lived ten years in a movement founded on one man's personal sin and rebellion, I am beginning to see Christ's relationship to sin. People can mingle the name of Christ with their sins as my father is doing, but it does not affect the Truth. It only proves to us why God had to send His Son. It only reveals deeper the depravity of man and his need for redemption.

I believe that is where God is in all the world's injustice, in the murders in Belfast, in the religious hypocrisy of the church, in the depravity of Moses David and the COG. He is there and He suffers. Yet through His suffering Christ has conquered all that is false, all that is a lie. Judgment will come. It must be that God will judge the world and its sin.

Until then we know that God's Truth is far stronger than any Inquisition, greater than the religious conflicts of Catholics and Protestants, and far deeper than the deceit of the Children of God. God's truth is greater than any sin. As the world lies in suffering, so Christ suffers. And through His suffering we can experience forgiveness, that bridge between a holy God and sinful man. Christ died for guilty individuals, and it is on this plane that we must meet Him. But this is an awesome perspective, for it places us face to face with God.

Notes

Chapter 1: The Coronation

[1]Moses David, "Prayer for a Queen," ML (Mo Letter) 181, pars. 1–2.
[2]Ibid., par. 20.
[3]"One Wife," ML 249, par. 13.
[4]Ibid., pars. 1, 5, 20–21, 23.

Chapter 2: The Inheritance

[1]Oswald Chambers, *My Utmost for His Highest* (New York: Dodd, Mead, n.d.), p. 74.
[2]Virginia Brandt Berg, *The Hem of His Garment*, pp. 5–6.
[3]Ibid., p. 8.
[4]Ibid., p. 52.
[5]"Survival," ML 172, pars. 72–73.

Chapter 3: The Gospel of Rebellion

[1]"Who Are the Rebels?" ML E, pars. 1–2.
[2]Ibid., pars. 5, 9, 12, 29.
[3]"Christmas 1968—Huntington Beach—The Lightclub," ML 1061, pars. 94–95.
[4]"Forsaking All," ML 314A, par. 4.
[5]"Millions of Miles of Miracles," ML 897, pars. 194–195.
[6]Ibid., pars. 196–198.
[7]Ibid., pars. 199–200.
[8]"Jesus People?—Or Revolution!" ML 148, pars. 9–10, 22–23, 37.

Chapter 4: The Conception

[1]"Terror by Night," ML 857, par. 40.
[2]"Millions of Miles of Miracles," ML 897, par. 207.
[3]Ibid., pars. 202–203, 208.
[4]"Real Love Never Fails," ML 639, pars. 18, 20, 22.

Chapter 5: The Birth of a Cult

[1]Samson Warner, "We Are the Children of God—Chapter 5," *Family News* 22, p. 115.
[2]"The Old Church and the New Church," ML A, par. 8.
[3]Ibid., par. 16.
[4]Ibid., pars. 1–2, 4, 11.
[5]"Millions of Miles of Miracles," ML 897, par. 2.
[6]"The Old Church and the New Church," ML A, pars. 16, 20.
[7]Ibid., pars. 21–22.
[8]Ibid., par. 28.
[9]"Prophecies of the Handmaiden of the Lord," ML 19, pars. 1, 11.
[10]Ibid., pars. 12, 15–16, 22.
[11]"The Old Church and the New Church," ML A, pars. 18–19.
[12]Roy Wallis, "The Social Construction of Charisma," *Social Compass* XXIX, 1 (1982), p. 35.
[13]Ibid., p. 36.
[14]Ibid., p. 37.
[15]Ibid., p. 31.
[16]Ibid., p. 33.

Chapter 7: A New Nation—TSC

[1]*New Nation News* (1971).
[2]"Where Are the Prophets of God?" ML 989, pars. 28–29, 39, 32, 35–36.
[3]"Abrahim the Gypsy King," ML 296, pars. 22–26.
[4]"Another Holy Ghost Story," ML 679, par. 55.
[5]"Madame M," ML 268.
[6]"The Goddesses," ML 224, pars. 3–4.
[7]"Mocumba," ML 554, par. 1.
[8]Dave Hunt, *The Cult Explosion* (Eugene, Ore.: Harvest House, 1980), p. 172.
[9]"Holy Ghosts," ML 620, pars. 10, 12, 16, 28.
[10]Hunt, *The Cult Explosion*, p. 170.
[11]"Holy Ghosts," ML 620, pars. 30–31.
[12]"More Precious Pearls," ML 540, par. 4.
[13]"Jesus and Sex," ML 525, par. 54.
[14]"Holy Ghosts," ML 620, pars. 45, 48.
[15]Ibid., pars. 63–65.
[16]"More Holy Ghosts," ML 621, par. 26.
[17]"I Gotta Split," ML 28.

Chapter 8: Sin in the Camp

[1]Ronald M. Enroth; Edward E. Ericson; and C. Breckinridge Peters, *The Jesus People* (Grand Rapids: Eerdmans, 1972), p. 27.
[2]Ibid.
[3]Ibid., pp. 52–53.
[4]"Sex Questions and Answers! Part 1," ML 815.

Chapter 9: "World Conquest Through Love"

[1]"The Great Escape," ML 160, par. 16.
[2]"Flee as a Bird," ML 160B.
[3]"Wonder Working Words," ML 207, par. 6.
[4]Ibid., par. 7.
[5]Ibid., par. 18.

⁶Ibid., par. 22.
⁷"Shiners? or Shamers?" ML 241.
⁸"Rags to Riches," ML 211.
⁹MLs 258, 250, 260, 249, 240, 224 respectively.
¹⁰"Come On Ma!—Burn Your Bra!" ML 286, par. 5.
¹¹Ibid., par. 11.
¹²Ibid., par. 20.
¹³"Techi's Story!—Chapter 7: Where Do Babies Come From?" ML 794, par. 1.
¹⁴"Gaddafi—And the Children of God," ML 246, pars. 15, 30.
¹⁵"Islam!—Chapter 2," ML 709, par. 15.
¹⁶"Gaddafi's Third World," ML 245, par. 32.
¹⁷"King Arthur's Knights! The Cost of Flirty Fishing," ML 501, pars. 33–34.
¹⁸"The FF Explosion," ML 576, par. 50.
¹⁹"The Latest News," ML 833, par. 9.
²⁰"The FF Explosion," ML 576, par. 20.

Chapter 10: "If the Truth Kills, Let It Kill"

¹"If the Truth Kills, Let It Kill," ML 678, pars. 1, 10, 13–14, 31, 39–41.
²"Alexander the Evil Magician," ML 666, par. 21.

Chapter 11: "The Lord Will Go On, With or Without You!"

¹Bill Gothard, *Research in Principles of Life,* Institute in Basic Youth Conflicts, p. 11.
²Carroll Stoner and Jo Anne Parke, *All God's Children: The Cult Experience* (Old Tappan, N.J.: Spire Books, 19), p. 124.

Chapter 12: "If We Have an Order to Believe, We Will Believe"

¹Richard Wurmbrand, *With God in Solitary Confinement* (Glendale, Calif.: Diana Books, 1979), p. 87.

Chapter 13: "Brainwashing? That's Ridiculous!"

¹"Brainwashing," *World Book Encyclopedia,* Vol. B (1976), p. 462.
²Stoner and Parke, *All God's Children,* p. 240.
³Ibid., p. 127.
⁴Stoner and Parke, *All God's Children,* p. 127.
⁵Ibid.
⁶Chambers, *My Utmost for His Highest,* p. 279.
⁷E. Stanley Jones, *Abundant Living* (Nashville: Abingdon, 1976), p. 176.
⁸Stoner and Parke, *All God's Children,* pp. 127–128.
⁹Ibid., p. 248.
¹⁰Chambers, *My Utmost for His Highest,* p. 175.

Chapter 14: "All Things Are Lawful"

¹"The FF Explosion," ML 576, par. 138.
²Lewis Sperry Chafer, *Systematic Theology,* Vol. 2 (Grand Rapids: Zondervan, 1948), p. 31.
³Ibid.
⁴Ibid., p. 35.
⁵Ibid., p. 36.
⁶Ibid., p. 251.

⁷ML 576, par. 14.
⁸Ibid., pars. 14, 32, 101.
⁹Ibid., pars. 172, 175.
¹⁰"A Prayer for the Poor," ML 681, pars. 23, 34, 67, 101–103.
¹¹Ibid., par. 97.
¹²"More Childcare Jewels," ML 990, par. 75.
¹³"Dad's Little Diamonds," ML 994, par. 47.
¹⁴"My Childhood Sex," ML 779, pars. 29, 31–32, 56–57.
¹⁵Gothard, *Research in Principles of Life,* p. 116.
¹⁶"RNR Rules," ML 663, par. XI:2.
¹⁷Ibid., pars. XII:1–2.
¹⁸*Matthew Henry's Commentary on the Whole Bible* (Grand Rapids: Zondervan, 1961), p. 1756.

Chapter 15: A Wonderful Servant, a Terrible Master!

¹Jones, *Abundant Living,* p. 131.
²Ibid., p. 132.
³Napoleon Hill, *Think and Grow Rich* (New York: Fawcett, Crest, 1979), pp. 184–185.
⁴Ibid., p. 185.
⁵Ibid., p. 188.
⁶Ibid., p. 189.
⁷Jones, *Abundant Living,* p. 130.
⁸Ibid., p. 131.
⁹Ibid., p. 129.
¹⁰Ibid.
¹¹"Terror by Night," ML 857, pars. 3, 5, 25–26.
¹²Jones, *Abundant Living,* p. 127.
¹³"King Arthur's Knights! The Art of Flirty Fishing," ML 501.
¹⁴"Women in Love," ML 292.
¹⁵Moses David, *The Story of Davidito*
¹⁶"Homos," ML 719.
¹⁷"The Real Meaning of the Lord's Supper," ML 781.
¹⁸"The Devil Hates Sex," ML 999.

Chapter 16: "God, How Could You Do This to Me?"

¹Howard Taylor and Mary G. Taylor, *Hudson Taylor's Spiritual Secret* (Chicago: Moody, n.d.).
²Richard Wurmbrand, "Church Triumphing Under Communism" (Glendale, Calif.: Diana Books).
³Taylor and Taylor, *Hudson Taylor's Spiritual Secret,* p. 152.

Chapter 17: Alive at Any Cost

¹Patricia Hearst with Alvin Moscow, *Every Secret Thing* (New York: Doubleday, 1982).
²Ibid., pp. 75–76.
³Ibid., p. 87.
⁴Ibid., p. 103.
⁵Ibid., p. 129.
⁶Ibid., p. 142.
⁷Wurmbrand, "Church Triumphing Under Communism."

Chapter 18: Where Is God?

¹Chambers, *My Utmost for His Highest,* p. 281.